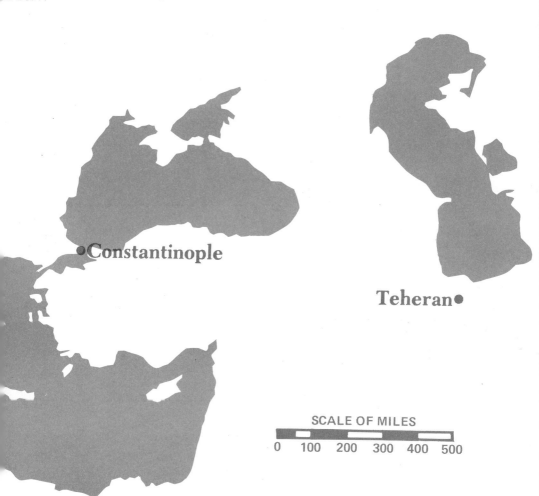

olm

•St. Petersburg

g

rsaw

•Constantinople

Teheran•

SCALE OF MILES

0   100   200   300   400   500

Napoleon's Diplomatic Service

WITHDRAWN

Edward A. Whitcomb

Napoleon's Diplomatic Service

Duke University Press

Durham, N.C.

1979

© 1979, Duke University Press

L.C.C. card no. 78–74018

I.S.B.N. 0–8223–0421–x

Printed in the United States of
America by Heritage Printers, Inc.

To

Bill and Edna

Mel and Ernie

and Alana

Acknowledgments

This study began as a Ph.D. thesis at the University of London, a project I was encouraged to undertake by Professor W. D. Smith, Dr. W. L. Morton, and the late Dr. C. W. Lightbody. I owe special thanks to the late Dr. Alfred Cobban under whose exacting standards and in whose challenging seminar the thesis took shape, and to Dr. Douglas Johnson who, although inheriting both me and the topic, contributed enormously to its completion. Acknowledgment is due to those librarians and archivists who assisted me, particularly at the Archives des Affaires Etrangères, the Archives Nationales, the Archives de la Guerre, and the Bibliothèque Thiers.

It would not have been possible to convert the thesis to a book without the generous assistance of Professor Harold Parker and Dr. James K. Kieswetter, both of whom read the entire manuscript and provided excellent advice and criticism. I should also like to thank those numerous unknown critics who read the text for university presses and research councils—hopefully they will recognize the benefits of their criticisms and suggestions. Finally thanks are due to Mr. Ashbel G. Brice and Reynolds Smith of Duke University Press for their many excellent editorial suggestions and patience.

Financial assistance came from a great many sources: the University of Manitoba's Adalsteinn Kristjansson Fellowship, research grants of the University of London's Institute of Historical Research, the I.O.D.E., the Canada Council, St. Francis Xavier University, and Sir George Williams University. Finally this book has been published with the help of a grant from the Humanitites Research Council of Canada, using funds provided by the Canada Council.

The combined assistance of these individuals and institutions made possible this book, and to them I am most grateful. I alone am responsible for whatever errors or weaknesses it might still contain.

Belgrade, Yugoslavia
January 1979

Table of Contents

Introduction

If 200,000 volumes on the Napoleonic period have been published, as Jacques Godechot claims, then the first task of this author must be to justify further research into Napoleonic studies.[1] That it is impossible to read all the Napoleonic historiography is an old cliché. That it would be fruitless to read it is a truism that is more to the purpose, for the study of Napoleonic literature reveals that it has three dominant characteristics: an absence of archival research, excessive repetition, and overconcentration on military, diplomatic, and political history and on Napoleon and his family. This concentration has led to the relative neglect of administrative, social, and economic history.

The general absence of research in French administrative history has been noted by Harold T. Parker: "The history of the center—of the growing central administration in France since the Middle Ages—has never been told." Parker discusses this weakness both for the general administrative history of France and for the specific administration of the ministries at the time of Napoleon.[2] A similar opinion is voiced by Jacques Godechot: "The political institutions of the Consulate and Empire are still poorly understood. The Ministries . . . have not been studied."[3]

This study, however, is relevant to the field of diplomatic history as well as Napoleonic administrative studies. The term "diplomatic history" can have two applications. It can mean international affairs as in the relations between two states, their foreign policies, and negotiations; or it can refer to the history of diplomatic institutions. Of these two fields, the former has attracted the attention of many of the best historians of every generation. For the Napoleonic period there are the great interpretative works of Sorel, Driault, Bourgeois, Fugier, and Mowat, and the many excellent monographs on France's relations with various states, plus innumerable studies of specific problems in diplomatic history.

Unfortunately, this diplomatic history has often been written in ignorance of the institutions or personnel responsible for the conduct of diplomacy. Some administrative history is available, but the accounts of Lévi-Mirepoix, Chastenet, Masson, and Outrey are far too superficial to explain adequately the nature of Napoleon's diplomatic service.[4] No one would attempt to explain wars without understanding the armies and generals. Similarly, we cannot understand diplomacy without understanding the diplomats and the organization of the diplomatic services. And, as Jules Cambon has said, "Diplomatists, unlike soldiers, are not as a rule the spoilt children of historians."[5]

The purpose of the present study is to provide a detailed and thorough account of the Ministry of Foreign Affairs and the French diplomatic service at the time of Napoleon. The first task is to discover who the diplomats were; their political, functional, geographical, and social backgrounds; their age, education, and experience; and how the personnel changed over the years. One should understand how they entered diplomacy, who appointed and dismissed them and why, and what training or preparation they had for their career. Did they enter a career open to talent, and if so, how was talent rewarded? The study of rewards will help explain why they entered diplomacy; the study of conditions will reveal what life was like in early nineteenth-century administration. Having entered the diplomatic service, they could work in one of the external missions or in one of the divisions or sections of the Ministry in Paris. Once we know who the diplomats were, who appointed them, what the career was like, and where they worked, we can then discover what they did and how the diplomatic service operated.

A more difficult challenge is to attempt to determine how well the diplomats accomplished their tasks, to draw some conclusions as to the general quality of the service. There is no question whatsoever about the state of historiography on this subject. Historians have repeatedly asserted that Napoleon's entire government deteriorated. In almost any study of Napoleon one can read of the able, brilliant, and independent-minded advisors of the early years being replaced by second-rate flunkeys who told Napoleon only what he wanted to hear. This has a far wider application than Napoleonic or diplomatic studies, for liberal and Marxist historians and social scientists have a tendency to assume that all dictatorial governments will deteriorate through the corruption of power. Often the example used is the alleged decline of the Napoleonic government. This assumption of decline is so widespread that it can be identified as the theory of deterioration in dictatorial government.

It is easy to assert that Napoleon's government declined, and the assertion has always found a ready audience which, for a variety of reasons, is willing to believe it without much reflection. But how does one prove that a government declined? The evidence offered by scores of historians is unacceptably fragile. In fact, it usually consists simply of the statement that several able ministers such as Talleyrand and Fouché were replaced by several inferior men such as Champagny and Savary. A number of questions can be raised about these examples, but even accepting them as valid, would two changes of portfolio prove that an entire government declined? The argument for decline is shot through with weaknesses. Not enough cabinet ministers have been studied. The examples used are questionable. No one has proven that changes in cabinet ministers produced similar changes in the ministries or subordinate personnel. More important, no one has ever proved that Napoleon actually received better advice in the early years of his government.

We can reject the present conclusions about deterioration because of the inadequacy of the evidence, but how does one reach conclusions about the quality of government? This study will offer two criteria. One is to identify the characteristics of a developed government or bureaucracy, and determine to what extent the Napoleonic diplomatic service conformed. The second is to analyze the advice Napoleon actually received to see if the diplomats eventually substituted flattery for good advice. Conclusions drawn from a study of one branch of government are not necessarily valid for the whole government, but they might suggest the lines for possible reconsideration of our opinions about that government.

Napoleon's Diplomatic Service

Chapter 1

The External Service

The modern diplomatic service is the product of centuries of evolution. During the Renaissance, the temporary missions of medieval times were replaced by permanent resident missions. Then in the last four centuries this system of resident embassies, Italian in origin, developed throughout the world.[1]

Before the Revolution France had the most fully developed diplomatic service. The wars of the Revolution, however, led to the destruction of this organization. On the day of Napoleon's coup d'état, France's foreign policy and diplomatic service lay in ruins. The external service consisted of small missions in Spain, Cassel, Ratisbon, and Dresden, and secretaries in Denmark, Holland, and Berlin. Fourteen years later France's foreign policy and diplomatic service once more lay in ruins. The external service consisted of a minister and secretary each in Denmark and the United States, an ambassador in Turkey, and a secretary in Switzerland. The career diplomat Latour-Maubourg expressed the position of all French diplomats: "I can now regard my presence in foreign countries as useless."[2]

Between 1800 and 1814, however, Napoleon had developed the most extensive diplomatic organization the world had yet witnessed. It contained thirty-nine missions reaching from the New World to Asia. They ranged in importance from residences to embassies, in size from a single diplomat to an official household of twenty-three, and in duration from a few months to fourteen years. They were staffed by a regular hierarchy of diplomats of various ranks assisted by secretaries, attachés, students, and miscellaneous staff.

At the Vienna Conference of 1814 the question of rank was settled and diplomats were graded as ambassadors, envoys or ministers plenipotentiary, residents and chargés d'affaires. This four-level classification was the result of centuries of evolution in diplomatic terminology. In the sixteenth century Venice had employed the ranks of ambassador, resident, and agent with or without the qualifying word "ordinary." The resident had only recently surpassed the agent in importance, and was in turn passed in the seventeenth century by the envoy, while both ambassadors and envoys began to attach the term "extraordinary" to their titles. In the eighteenth century the rank of resident dropped to fourth place with the introduction of ministers, ministers resident, and ministers plenipotentiary. At the Peace of Nijmwegen of 1678, the second and third levels were united in the term envoy extraordinary and minister plenipotentiary.[3] This confusion in diplomatic terminology survived into the nineteenth century with at least ten different grades employed in the Napoleonic diplomatic service.[4] They fall, however, into three broad categories depending on the nature of the mission. An embassy was headed by an ambassador or an ambassador extraordinary; a legation by a minister, minister plenipotentiary, minister extraordinary, minister plenipotentiary and envoy extraordinary or, in the absence of one of these, a chargé d'affaires *ad interim*; and a residence was headed by a resident or a chargé d'affaires *en titre*.

Throughout the period the French missions in England, Austria, Spain, and Turkey were headed by ambassadors. Those in Portugal, Poland, and Russia were upgraded to embassies, the former in 1805 in an attempt to prevent Portugal from joining the Third Coalition, the second in 1812 to win greater sacrifices from the Poles. When relations were reestablished with Russia in 1807, Alexander was given the choice of exchanging ministers or ambassadors,[5] and the final title was ambassador extraordinary. By tradition France maintained ambassadors in Holland, Rome, and Naples, but there was considerable fluctuation in the rank of these missions due to their changing status and favor within the Napoleonic system.

Legations, the second level of diplomatic position, were normally headed by ministers plenipotentiary. In Germany they were in charge of missions in Cassel, Dresden, Hamburg, Ratisbon, Salzburg, Stuttgart, and Würzburg. In Italy they represented France in Genoa, Milan, Turin, Lucca, and Malta. The representative in Florence was originally titled minis ter; but Beauharnais signed himself minister plenipotentiary and complained to Talleyrand in a private letter that Florence wanted the latter rank since "Here they believe that the title of minister is inferior to that of minister plenipotentiary."[6] Ministers plenipotentiary were also exchanged with the United States, Switzerland, the Valais, and Persia. Sometimes the prestige of a minister plenipotentiary was raised by adding the title "envoy extraordinary" which presumably implied powers to negotiate. This was true of the more important legations such as Berlin, Munich, or Copenhagen. Clearly there was a great deal of confusion in the ranks of those in charge of legations, a confusion affecting the Ministry, Napoleon, the diplomats themselves, and even the decrees of nomination.

The third level of permanent mission was the residence, headed by a resident or a titular chargé d'affaires. Four missions—Parma, Danzig, Ragusa, and Mecklenburg—were residences throughout their existence. As the embassy network was reestablished, relations were often begun with a chargé d'affaires. Then, if relations improved, a minister could be sent. Frankfort was a residence until 1807, when it became the capital of the Confederation of the Rhine and the mission was upgraded to legation status. France was represented in Hesse-Darmstadt by a chargé d'affaires until 1811, when the Duke of Darmstadt complained that the French diplomat at his court was not of the same rank as those at Baden and Frankfort.[7] The chargé d'affaires was replaced by a minister plenipotentiary.

During the absence of a minister from an embassy or legation, the first secretary became chargé d'affaires *ad interim*. The chief technical difference between a chargé d'affaires and a minister was that the minister was accredited to a sovereign while a chargé d'affaires was accredited to the Minister of Foreign Affairs and could have direct contact with the sovereign only during the relaxed protocol of a military campaign.[8] Four situations could lead to the appointment of a chargé d'affaires *ad interim*: a minister's leave, the temporary break between the recall of a minister and the appointment of another, the establishment or down-grading of an embassy, or the near rupture of relations effected when a minister was recalled and not immediately replaced.

The accredited secretaries took their titles from the missions; an embassy having secretaries of embassy, a legation having secretaries of legation. Napoleon was careless in the use of this terminology when he requested that Mériage be appointed secretary of legation in the Austrian embassy; but even the official decrees were sometimes incorrect.[9] Normally a residence did not have a secretary. Maret suggested that this was a rule;[10] but there were exceptions, such as Parma.

The number of secretaries attached to a mission depended on the importance of that mission. Two embassies, Vienna throughout the period and Russia from 1808 until 1812, had three secretaries. Constantinople began with three secretaries but the number was reduced to two in June 1806, to one in June 1808, and after August 1813 the ambassador was left with no secretaries at all. Teheran was the only legation to have three secretaries. The legations in Amsterdam, Berlin, Copenhagen, Madrid, Philadelphia, Stockholm, and Florence began with two secretaries, but the number was later reduced to one. Seventeen legations had one secretary virtually throughout their existence. In relation to the number of missions, the number of secretarial positions was gradually reduced. This policy reflected two of the principles of Napoleonic administration, the elimination of unnecessary positions and the reduction of costs.

The thirty-nine missions were headed by seventy-one ministers. Forty-seven ministers served in only one mission; fifteen in two missions; eight had three missions; and Alquier had five. Most of the transfers occurred within the same geographical area. Only four ministers served in both northern and southern Europe. The ministerial corps was highly unstable. Twenty-three ministers served less than two years, only nine served more than eight years. On average a minister remained in one post for two years ten months, and their total diplomatic service averaged four years and two months. This ministerial instability was a reflection of the international situation, of the constant ruptures of diplomatic relations, of the use of generals on quasi-military missions, of the constant changes in the embassy network in Italy and Germany, and of normal transfers.

The secretarial corps was more stable than that of the ministers. They were transferred less frequently—forty occupied only one position, and only nine occupied three or more, including promotion within the same embassy. On average the secretaries served Napoleon for four years and eleven months, remaining in each position for over three years. Sixteen secretaries served less than two years; thirteen for over eight. Most transfers of secretaries occurred within the same geographical area; but the more professional ones were freely transferred between northern and southern Europe. As the Italian legations were closed down, three of the secretaries were transferred to Germany. Eleven times the secretaries were changed when a new minister was appointed; but in other cases secretaries were deliberately left in the legations to ensure continuity of policy.

Diplomatic students were given several ranks in the service. According to the *arrêté* of the Year VIII, there were to be two ranks of diplomatic students. Those just beginning in the career would be called aspirants. Then, if they were recommended for a permanent position, they would become *élèves*. In fact, the diplomatic students were never clearly divided into these two categories, and the two terms were used interchangeably. Alquier asked that his son be appointed *élève*; he became an aspirant. In the letter informing Laville and Doucet of their appointments, the word aspirant was crossed out and replaced by *élève*. The diplomats themselves clearly did not know the difference between the two terms, as Clarke referred to his "two students or aspirants," and Larochefoucauld called his diplomatic student an *aspirant élève*.[11] Similarly, there is little difference in the use of these two terms and that of attaché. An attaché was anyone attached to a mission. Normally the term referred to a diplomat's private secretary, but diplomatic students were often called attachés. Consequently, throughout this study, aspirants, *élèves*, and attachés have been classed together as diplomatic students. Approximately forty-five students served in the external service, but there was no pattern to their distribution throughout the missions.

Sometimes a minister had a private secretary as well as a secretary *en titre*. At least ten ministers are known to have had private secretaries, and they served in both large and small missions. Unfortunately practically nothing is known about them. There were various miscellaneous personnel in the embassies in addition to the ministers, official and private secretaries and students. At least nine generals took their aides-de-camp with them. In Persia, Gardane had ten military attachés who had the hopeless task of making an efficient fighting force out of the Persian army.[12] De Pradt in Poland was assisted by four *auditeurs* who were experienced administrators. At least three embassies, Madrid, Warsaw, and Constantinople, employed secretary-interpreters. In Constantinople, Bernard was *chef de dépêches* and *secrétaire expéditionnaire*, grandiose titles for a filing clerk.[13] In Rome, Fesch had an *expéditionnaire* in charge of correspondence and archives.[14] Mattelay claimed that he was *secrétaire géographe* in Constantinople, but added that the title had been invented and was quickly suppressed, and that he had really filled the functions of a fourth secretary![15] Throughout the period Ruffin occupied the position of embassy chancellor in Constantinople. This was a unique appointment in the service involving a combination of consular, political, and diplomatic offices, and reflecting the unique situation of Turkey as well as Ruffin's special qualifications.

Rarely does one find a document that gives the overall size of an embassy, and the picture of the size of the external service has to be painstakingly drawn. Fortunately, several ministers did state how many employees they had. In Switzerland, Verninac had a secretary of legation, a private secretary, and a student. This he claimed was adequate, and an attaché was not needed.[16] In Florence, Clarke's staff included two secretaries, two aides-de-camp, two students, a private secretary, and an *homme d'affaires*.[17] Narbonne had three secretaries, three aides-de-camp, two *auditeurs*, plus the former ambassador's staff.[18] The short-lived Persian legation was the largest in the network. It numbered twenty-four, including the minister, three secretaries, three translators, two missionaries, a doctor, two language students, two aides-de-camp, and ten military attachés.[19] The Russian embassy was, by necessity, one of the largest. Hédouville had two secretaries, three aides-de-camp, three or four private secretaries, eight students, his wife, one of his wife's relatives, and a "proportionate number of domestics." Caulaincourt, according to Adams, "has a family of 65 persons,"[20] and Lauriston, who replaced Caulaincourt, said he was bringing two aides-de-camp, a private secretary, a *maître d'hôtel*, a *chef de cuisine*, and several other domestics.[21] These examples give some idea of the personnel of a French embassy at the beginning of the nineteenth century, but it is impossible to generalize on the size of the embassies.

The French diplomatic network extended throughout central Europe, northern Europe as far as St. Petersburg, and southern Europe from Lisbon to Constantinople. Outside continental Europe, there were missions in England, the United States, Malta, and even Persia. In 1812 the Ministry made plans to establish missions in the soon-to-be independent states of Latin America and Asia, but none of these was opened at the time. The existence, size, and nature of each mission reflected accurately Napoleon's foreign policy. These missions can best be described by tracing the route of the couriers as they delivered their portfolios to the far corners of Europe.

For the couriers on the central European route, the immediate destination would be Bern. Switzerland had been a confederation of independent cantons, but French intervention had led to political unification in the Helvetic Republic. This in turn led to near continuous civil war between the supporters of unified government and the supporters of the federal system. During the first four years, the instability of Swiss politics was reflected in the French legation—five ministers in five years attested the involvement of French diplomats in local politics. By 1802 Napoleon had decided to end the instability of Swiss affairs because the volatile situation interfered with the recruitment of Swiss troops and offered an opportunity for English and Austrian intervention. In preparation for the Act of Mediation, General Ney led a French army into Switzerland. Ney then became French minister, combining military and political control. It took a year to ensure the application of the Act, which, in effect, restored the federal system. Then Ney, on his own request, was recalled. The legation then became stable under ministers Vial (1804–8) and Auguste Talleyrand (1808–14).

The Act of Mediation also led to the creation of a new state and, therefore, of a new diplomatic mission. The Valais, the southernmost canton in Switzerland, included the Simplon pass, vital to France's communications with Italy. To ensure French control, the Valais became "independent" in 1804 with a French chargé d'affaires wielding effective power. By December 1810 Napoleon had grown tired of the façade of independence in the Valais and had arrived at a position where such appearances were no longer thought necessary. On 1 January 1811 the Valais became the French Department of the Simplon; the chargé d'affaires became the prefect.

After delivering his dispatches to the ministers in Switzerland, the courier would set off for the lands of the Hapsburgs. Vienna had long been one of the largest and most important embassies in the French service. The first mission lasted from October 1801 till the beginning of the War of the Third Coalition. After the Treaty of Pressburg of 1806, the war against Russia and Prussia continued, and since Austria presented a threat to Napoleon's southern flank, a general was appointed. His mission ended with Austria's declaration of war in 1809. The third period of diplomatic relations ended in Austria's final declaration of war in 1813. In spite of the three ruptures in relations, the personnel of the embassy was relatively stable, and four of the secretaries were in Vienna for over seven years. The embassy also had a distinct military flavor as two of the ambassadors and four of the secretaries were from the army. As the couriers passed through Austria, they usually encountered a suspicious if not hostile attitude. Crossing into Prussia they experienced, before 1806, a much more friendly reception, one which changed dramatically by 1808.

Prussia had been friendly towards France since 1795, but Napoleon's coup resulted in a change of staff in the Berlin legation. This new diplomatic mission ended abruptly with Prussia's declaration of war in 1806. Prussia had virtually replaced Poland in the old French alliance system, and Napoleon was determined to punish Prussia severely for her defection. By the Treaty of Tilsit, Prussia lost her share of the partitions of Poland plus territories in western Germany, and continued to be administered as a French province. Eventually a French legation was appointed (December 1808) indicating the achievement of a slight degree of Prussian independence. This mission remained until Prussia's final defection in March 1813.

Moving eastward over increasingly treacherous roads, the courier came to the last major outpost of French influence, Warsaw. Napoleon never decided on a Polish policy and his mission in Warsaw reflected this indecision. In 1806–7 Napoleon was faced with the problem of whether or not to restore Poland. Talleyrand argued against it, feeling the Poles too unstable; and a condition of the Tilsit alliance was that Poland would not be restored. But the Russian alliance might not work, and if not, Napoleon wanted an advanced position in central Europe. Therefore in 1807 he compromised by creating the Duchy of Warsaw, which he placed under his ally, the King of Saxony. A chargé d'affaires was maintained in Warsaw from February 1808 until June 1812. The campaign against Russia led to great changes in the Polish mission, upgraded from a residence to an embassy. It actually became one of the largest embassies in the network, with an ambassador, two secretaries, and four *auditeurs*. At Tilsit Prussia had also lost Danzig, which became a "free city." At first diplomatic relations were handled by the French resident in Warsaw. Then, from 1808 until 1813, France was represented in Danzig by a chargé d'affaires. From Danzig the rider continued his seemingly endless journey to St. Petersburg.

An embassy was maintained in St. Petersburg during the short periods of peace between the Second and Third Coalitions and during the period of the Tilsit Alliance. In both cases relations were opened by Napoleon's aides-de-camp, Caulaincourt and Duroc in 1802 and Savary in 1807.

In both cases the missions were headed by generals. The first embassy (1802–4) had two secretaries and eight attachés. The second embassy (1808–12) was designed to cement the Tilsit Alliance. It consisted of Ambassador Caulaincourt and two secretaries who had previously been in Russia, another secretary, and an attaché. Caulaincourt and his successor, Lauriston, did everything possible to prevent the breakdown of the alliance. They failed—in July 1812 the mission was recalled.

The couriers on the northern route passed through Amsterdam, Hamburg, and Copenhagen on their way to Stockholm, capital of one of France's traditional allies. This tradition was rapidly drawing to a close. France was at peace with Sweden for only two short periods between 1799 and 1814. The first followed the general peace of Lunéville and Amiens. Bourgoing, minister in Copenhagen, negotiated the reestablishment of relations and was appointed minister. However, relations quickly deteriorated because of Sweden's reluctance to join the Continental System, and in August 1804 the mission was ordered to return to France.[22] In 1810 Sweden began to favor France, as was indicated by the election of the French Marshal Bernadotte as Crown Prince. From the first the French were sceptical of the success of a diplomatic mission to Stockholm. Four days after his nomination as minister, Alquier was ordered to stay in Paris while relations were opened by the second secretary from Copenhagen acting as chargé d'affaires.[23] Relations were finally broken in 1812 when Sweden decided to join in the "liberation" of Europe, her chief contribution being the conquest of Norway from Napoleon's ally, Denmark.

Since Denmark was as friendly towards France as Sweden was hostile, the legation in Copenhagen was one of the few to be permanently occupied. France desired a Danish alliance because Denmark controlled the Kattegat and Skagerak and was therefore important to the Continental System, and because Denmark had a few ships to offer. Denmark accepted France because of the English threat—Denmark had joined the armed neutrality leagues of 1780 and 1795—because France accepted Danish control of Norway, and perhaps because of the fear of a French attack. Both sides remained loyal to the alliance even in 1812–13 when Denmark might have saved Norway by joining the Allies and when France might have gained a Swedish alliance by offering Norway to Sweden. In spite of the continuity of diplomatic relations, the legation was headed by six different ministers and five times by a chargé d'affaires. The continuity of the legation was maintained by the two Desaugiers brothers, who were first and second secretaries from 1796 to 1811.

The embassy in Amsterdam survived from the period of the Directory until Holland's absorption into the Empire. In September 1799 the Directorial staff, in spite of protests of loyalty to the Consulate and pleas for continuing employment, was replaced. The new mission included a minister who was promoted to ambassador in 1802, two secretaries, and two students. This mission was recalled in 1805 and replaced by an ambassador and a secretary. In 1806 the creation of the Kingdom of Holland under Louis Bonaparte necessitated the appointment of a new ambassador, Larochefoucauld. By 1810 Napoleon had decided to annex Holland. An incident involving an attack on Larochefoucauld's coachman was used as a pretext for recalling the ambassador, and Amsterdam became just another imperial city.

Relations with England were established following the successful negotiations of a preliminary treaty by Otto and the completion of these negotiations at Amiens. The French diplomatic mission, consisting of General Andréossy and a secretary, was in England from November 1802 until June 1803, when relations were again broken. The Peace of Amiens led to two other diplomatic missions. Malta had acquired an immediate importance as a result of the Franco-English duel for the Mediterranean. Napoleon conquered it on the way to Egypt, but inevitably lost it to the English fleet. By the terms of Amiens, England was to withdraw its forces from Malta, so the French opened a diplomatic mission to ensure the neutrality of the fortified island. In fact, the English did not evacuate the island until the 1960s. Their failure to honor the Treaty of Amiens was the pretext for renewed war, and war ended the French mission. The French also opened a mission in Lisbon. All the minister's dispatches confirmed the French opinion that Portugal was England's only European colony. War with England ended this mission.

France maintained only one diplomatic mission in the new world, that in the United States. This mission, located first at Philadelphia and later at Washington, was one of the few to remain stable throughout the period. It was originally headed by a chargé d'affaires, but he was recalled to make way for a permanent minister, Turreau. After eight years in the United States, and after several requests for a recall, Turreau was replaced by Serurier, who had been secretary for ten years and was to remain in the United States under the Bourbons. In addition to this permanent diplomatic mission, Napoleon employed a diplomatic agent in Buenos

Aires. This mission was in anticipation of the independence of the Latin American states, a development Napoleon foresaw.

A mission was maintained in Madrid throughout the period, but the instability of Spanish politics led to instability in the personnel of the embassy. Shortly after the coup, Talleyrand reported that the entire embassy would have to be replaced because the diplomats had become identified with the various Spanish factions. The first mission arrived in March 1800. Nine months later it was replaced by Lucien Bonaparte and his secretary. France and Spain had decided to attack Portugal and force her to break relations with England. The Franco-Spanish army was commanded by General Gouvion St. Cyr, who, upon Lucien's recall, became ambassador. The successful completion of this war ended Gouvion's mission, and the embassy passed to Beurnonville (1802–6), then Beauharnais (1806–8). Throughout this period the King was too stupid to rule and too greedy to abdicate, so effective power was wielded by the Queen's lover, the unpopular Godoy. Equally greedy for power was the King's son, whose incompetence had not yet been demonstrated. Under such government Spain could hardly be an effective satellite. The situation led to Napoleon's intervention in Spain, and the appointment of Joseph Bonaparte as King. The Spaniards, however, preferred old French Bourbons to new French Bonapartes. But while the guerilla war raged, the diplomatic situation was stabilized. Laforest remained ambassador from 1808 until 1813, when he negotiated the withdrawal of the French and the restoration of the Spanish Bourbons.

At the beginning of 1800 Naples was at war with France. Napoleon's victories made a continuation of the war impossible for the Neapolitan Bourbons. Peace negotiations were conducted by Alquier and Durant, who were then appointed minister and secretary in Naples. This mission ended when Naples joined the Third Coalition in violation of her treaties with France. The Neapolitan Bourbons would not serve as French satellites, so they were replaced by someone who would, namely Joseph Bonaparte and later Caroline Bonaparte and her husband, Marshal Murat. Murat proved a little too independent, expecially in launching a disastrous attack on Sicily without Napoleon's approval. Relations deteriorated to the point that the French minister was recalled. A chargé d'affaires headed the embassy for two years, and the last minister stayed in Naples until the spring of 1814.

Some of the couriers who went to Vienna turned southeast towards the Ottoman Empire. After 1806 their first stop was Ragusa, today's holiday resort of Dubrovnik. By the Treaty of Pressburg with Austria, France gained control of the Adriatic coast as far as Ragusa, earlier an independent merchant republic, which had become an important Mediterranean port during the Revolutionary and Napoleonic wars. Napoleon decided to establish a diplomatic post, and in 1806 a chargé d'affaires was appointed. This mission ended with the absorption of Ragusa into the Empire.

Immediately south of Ragusa, the courier entered the lands of the Ottoman Empire for the dangerous and long trip to Constantinople. In November 1799 France and Turkey were at war because of the Egyptian campaign. After peace negotiations, French influence was re-established by General Brune with a mission of three secretaries, consular agents, and various miscellaneous staff. After two years Brune was recalled because Turkey would not recognize Napoleon as Emperor. The entire embassy was changed when General Sébastiani was appointed in 1806 to bring Turkey into the war against Russia. Sébastiani was successful, but his work was destroyed by Napoleon's change of policy at Tilsit. Sébastiani was recalled in 1808, the first secretary went to Persia on mission, and the embassy was conducted by the second secretary as chargé d'affaires. This situation revealed the disastrous consequences to the diplomatic service of the rapidly changing policies of Napoleon, and in turn, the disastrous consequences to foreign policy of the confused situation in the diplomatic service. For in 1812, when France desperately needed a Turkish alliance, she was represented in Constantinople by a thirty-one year old secretary. He pleaded for the dispatch of a fully accredited ambassador, but the ambassador did not arrive until it was too late to bring Turkey into the war. He was still in Constantinople at the time of the first abdication, usefully spending his time in geological research.

The worst route for the couriers had always been the one to Constantinople. After 1807 it was rendered doubly dangerous by extending it to Persia. The exigencies of the war against England and Russia led Napoleon to contemplate a Persian alliance, the purpose of which was to produce a military diversion on Russia's Georgian frontier and possibly to serve as a base for an overland attack on India. The mission was entrusted to General Gardane, Napoleon's aide-de-camp. He had as secretaries his brother Paul and Rousseau, both consular agents from the Middle East, plus twenty other persons. The *raison d'être* of the mission, the war with Russia, disappeared before the mission ever arrived. Gardane had to emphasize the anti-English aspect of the alliance, the part to which the Persians were totally indifferent. After a year's effort Gardane returned without a recall, and the embassy gradually straggled back across the deserts to Europe. The mission was indicative not only of the imagination and force which characterized Napoleon's conduct of foreign policy, but also of the instability and waste resulting from Napoleon's rapidly changing policies.

At the time of the coup d'état of 18 Brumaire, the armies of the Second Coalition were triumphant in northern Italy. The French had been driven out of the peninsula except for Massena's army under siege in Genoa, and the French-inspired republics had collapsed one by one. Austro-Russian control was broken by the campaign of 1800 and the republics were restored. On 2 June Milan was occupied, on 4 June an administration was created, and on 24 June Petiet, the Revolutionary Minister of War who had accompanied the French armies as intendant-general, was appointed minister. Petiet was minister until March 1805, when the Italian Republic, as it had been called since 1802, became the Italian Kingdom and effective power passed from the hands of the French minister to those of the French Viceroy.

Until September 1800 Piedmont shared the same fate as the Cisalpine Republic. It was taken from Austrian control in July 1800. On 24 July General Jourdan was appointed minister with a role and powers similar to those of Petiet. In April 1801 the façade of independence was ended. Piedmont became a French military division, and, although Jourdan's position remained the same, his rank changed from minister to administrator-general.[24] The history of the diplomatic mission in Genoa, or the Ligurian Republic, was similar. Massena, under siege in Genoa, capitulated on 6 June 1800, and Austria imposed a government which survived for two weeks. On 23 June the French established an administration; on 29 June General Dejean was placed in control with the title of minister plenipotentiary. This satellite was governed by the French minister until 1805, when it, too, was absorbed into the French Empire. Similarly, Lucca and Parma experienced short periods as satellites before absorption into the Empire.

Tuscany, under the Archduke Ferdinand, brother of Francis II of Austria, had supported Austria in the War of the Second Coalition. Napoleon was determined to destroy the influence of the Hapsburgs in Italy, and at Lunéville Ferdinand lost Tuscany to become Elector of Salzburg. At the time Napoleon was attempting to dominate Italy through the old Bourbon "pacte de famille," with himself playing the part of French Bourbon. By the Second Treaty of San Ildefonso, a Bourbon became King of Tuscany. Thus a French legation was maintained in Florence from September 1801 until October 1807, when Tuscany joined the Empire.

A legation was maintained in Rome during the same period. Cacault, a French diplomat with years of experience in Italy, became minister in April 1801, after negotiating the reestablishment of relations. By mid-1803 the Concordat and the general peace had led to such an improvement in relations that Cacault was replaced by Cardinal Fesch. This period of harmonious relations did not survive the strains placed on the Pope's temporal power by the Continental System and the Wars of the Third and Fourth Coalitions. Early in 1806 Fesch was replaced by Alquier, and in the spring of 1808 the Papal states entered the Empire.

When Napoleon came to power all but three of the French legations in Germany had disappeared. The three exceptions were Cassel, Dresden, and Ratisbon, seat of the German Diet. Napoleon immediately set to work to reestablish the diplomatic service in Germany, a task made possible by the defeat of Austria and the Treaty of Lunéville. In the north a mission existed in Cassel when Napoleon assumed power. Unfortunately, Cassel joined Prussia in the war of 1806. Such "disloyalty" could not go unpunished. The Duke was deposed; his land was joined to Hanover and some Prussian territory to form the Kingdom of Westphalia under Jerome Bonaparte. Diplomatic relations were established in November 1808 with a legation that included the experienced diplomats Reinhard and Lefebvre. To the north and west of Cassel lay the Circle of Lower Saxony or the Hanseatic Cities of Hamburg (site of the French residence), Lübeck, Bremen, and the Dukes of Brunswick and Mecklenburg. A permanent French mission was established in Hamburg in 1802. Later on it became impossible to prevent smuggling through Hamburg, so the execution of the Continental System dictated the absorption of the Hanseatic Cities into France (December 1811). However, Mecklenburg, which was not absorbed, had been included with the Hanseatic Cities, so a new legation was created for the Baltic Coast of Germany. This mission collapsed in March of 1813 when Prussia joined the Fifth Coalition.

The first new mission opened in 1800 was to the Circle of Swabia, which consisted of Baden and Württemberg, with residence in Karlsruhe. The minister, appointed even before the Austrians had withdrawn, claimed that only an army could deliver him to his residence.[25] As Napoleon's German policy developed, this mission was divided, the former minister staying in Karlsruhe, a new one being appointed to Stuttgart, Württemberg. Just north of Karlsruhe a new legation was established in Darmstadt, but again the new minister had to wait until the Austrian army retreated before taking up his position. These three legations remained permanently occupied until the autumn of 1813.

The French legation in Dresden, Saxony, had not been affected by the War of the Second Coalition, though Napoleon did change ministers, a career diplomat being replaced by General La Valette, one of Napoleon's comrades from the Army of Italy. In 1806 diplomatic relations were broken when Saxony was forced to join Prussia. Saxony was not punished for her defection, but gained in territory while her Elector became King. In southern Germany, Bavaria had fought against France in 1799 and 1800. Peace negotiations were conducted by Laforest and Marandet, who then became minister and secretary to Munich in July 1802. After that Bavaria became a loyal French ally and was rewarded with vast increases in territory and promotion from Electorate to Kingdom. In 1813 Bavaria changed sides in time to retain many of the fruits of subordination to Napoleon. Saxony, unfortunately, remained loyal, at great cost in population and territory. The French left Dresden in September 1813 and Munich in November.

In addition to these legations, there were five minor missions in central Germany. Since the Diet of the Holy Roman Empire met at Ratisbon, France had a small mission there. Curiously, it contained both a minister and a chargé d'affaires, a situation unique in the diplomatic service. The Empire was suppressed by Napoleon in 1806 and replaced with the French-dominated Confederation of the Rhine. The French diplomats were transferred from Ratisbon to Frankfort, the capital of this Confederation, where they joined a legation which had been open since 1801. A new minister was appointed to Salzburg when, during the secularization of Germany, that bishopric was given to the Hapsburg Archduke Ferdinand of Tuscany. In 1806 the Archduke and the legation were transferred to Würzburg. The last mission established in Germany was attached to the Saxon Princes of Weimar, Gotha, Koburg, and Meringen. The mission, with main residence in Weimar, was established in 1811 when Napoleon began exerting his influence over Germany in preparation for the Russian campaign. These legations—Frankfort, Würzburg, and Weimar—ended during the German campaign of 1813 when, from east to west, the German rulers changed sides in direct proportion to the proximity of the Russian and Prussian armies.

By the time of the Napoleonic period the French diplomatic service had evolved a fairly sophisticated organization. In the north it included permanent missions in Copenhagen, Stockholm, and St. Petersburg; in western Europe there were missions in Amsterdam, London, Lisbon, Madrid, and in the United States in Washington. It contained large missions in Rome, Naples, and Florence, plus minor ones in the small northern states around the cities of Turin, Genoa, Milan, Parma, and Lucca. There was a permanent embassy in Constantinople, and temporary legations in Malta, Ragusa, and Teheran. There were four missions in the non-German areas of central Europe, in Berne, the Valais, Warsaw, and in Danzig after 1808. Fifteen German states were acknowledged by the exchange of diplomatic relations, the French representatives residing in the cities of Berlin, Hamburg, Mecklenburg, Cassel, Dresden, Frankfort, and Weimar in northern Germany, and in Vienna, Karlsruhe, Stuttgart, Darmstadt, Würzburg, Munich, Ratisbon, and Salzburg in southern Germany. These missions were staffed by about seventy heads of mission using at least ten different ranks, who were assisted by sixty secretaries plus numerous private secretaries, students, and attachés of various kinds. The Napoleonic wars and the constant changes in policy rendered this network highly unstable. Nevertheless, the thirty-nine missions represented a well-organized diplomatic service stretching over the entirety of Europe as well as the United States and Persia.

Chapter 2

The Ministry in Paris

Change, turmoil, confusion—such was the fate of the Ministry of Foreign Affairs as a result of the French Revolution.[1] Every new political faction, every new Foreign Minister had ideas to test and friends to place. When Foreign Minister Talleyrand resigned in 1799, his successor, Reinhard, introduced still another reorganization to the Ministry. Curiously this organization was quite reminiscent of the pre-Revolutionary days. It was, as Frédéric Masson said, "the system of 1789."[2] The Ministry, like so many aspects of the Revolution, had come full cycle. And, since Napoleon's Foreign Ministers changed little, "the system of 1789" was inherited by the restored Bourbons. Some change was inevitable, for the restless genius of the Emperor constantly sought improvements in all French institutions. One such change was of name, from the Ministry of External Relations to the Ministry of Foreign Affairs. One suspects that changes of this nature are effected by bureaucrats who relieve the monotony of their routines by changing the letterheads on their stationery. Since both these names are rather long, and since the popular name "Quai d'Orsay" was not then applicable, it will be referred to here simply as the Ministry.

At the time of Napoleon's coup d'état, the Ministry of Foreign Affairs in Paris consisted of six divisions—two political ones, Archives, Consulates, Finances, and Codes.[3] This six-division organization was maintained essentially throughout the Napoleonic period. The two political divisions were named the North (First) and South (Second) Divisions. The demarcation between the two was mainly, but not entirely, geographic. Besides the six regular divisions with their salaried personnel of *chefs, sous chefs*, and *commis*, there were a variety of miscellaneous personnel in the Ministry, including geographical engineers, a bureau for military statistics, translators, couriers, *garçons*, supernumeraries, a doctor, a surgeon, an architect, and a clock-maker.[4]

A clear statement of the duties and functions of the members of the political divisions was made in Article 2 of the *arrêté* of 9 January 1812 on the organization of the Ministry.[5] The employees had to analyze all dispatches from French missions abroad and those from foreign missions in Paris. They had to write the ministerial dispatches, draw up instructions for the external agents and negotiators, and write notes to foreign governments. They were responsible for drafting memoirs on those legal points necessary for foreign affairs, for examining complaints and petitions, and for making reports on regulations for the conduct of the external agents. Finally, they had to write an annual résumé of all the affairs treated in the previous year and of those not yet completed.

In 1799 the North Division handled all political correspondence with England, Holland, Austria, Prussia, Russian, Denmark, Sweden, and the German states. The South Division was concerned with Spain, Portugal, Turkey, Switzerland, and the states of the Italian peninsula. The United States was handled by the North until 1802, then by the South.[6] The division was political as well as geographic, for the most important countries were handled by the North Division. In May 1803 England was transferred from the North to the South. The main reason given was that since Hauterive, *chef* of the South, was an expert on English affairs, England should be in his division.[7] At the same time Switzerland was transferred to the North. This change reestablished the exact demarcation existing in 1797 when Talleyrand first became minister.

In 1812 an attempt was made to divide the two political divisions into four: for the North, Center, East, and West.[8] Possibly the chief interest of this plan was the anticipation of diplomatic missions in Asia and Latin America. It represented both the foresight and the impracticability of Napoleon's schemes. The plan was never fully applied and had disappeared by 1814. The First Restoration found the political divisions organized as they had been in 1797 or 1789.

The two political divisions were relatively unstable in both size and personnel. The North Division consisted of a *chef*, a *sous chef*, and between four and seven *commis*. Three persons held the position of *chef*. Hauterive, who had been in the Ministry for eleven years, was transferred

almost immediately to the South Division. The second *chef* was Joseph
Durant, a diplomat of six years experience. In 1805 Durant became minister at Stuttgart, allegedly an exile for accepting bribes during the reorganization of Germany.[9] Durant was replaced by Labesnardière, promoted
from *sous chef* of the Consulates Division, where he had been since 1797.
The North also had three *sous chefs*. Of the *commis*, Barthel served
throughout the period, Duault for over thirteen years, and five *commis*
served for over six years.

The South Division was as unstable as the North. It consisted of a *chef*,
a *sous chef*, and from three to eight *commis*. The size varied between five
and ten. Jacob, *chef* at the time of the coup, was soon appointed secretary
in Spain, being replaced by Hauterive from the North Division. When
Hauterive was appointed *chef* of the Archives Division in 1807, Roux,
first *commis* until 1800 and *sous chef* since then, was promoted to the top
position. Fifteen *commis* served in the Division, but only four lasted more
than eight years. Of the twenty who worked in the South, only Roux
remained there from 1799 to 1814.

The Consulates Division had belonged to the Ministry of Marine until
14 February 1793, when it was transferred with all of its staff to Foreign
Affairs. This transfer marked the growing importance of economic matters in foreign affairs and the tendency to concentrate all relations with
foreign countries in one Ministry.[10] It also reflected the clarity in ministerial responsibilities that came about during the Revolution. The division handled all correspondence with the consular agents, political
litigations over captured foreign ships, passports, the execution of the
Continental System (certificates of origin, permits, licences), correspondence relative to external commerce, the application of the principles of
maritime law, the keeping of tables of external commerce and navigation,
and the training of interpreters. The division remained unchanged until
the administrative reorganization of 9 January 1812, when it was divided
into two sections headed by the *chef* of the division and a *chef adjoint*.
This plan was never fully applied, and is significant only in identifying
the execution of the Continental System as a distinct and important function of the Ministry.[11]

At the time of the coup, the Consulates Division consisted of seven
employees. The *chef*, d'Hermand, a former consular agent, was still in office in 1814. Two men held the position of *sous chef*. In June 1806 the
division was enlarged with the appointment of three additional *commis*,

an increase probably dictated by the expansion of the Continental System. Of the eighteen persons who served in the division, six stayed for fourteen years, two for ten years, five for five or more years. The size of the division after 1800 varied between eight and ten until 1806 and was twelve after that date. The ranks were always the same: a *chef*, a *sous chef*, Brulé at the passports section, and from five to nine *commis*. The Consulates Division was highly stable and quite isolated from the other divisions.

The Codes Division was the smallest section in the Ministry. It was headed throughout the period by Campy. The division operated without a *sous chef* until August 1807. Between 1809 and August 1811 Baudard occupied the position of *chef adjoint*, a rank unique to this division. The limited size and unique function of this division rendered it slightly inferior to the other sections of the Ministry. The division achieved, as Masson remarked,[12] absolute stability, centering upon Campy (serving from 1772 to 1825), and the three *commis* Cornillot (1766 to 1814), Lebartz (1756 to 1807), and Desnaux (1798 to 1808). From 1799 to 1814 Finet was *colleur de chiffre*, the functions of which are unknown.

The Finances Division handled all of the financial matters of the Ministry, the records, budgets, internal and external salaries whether diplomatic or consular, the endorsement of treaties, plus the laws and decrees of the government.[13] The Finances Division consisted of a *chef*, *sous chef*, and between four and seven *commis*; and after the first year the size never varied from six to seven employees. Ten days after Napoleon's coup, the *chef*, Laforest, was transferred to the postal bureau and then the external service, being replaced by Bresson, *chef* throughout the period. The stability is indicated by the fact that three persons served throughout the period, and a further four for over eleven years. Most of the personnel changes occurred within the first year, and after December 1802 there was only one retirement and one compensating appointment. The Finances Division, like the Consulates and Codes divisions, was quite isolated from the other divisions.

The Archives Division was relatively unstable both in its organization and in its personnel. There were three *chefs*: Resnier, who was replaced shortly after Napoleon's coup, Caillard, *chef* until his death in 1807, and Hauterive, who remained *chef* until 1830. There was one *sous chef* till 1802 and between 1807 and 1811, none between 1802 and 1807, and two after 1811. The position of *sous chef* in Archives depended on the personnel available and was not a regular position. The Archives section

contained a number of ranks unique to itself. Tessier, and later Hauterive, was director of diplomatic students. Rosenstiel and Mathieu were
publicists, presumably engaged in propaganda; Mathias was the librarian;
Sautereau was *analyseur*; and there was a geographer. Of the twenty employees who worked in the division, only three remained from 1799 to
1814. The total size of the division rose steadily as the propaganda functions of the Ministry increased: it counted six employees in 1800, eight or
nine from 1802 to 1809, and eleven or twelve after that date. The personnel of the Archives was closely related to that of the two political
divisions, six employees being recruited from them, one from the Codes
Division. No persons were transferred out of Archives. It contained the
older and more experienced members; it was a repository for experience
as well as records.

Propaganda was a major weapon in Napoleon's struggle for Europe.
Much of that propaganda originated in the Archives Division of the Ministry. The senior employee, Hauterive, wrote a 350-page book on the state
of France in 1800 explaining the European situation, France's relations
with her allies, with neutrals, and with the enemy states, and discussing
the internal situation in France. The book was well written and well
argued with that excellent balance between truth and exaggeration that is
the hallmark of good propaganda. A similar work was the annual report
Talleyrand gave to the Legislative Corps on the state of Europe and
French policy. The main organ of Napoleonic propaganda was the *Moniteur*, the official government newspaper. By a decree of 27 November
1810, the Foreign Minister was to write daily articles for the *Moniteur*
on European ruling families, foreign policy, military movements, or trade.
These articles were designed to destroy the "false" information in the
foreign press, and would be "non-official."[14] In addition to this regular
news service, the Foreign Minister inserted articles in the *Moniteur* on
Napoleon's instructions, and the ambassadors and ministers had to provide information to the foreign newspapers.

Within the Archives Division much of this propaganda came from
the *bureau historique*, formerly known as the *bureau des analyses histori-
ques*. This bureau, headed by Tessier, had been summarizing the most important correspondence and negotiations of the eighteenth century, a
project which had been used as a method of instruction for the diplomatic
students. In 1812 this activity was transferred to the bureau responsible
for the collection, classification, and analysis of newspapers, pamphlets,

and all other information on the commerce, power, politics, and policies of England, information which was used in anti-English propaganda for the Continent. In addition, the new bureau of historical analysis included the other employees in various parts of the service who were working on England and even persons outside the Ministry who were collecting information on England. The new bureau drafted works in which the cause and interest of the government was defended against the "malicious" attacks of jealous countries and of France's enemies. It was, in short, a reorganization of the entire propaganda wing of the Archives indicating the new importance given to propaganda by the Napoleonic government as well as the identification of England as the chief enemy of France.[15]

In addition to the six regular divisions, the Ministry contained several specific sections. One of these comprised the regular couriers. The interpreters for Oriental languages, known as *drogmans*, were trained by and attached to the *École des Jeunes de langues*. There had long been a *bureau des ingénieurs géographes* responsible for obtaining technical information on maritime and military matters. More important, especially under Napoleon, was the bureau of statistical information and naval movements. This section, which had existed at least since 1805, was formalized by a decree of 7 November 1810. It was responsible for obtaining and organizing information on foreign military and naval forces and movements, and consisted of one *auditeur* from the Council of State and two *commis*. During the campaign of 1812 and 1813 the *auditeur* Lelorgue was attached to Napoleon's headquarters where he spent half a million francs from the secret service fund.[16] Napoleon may have thought the bureau useful, but Picard claimed in 1814 that he had vegetated in *"un emploi médiocre."* This statistical bureau was suppressed in 1814, reestablished in 1817, then suppressed, and established again in 1833.[17]

Finally there was a section to handle relations between the Ministry and the Office of External Relations in the Council of State. The Council of State, as recreated in December 1799, consisted of five sections—War, Marine, Finances, Interior, and Legislation. There was no section for foreign affairs because the Council was concerned with administration and the formation of internal policy. The administration of the diplomatic service required few changes, and external policy was a matter for Napoleon and the Foreign Minister to decide. When Hauterive, the senior member of the Ministry, was appointed to the Council in 1805, he was attached to the interior section but was told that he would remain at the

Ministry.[18] The Ministry would then have a representative on the Council of State, but he would not be a full-time member. All of the *auditeurs* attached to the Ministry were members of the Office. The only activity of this Office came when administrative matters relevant to the diplomatic service were debated in the Council of State; it had no influence over the diplomats or foreign policy.[19]

On 18 Brumaire, Year VIII, the Ministry consisted of the Foreign Minister, Reinhard, and forty-two employees. Reinhard, a Württemberger, entered France in 1787 as tutor to a Protestant's children in Bordeaux. He joined the Girondins and, through their influence, entered diplomacy as first secretary in England where Talleyrand was also employed in French diplomacy. During the Revolution, Reinhard also held the positions of secretary in Naples, *chef de bureau* in the Ministry, and minister to Hamburg and Florence. When Talleyrand resigned the Foreign Ministry in July 1799, Reinhard replaced him—the only time in French history that a German held the position of Foreign Minister. There was no diplomatic activity during Reinhard's Ministry because of the War of the Second Coalition, but as mentioned, Reinhard did effect a reorganization of the Ministry. Shortly after the coup (21 November) Reinhard was appointed to the external service, where he served for the next thirty years. He was replaced by Talleyrand, whose career began in 1792 with a short and unsuccessful mission to England. As Minister of Foreign Affairs for the Directory, Talleyrand presided over a disastrous foreign policy; but under him as Napoleon's Foreign Minister (22 November 1799 to 8 August 1807), French diplomacy went from triumph to triumph. His greatest success was in negotiating the Treaties of Vienna of 1814 and 1815. After 1830 he came out of retirement to negotiate with England the independence of Belgium.

The Ministry which Talleyrand was called to in November had reverted to the basic organization of 1789, but the effects of the Revolution on personnel were more difficult to erase. In his introduction to the *arrêté* of 3 Floréal, Year VIII, for the stabilization of the personnel, Hauterive described the sorry state of the employees of the Ministry. Through their attempts at reorganization, the Revolutionaries had destroyed the old administration. These attempts had caused instability, uncertainty, insufficient funds, abuses in expenses, audacity and insolence on the part of the factions, and fickleness in the government. Hauterive called for stability of personnel and organization, for an end to experimentation and political interference, for discipline, for more control from above and less confusion below. He wanted a stable system of pay, security of employment, promotion through four established ranks, and reward for excellence. His proposals were never applied,[20] so the achievement of a stable administration must be indicated by an examination of the personnel of the Ministry. Hauterive's report, however, is extremely important in another respect. Napoleon is often given credit for bringing stability to the French administration or, alternately, is condemned for introducing too much authoritarianism. This report makes it clear that the tendency towards stability, discipline, and authority was encouraged by and welcome to the administration. In fact, it would not have been possible without the active support of the bureaucracy.

The most profound change of personnel occurred immediately after Napoleon's coup. At that time there were forty-two employees in the Ministry: within ten months twelve had been removed and eight new ones appointed. At the top level three *chefs* were replaced, one was transferred, only two held their positions. Two of the *commis* became secretaries of legation, and six others left the service altogether. Thus only thirty of the original forty-two employees survived the first year of the Napoleonic administration. The appointment of eight new employees brought the Ministry to thirty-eight at the end of the Year VIII.

By September 1800 comparative stability had been attained. There were six appointments in the first month, plus two retirements, leaving the Ministry with forty-two employees. In the Year X there were three new appointments and one retirement. The size of the Ministry again increased in the Year XI—eight appointments and one dismissal—bringing it to forty-eight persons. Eight of the appointments of the first four years were simply the reappointment of persons who had previously been in the Ministry, and marked the deliberate attempt to recruit the personnel of the Old Regime and of the Revolution. The Ministry continued to grow, numbering fifty-three by 1806. Other personnel changes constituted normal retirement and a few transfers between divisions.

The greatest change in personnel, apart from those of the first year, occurred in 1807. On 9 August Talleyrand became Vice Grand Elector. Historians have never agreed on whether this was a promotion or a dismissal or whether Talleyrand desired it or not.[21] One common fallacy is to regard his departure from the Ministry as a departure from the government. In fact, he remained one of the chief members of the government and was still advising Napoleon as late as 1813. At any rate, he was re-placed by Jean Baptiste Nompère de Champagny (1756 to 1834). After twelve years in the Royal Navy, Champagny entered the Estates General as a deputy for the nobility. Joining the Third Estate, he played a great part in the reorganization of the navy. In 1800 Napoleon appointed him to the Council of State in the Marine Section. His diplomatic experience consisted of three years as ambassador to Vienna, and he came to the Ministry of Foreign Affairs after three years as Minister of the Interior. His social, military, political, diplomatic, and administrative background was excellent for the post, and he presided over the most successful years of Napoleonic diplomacy. The period when he was Minister coincided with the peak of Napoleon's power, with France dominant from Spain to Poland. It was also a period of relative peace, marred only by the develop-ment of the Spanish insurrection, which arose out of policies adopted be-fore Champagny's appointment, and by the war of 1809 with Austria, which resulted from the failure of the Erfurt Congress, a failure for which Talleyrand must take the main responsibility. Administratively, there were no major changes under Champagny, but only the continuation of or working out of policies adopted before 1807.

Only one change of personnel resulted directly from the appointment of a new Foreign Minister. Osmond had been Talleyrand's chief secretary with the rank of *sous chef*. On the same day Champagny was appointed, Osmond left the Ministry and was replaced by Posuel de Verneaux, who had been Champagny's secretary in Austria and at the Ministry of the In-terior. A change at the top was necessitated by the death of Caillard, *chef* of the Archives, in April. Hauterive was transferred to Caillard's position, and was replaced as *chef* of the South Division by the direct promotion of his *sous chef*, Roux. Three new *sous chefs* were appointed, there were two other transfers, two other appointments, and Lebartz retired after fifty years of service. These changes left the Ministry with a new Minister, six *chefs*, six *sous chefs*, eight other ranks, and thirty-three *commis*, a total personnel of fifty-three. The Ministry was then relatively stable until 1811.

On 17 April 1811 Champagny was replaced by Maret, Duc de Bassano. The change was probably dictated by the new policy towards Russia (Alexander I also changed Foreign Ministers), and Champagny would have us believe that he opposed the anti-Russian policy. It is also evident that Napoleon was increasingly critical of Champagny's administration of foreign affairs.[22] Again the change represented a cabinet shuffle—Maret had been Secretary of State or chief executive in the government since 1799, a position of cabinet rank. During the Revolution Maret had been mainly involved in diplomacy. As Secretary of State he had accompanied Napoleon everywhere and had been involved in foreign affairs at the negotiations of Tilsit, Bayonne, Erfurt, and Vienna, and, as the intermediary between Napoleon and the Foreign Minister, was perfectly familiar with foreign affairs.

The change in ministers does not appear to have affected the personnel very much. There were no changes in the *chefs*, *sous chefs* or ranks other than *commis*, and only one minor transfer took place. Two minor appointments were made, and seven *commis* were dismissed. Two of these had only recently been appointed. Guillois, seventy-six years of age and with fifty-three years of service, probably took the opportunity of retiring, as did Guyétard, aged sixty-six. Only Posuel was directly affected by the change at the top for as the Minister's private secretary he left with Champagny. The dismissals and transfers reduced the Ministry to forty-nine. There were few changes in 1811–12. Then in June 1812 the Ministry underwent the only fundamental reorganization during the Napoleonic period, as explained in the previous sections. Apart from a few changes in names and ranks, only two new persons were added to the Ministry. By 1814 the old organization had reappeared and the two new *sous chefs* had left, reducing the Ministry to forty-six.

The disasters of the campaign of 1812 and 1813 finally forced Napoleon to negotiate for peace. The change in policy dictated a change in Foreign Minister. Maret returned as Secretary of State, and the Ministry passed to Caulaincourt, a general, Napoleon's aide-de-camp, Grand Equerry since 1806 and Grand Marshal since 1813, Duc de Vicence, ambassador to Russia 1807 to 1811, and, what was most important, a staunch proponent of peace, personal friend of Alexander I of Russia, and known opponent of the policy of 1812. In fact, the change is less dramatic than has often been suggested, for Caulaincourt had already performed the functions of minister in April and May of 1813 when he was with Napoleon on campaign and Maret was in Paris.[23] He had been negotiating with the Allies since the summer of 1813 (the Armistice of Pleswitz and the Congress of Prague), and as Foreign Minister, he had negotiated the Treaty of Châtillon which was favorable to France but which Napoleon refused to sign. In the absence of pay records for 1813, we do not know of any personnel changes resulting from Caulaincourt's appointment, but by January 1814 Maret's reorganization had disappeared, the Ministry had gained two *commis* plus a Secretariat Division consisting of a *chef* and four *commis*. The *chef* was Rayneval, Caulaincourt's first secretary in Russia. The final size of the Ministry at the time of Napoleon's abdication was fifty-three, eleven more than in 1799 and two less than the fifty-five employees of 1809. The First Restoration accommodated its followers by making new appointments rather than by replacing Napoleonic employees, so that the Ministry grew to seventy-three by June 1814, and still numbered sixty-four in January 1819.

Movement between divisions and between the internal and external service has already been mentioned in individual cases, but it remains to establish the degree and nature of this mobility. Within the Ministry there were seventeen transfers between divisions involving fourteen persons. Two of them, in the Year VIII, involved persons who shortly left the Ministry, and were therefore of no consequence, except in further illustrating the instability of that year. Five of the transfers occurred between the two political divisions, and six more represented the recruitment of persons for the Archives. The other four transfers involved senior employees of the Ministry. Three of the divisions, Consulates, Finances, and Codes, were, therefore, almost completely isolated. Aside from the diplomatic students who were trained in the Ministry before appointment to the external service, there was very little contact between the internal and external personnel, in sharp contrast to modern practice. During the War of the Second Coalition a number of unemployed external agents were given positions in the Ministry, but as legations were established, they were sent back to the external service. André Durant was the only employee who transferred regularly between the two services. The internal and external services were distinct careers, and transfers between them were exceptions to the rule.

One of the main themes of Masson's study of the Ministry is the stability of personnel and the fact that the bureaucracy, while tampered with, came through the Revolution relatively unscathed. Masson's method, wholly narrative, consisted of tracing individual careers throughout the period and mentioning how certain *commis* were employed for great lengths of time. While this method is useful, we must ask more searching questions about the Napoleonic bureaucracy: how many employees served throughout the period? What proportion were they of the total staff? How many employees served for only a short time? How long was the average employee in the Ministry?

Ninety-three men worked in Napoleon's Ministry of Foreign Affairs. Of them, one-quarter served throughout the period, almost 60% for over seven years, and a further 20% for three to six years. Of the fifteen who served less than one year, twelve were dismissed during the first year of reorganization. There were only seventeen transfers between divisions, roughly one per year. The overall stability is even more impressive. Of these ninety-three employees, over one-quarter were in the Ministry for more than thirty years, and half for over ten years, the average length of service being seventeen years.[24] These figures do not include years of service in other branches of government or in the consular or external service. During the period each employee served an average of almost eight years, and transfer or promotion was so infrequent that the average stay in each position was six years. Personnel stability may have been a principle of Napoleonic administration—it was also a well-established principle of the French bureaucracy.

The *arrêté* of 3 Floréal, Year VIII provided for a regular system of promotion, but with the high degree of stability there was little vertical movement. In fact, twenty-eight of the employees held the same positions for over ten years, many of these lasting the entire period. Roux and Labesnardière moved up from *sous chef* to *chef*, both being fairly inexperienced with only eight or nine years in the Ministry. Five employees were promoted from *commis* to *sous chef*. Within the ranks of the *commis*, one can detect a definite trend of promotion in only eleven cases— Guérard, for example, being fifth or sixth *commis* in the Year VIII, fourth in the Year IX, third in the Year XI, second in 1806, and first *commis* after 1807. A few exceptional high-ranking appointments were made from outside the Ministry, but in general the more able employees could expect a gradual promotion through the ranks to *sous chef* or *chef*.

The Napoleonic Ministry of Foreign Affairs consisted of six divisions: two political ones handled the correspondence with northern and southern Europe, a Consulates Division responsible for all consular affairs, and three supporting divisions for Codes, Finances, and Archives. Besides these there were bureaus for geological engineers, European military and naval movements, and translators. This was essentially the organization of 1789, of 1799, and of 1814, and there was no basic change in this organization by the Napoleonic government. Napoleon employed four

Foreign Ministers, but their appointments resulted in no significant changes in either organization or personnel, with the exception of the minor and short-lived reorganization of June 1812. The personnel were as stable as the organization and size of the Ministry—there was a considerable change in the first year, but after that the Ministry experienced only normal personnel changes—retirements, transfers within and to the external service, a few dismissals, and compensating appointments. The Ministry's growth up to 1809 reflects the increasing importance of propaganda and the Continental System. Thereafter the size remained around fifty. In terms of organization, the Ministry could be classified as "modern" in the sense that it was highly organized with a strict and functional division of labor and personnel among the six divisions. The stability of personnel could also be defined as "modern" in administrative terms. For the employees, the Ministry was a career. They entered it about the age of twenty, worked there all their lives, and were then pensioned or attached to an advisory Council.

Chapter 3

The Diplomats

The officer corps of the French army was one of the main sources of recruitment for diplomats.[1] There were several reasons for this. Military duties dictated the selection of several generals: Sébastiani supervised the defense of the Straits in Turkey, Gardane was to organize the Persian Army, Macdonald helped with the defense of Copenhagen. Two generals, Gouvion St. Cyr and Ney, became ambassadors while commanding armies in Spain and Switzerland. Generals were often employed as ministers to the states on the periphery of French power—Portugal, Turkey, Russia. A close personal relationship with Napoleon was also a factor in the selection of many of the generals. La Vallette, Napoleon's aide-de-camp, was with him in Italy and Egypt, and at the coup d'état of 18 Brumaire, and Napoleon had arranged his marriage to Émilie de Beauharnais, Josephine's niece. Andréossy, Lannes, and Sébastiani were in the armies of Italy and Egypt and at Napoleon's coup.

A total of twenty-two generals were employed in the ministerial corps.[2] They tended to serve in the earlier years of the period—fourteen completed their diplomatic service before 1807. They accounted for between one-quarter and one-third of the ministers before 1808, less than one-sixth after that date. This fact is in direct contradiction to both Deutsch and Mowat who state that generals came to be employed more and more.[3] These figures must be qualified by the fact that since generals were usually appointed to the most important missions, they occupied a position of importance within the service greater than their numbers would suggest.

The second significant source of recruitment for the ministerial corps was the subordinate levels of the service. Included within this group, who have been defined as professional diplomats, are those diplomats who were already in the service in November 1799. Nine professional diplomats were inherited from the Revolution.[4] Ten were promoted from secretary;[5] Pichon and Durant from the Ministry. Saint Marsan and Serra were recruited from the diplomatic services of Piedmont and Genoa. These diplomats were concentrated in the minor positions in the service. Ten of them served exclusively in Germany; five more in central Europe. Only Laforest and Durant served in both northern and southern Europe. There was a marked increase in the number of professionals in the service during the period. Between 1800 and 1806 they accounted for about one-third of the ministers, for one-half between 1807 and 1809, and two-thirds after 1810. Their absolute number rose from less than eleven before 1807 to more than thirteen after that date.

In addition to these twenty-three professional diplomats, ten other ministers had had some diplomatic experience before their ministerial appointments. Some of the ministers, who have not been defined as professional diplomats, remained in the service for considerable lengths of time, eleven serving for over six years.[6] A few ministers spent an entire lifetime in diplomacy. At the time of retirement or at the end of the Napoleonic period, Bacher, Otto, and Laforest had over thirty-five years service; Cacault, Bourgoing, and Helflinger over twenty-five; and Durant, Reinhard, Demoustier, and Serurier were well advanced towards equally distinguished careers.

The increasing professionalization of the service is seen in the increasing proportion of career diplomats among the ministers. It can also be shown by the average amount of diplomatic experience shared by the ministers as of the first of January of each year. For the first six years this average fell progressively from about eleven years to about seven. This decline was caused by the continuous appointment of new and inexperienced diplomats. Then, beginning in 1806, the average amount of experience of the ministers increased—8.1 years in 1806, 9.6 years in 1807, 11.1 years for 1808 to 14.5 years in 1811. This stability reflected the Peace of Tilsit. Then, in 1812–13 the average decreased as new ministers were appointed to the positions.

Napoleon's only pronouncement on recruitment was his advice to Roederer: "It's best to enter the Council of State . . . it is there that I will recruit my ambassadors and ministers . . ."[7] Napoleon did in fact recruit some of his plenipotentiaries or negotiators from the Council—men such as Jollivet who conducted the negotiations on the Rhine frontiers—but these men did not belong to the salaried diplomatic service. But Napoleon did not recruit ambassadors from the Council of State. Saint Marsan, an Italian diplomat, was called to the Council of State for a short period before his appointment to Prussia. As early as 1802 Napoleon had indicated his desire to employ him,[8] and Saint Marsan's appearance on the Council may have been a sort of French apprenticeship—an opportunity to meet the members of the Imperial government and Foreign Ministry and to familiarize himself with French politics. Champagny is the only diplomat who may have been recruited from the Council. He had considerable administrative ability, and his work in the Marine Section of the Council between 1799 and 1802 may have brought him to the favorable notice of Napoleon.

Eighteen of Napoleon's ministers had been involved in politics before their diplomatic appointments. Narbonne, Petiet, and Beurnonville had been Ministers of War; Reinhard was Minister of Foreign Affairs at the time of Napoleon's coup. Lucien Bonaparte had been Napoleon's second Minister of the Interior. Seven ministers had been in the Estates General: de Pradt in the First, Champagny, d'Aguesseau, and Beauharnais in the Second, and Moreau, Salicetti, and Alquier in the Third. Eschasseriaux, after sitting in the Legislative Assembly, joined Alquier and Salicetti in voting against Louis XVI in the Convention. These three were reelected to the Council of 500 where they were joined by Jourdan, Petiet, Cacault, and Lucien Bonaparte.

Five ministers were recruited from the administration. Larochefoucauld, Verninac, and Didelot had been prefects, Didelot was also Prefect of the Palace, and Bourrienne had been Napoleon's private secretary. Lamoussaye, an *auditeur* in the Council of State, had been intendant of Upper Austria, Carniole, and Carinthia between 1809 and 1811, excellent preparations for his appointment to Danzig in 1813. There is no pattern in either time or place to the appointment of these administrators —they served throughout Europe between 1802 and 1813.

The Imperial Household proved a fruitful source of recruitment for ministers. Napoleon's chamberlains Auguste Talleyrand, Mercy d'Argenteau, Nicolai, Germain, Montholon, and Saint Aignan were appointed. Aubusson de la Feuillade had been Josephine's chamberlain. The Abbé de Pradt, self-styled *aumonier du Dieu Mars*, was appointed from the Imperial court to the Polish embassy. Except for Aubusson in Italy and

Talleyrand in Switzerland, these ministers served in the minor courts of Germany. By 1812–13 they accounted for one in every five of the ministers. They were quite young and all were of noble birth. Besides these, Caulaincourt was Grand Equerry, Cardinal Fesch had been Almoner, and General Gardane had been Governor of the Pages. Two ministers, Cardinal Fesch and Lucien Bonaparte, were related directly to Napoleon; Beauharnais, La Vallette, and Lezai-Marnesia were related to Josephine.

Eight of the ministers had legal training or experience, but in only one case was this a factor in the diplomatic appointment. Alquier, Eschasseriaux, and Salicetti were also Revolutionary politicians. Verninac had been an advocate before the Revolution, but then went on to diplomacy and administration. Before the Revolution d'Aguesseau had been *avocat du Roi* and *avocat général*. After Napoleon's coup he became President of the Tribunal of Appeal in Paris, from which he was appointed to Denmark. Only de Pradt and Fesch had religious backgrounds, in contrast to the days of the Old Regime when the Church had been a major source of recruitment.

In general, the secretaries came from backgrounds both more humble and more professional than those of the ministers. Seventeen of them had been in the service during the Revolution; twenty-three had been diplomatic students or *auditeurs*; four came from the consular service; and four from the Ministry. That is, at least forty-eight of the sixty-two had diplomatic backgrounds. Three secretaries, Lacuée, LaGrange, and Mériage, were recruited from the army for quasi-military duties in Vienna. At least eleven other secretaries had been in the armies before 1800, but did not occupy any important positions. Nine secretaries claimed some administrative experience. Hué de Grosbois had introduced the metric system in several departments, Lamare was *commissaire national* in the Antilles, Desportes was mayor of Montmartre, the rest were in the bureaucracy. Jacob and Gandolphe were the only lawyers. Lamare claimed that he was a writer and had "accepted the Revolution with enthusiasm, but without taking part in its excesses."[9]

The high degree of professionalization within the secretarial corps is reflected in the amount of diplomatic experience of the secretaries. Most of the eighteen promoted from diplomatic student had been students for three years or less, but some had over six years and Bogne de Faye had over ten. Those inherited from the Revolution, or those who had been in the service during the Revolution, had from one to nineteen years service; eight of them had been in diplomacy for over six years. Unlike the ministers, few of the secretaries served for excessive periods of time—only seven attained over fifteen years in office,[10] and none of these served over twenty years. The reason for this is that the experienced secretaries were usually promoted to the rank of minister. Still, the secretarial corps was relatively stable. One-half of the secretaries served over eight years, compared to one-third of the ministers, in spite of the fact that ten of the ministers had been secretaries.

This stability and experience is reflected in the average amount of experience shared by the secretaries as of January first of each year. Beginning in 1802 with 4.2 years, the average amount of experience rose every year until 1812, when a secretary could be expected to have served over ten years, a remarkable figure which proved that diplomacy was a career for the secretaries, for in 1812 their average age was only thirty-four. In fact, there was almost absolute stability between 1804 and 1811 when eighteen secretaries held continuously eighteen of the twenty-one to twenty-five positions. Then in 1812–13 the amount of experience fell to ten years, a factor accounted for by the promotion of several of the *auditeurs* of the Council of State to secretarial positions and of the promotion of several secretaries to the ministerial corps.

The bureaucracy in Paris was a career in itself. On average the members entered the Department about the age of twenty-three; many of them remained there all their lives. At the time of retirement, or by 1 January 1814, seven had served for over forty years, eleven more for over twenty years, twenty-six for over ten years, and thirty-three of these forty-four continued to serve after Napoleon's abdication. The professional nature of the administrative career is shown in the average amount of experience of the bureaucrats as of January first of each year. In 1800 they had over eleven years service on average, and this figure rose to almost seventeen years by 1815. Increasing stability accounts for this rise plus the fact that the information is increasingly accurate after 1800.

Three members of the Ministry, Picard, Joly, and Beuscher, had been in the armies; Mathieu, Posuel, and Caillard had been in other branches of the administration. Buache and Barbie were geographers, and Resnier and Guyétard were writers. Only two members of the Ministry, Bresson and Mathieu, had been deputies during the Revolution, both, apparently, as moderates. For the rest, their working career began and ended with the Ministry of Foreign Affairs or with other branches of the diplomatic or consular service.

The social origins of the ministers, secretaries, and employees would, if examined in any depth, constitute an entire chapter if not a book. The question of who is and what is a bourgeois and what the term "bourgeoisie" means, are currently among the great controversies of French historiography. The question of the nobility is almost equally confused.[11] Once the Napoleonic nobility was created, practically all the senior diplomats were ennobled, but here we are concerned only with the nobility of the Old Regime. There is no limit to the depth to which the question of social origins can be studied; seemingly no limit to the number of books and archives that could be consulted. However, this is a study of the diplomatic service rather than of the social stratification of Revolutionary France. The matter of social origins is valuable to our understanding of the diplomats, but that value is limited. Consequently, the diplomats have been classified in only three social groups. First are those diplomats whose families were ennobled before 1790.[12] The second social group is the bourgeoisie, who have been defined here as the lawyers and merchants of various kinds, rich property owners, prominent non-noble military families, well-educated professional persons such as professors, doctors, or writers, and the higher commercial classes such as bankers. The third social group is the petite bourgeoisie which, for our purposes, includes the lesser military ranks, the lower ranks of the diplomatic and administrative corps, and clerks. Naturally there is no clear division between bourgeoisie and the petite bourgeoisie, but in general one can accept that an army officer or a lawyer was of a higher social class (bourgeoisie) than a lawyer's clerk or a government *commis* (petite bourgeoisie). This arbitrary classification, while subject to error and to criticism in detail, should prove sufficient for providing a general indication of the social origins of the three main groups in the diplomatic service.

Thirty-one of the seventy-one ministers or ambassadors were noble by birth. These included scions of some of the great French noble families —Talleyrand-Périgord, Larochefoucauld-Liancourt, d'Aguesseau, Beauharnais, and Caulaincourt. It also included some nobles of foreign origin such as Saint Marsan. The proportion of nobles in the ministerial corps increased over the years. During the first nine years, the nobles accounted for between 27% and 37% of the ministers. From 1809 to 1811 roughly one-half of the ministers were nobles, and after 1812 nearly two in three were nobles.

Eighteen of the ministers have been defined as bourgeois in origin.

This group includes the lawyers such as Alquier, Eschasseriaux, or Salicetti, merchants such as Derville-Maléchard or Vandeul, members of the
liberal professions such as the professor of fortifications, Cacault, and non-
noble military families such as that of Marshal Macdonald. The proportion of ministers drawn from this social group declined steadily from some
35% (1800 to 1802) to 30% (1803–7), 20% (1808–11), and finally
to 10% or two ministers out of nineteen by 1813.

The petite bourgeoisie has been defined as the educated administrative
personnel, clerks, or minor military persons. In this group could be found
sixteen of Napoleon's ministers. These include essentially the generals of
lowly origin such as Beurnonville, Ney, Lannes, and Victor, and the professional diplomats such as Hirsinger, Helflinger, or Desaugiers. This
group is less prominent in the ministerial corps than the bourgeoisie, but
it eventually outnumbered the bourgeois ministers because it contained
the nonnoble professional diplomats. From 1801 to 1803 approximately
30% of the ministers were petite bourgeoisie. Then, between 1804 and
1808 the proportion rose to about 40% but steadily fell after that date
to 20% in 1813.

In terms of social origins, the proportion of nobles increased from
35% to 60%, the proportion of bourgeois fell from 35% to 10%, and
the proportion of petit bourgeois rose 30% to 40% then fell back to
30%. Alfred Cobban explains this increase in the proportion of nobles
by saying that Napoleon "with the weakness of a new man for real gen-
tlemen, tended to appoint former nobles to office."[13] Other historians
have identified an aristocratic reaction beginning in 1810 and influenced
by Napoleon's marriage to Marie Louise.[14] This theory is nonsense as far
as the diplomatic service is concerned, for the proportion of nobles began
increasing sharply about 1805, and rose most dramatically in 1808
rather than 1810. In fact, the return of the nobility cannot be attributed
exclusively to Napoleon, for it began during the Directory, continued
gradually under Napoleon, and was completed by the Restoration. In
this respect, as in so many others, the Napoleonic period marks a stage in
the evolution away from the Republic, a mid-way point between Directory
and Restoration, or, in another analysis, a part of the Thermidorean Reaction which began in 1794 and ended after 1815.

There are several reasons for the decline in the proportion of bourgeois ministers and the appointment of nobles in the later years. To begin
with, Napoleon inherited a number of ministers of bourgeois or petit

bourgeois origin. The retention of these men gave the service a heavy bourgeois flavor in the early years. Throughout the period Napoleon appointed persons whom he knew personally. At first they were generals, most of whom were bourgeois. Later recruitment from Napoleon's immediate circle shifted away from the army to the Imperial Court, where nobles dominated. The change was a reflection of the political evolution of France. At first it would have been dangerous to appoint many nobles because of the power of republican opinion as exhibited in the opposition to the Concordat and the Legion of Honour. Later these forces weakened, France became more aristocratic with an Imperial Court and nobility, and this change in the social-political situation was reflected in the status of those persons who represented France abroad. Also during the Consulate France maintained relations with a number of republics in Italy, and bourgeois ministers usually represented France in these states. Later in the period, the prestige of many of the German states had increased, and their enhanced status was recognized when France appointed nobles to their courts. Essentially the change in the proportion of nobles reflects the fact that France was evolving towards a condition more in line with the general European situation, for the Europe of 1810 was aristocratic, and in appointing nobles, Napoleon was ensuring that France's representatives were drawn from the social class that dominated the rest of Europe.

The effects of this change in social origin can be overestimated. Many of the nobles were appointed to minor posts in Germany so that a higher proportion of nobles did not necessarily reflect greater influence or importance. In fact, after 1810 nobles were replaced by non-noble ministers in Dresden, Naples, Denmark, Warsaw, and even Austria, five of the most important French missions. The change in the social basis of the ministerial corps was therefore a logical and deliberate policy, reflecting the changed circumstances of both France and Europe, and constituting a trend which began before and continued after the Napoleonic period.

The social origins of the secretaries are substantially the same as those of the ministers, though there are some significant differences in the patterns of evolution. Twenty-one of the secretaries were nobles, a smaller proportion than in the ministerial corps. In the early years, members of some of the great noble families—Chateaubriand, Salignac-Fénélon, Latour-Maubourg, Courbon St. Genèst—entered the service as secretaries. Later, many of the *auditeurs* appointed as secretaries were nobles. In the first years of the regime, the proportion of nobles was about 30%. It began rising in 1805 and remained about 60% until 1812, when 70% of the secretaries were of noble birth.

Only nine secretaries have been classified as bourgeois in origin—seven of these having a legal background, Vandeul and Derville-Maléchard being merchants. The proportion of bourgeois among the secretaries was never more than one-third, and it decreased from some 20% before 1806 to less than 10% after 1807. A large number of the secretaries—eighteen of the forty-eight classified—were petit bourgeois in origin. Almost all the members of this group were professional diplomats or administrators, educated persons who might work up to a minor ministerial post, but who would never be promoted to ambassador. These professional diplomats provided the background of the secretarial corps, accounting for about 50% before 1806, 33% to 40% after that date. Unlike the secretaries of noble birth, they were unlikely to be promoted, so that the secretarial corps was their career, and they provided a degree of stability and depth to the external service.

Of the forty-five members of the Ministry whose social origins can be clearly identified, only four were nobles. Trained as a lawyer, experienced as an administrator, introduced into politics as a deputy in the Convention, Bresson entered the Ministry just before Napoleon's coup and was still there in 1815. Of the other nobles, Posuel de Verneaux came to the Ministry with Champagny and left when Champagny retired, and D'Asnières de la Châtaigneraye was paid by the Ministry but really worked for Ambassador Caulaincourt in Russia. The only noble to work as a *commis* was Rumigny, who was later transferred to the secretarial corps.

The Ministry contained at least fourteen persons whose backgrounds could be identified as bourgeois. The Archives Division required educated middle-class men such as Hauterive, the *sous chefs* Tessier and Galon-Boyer, the famous geographer Barbie de Bocage, and the publicist Rosenstiel. Seven members of the Ministry were lawyers or came from legal families, and several other persons such as the Protestant Minister Barthel could be classed as bourgeois. The social or perhaps educational background of these men and of the four nobles ensured for them many of the best positions in the Ministry. Of the eighteen nobles and bourgeois employees, six were *chefs* or *sous chefs*, two were private secretaries to the Minister, and three others had special positions. The proportion of bourgeois in the Ministry remained constant throughout the period, never less than 25%, never more than 32%, another indication of the profound stability of this bureaucracy.

The petite bourgeoisie was the greatest source of recruitment for the Ministry. Of the forty-five employees whose social origins have been discovered, twenty-five or 55% were petit bourgeois. Within this group, there were eleven junior members of the administration, eight who were clerks in legal or commercial firms, four who held minor positions in the army. Only one employee, Jorelle, can be clearly identified as lower class in origin, his family being poor farmers. Of the remaining forty-three members of the Ministry, the majority would unquestionably be petit bourgeois as they were well enough educated to obtain the positions, but not of sufficient importance to have left much evidence of themselves. The proportion of employees recruited from the petite bourgeoisie fell somewhat during the period. At first about 70% were petite bourgeoisie, their proportion falling to about 65% (1803–7), to 60% (1808–11), then rising again to 65% in 1812. These figures are all conservative. Assuming that the majority of the forty-three employees not classified were petite bourgeoisie, then the proportion of petite bourgeoisie in the Ministry was probably over 80%.

This analysis might leave the reader with a false impression of the degree of social mobility within the diplomatic service. In the bureaucracy it was easier for someone of noble or bourgeois background to become *chef*, but invariably these people also had better educations than the petit bourgeois. In the external service the nobles such as Serurier, Latour-Maubourg or Demoustier received the most rapid promotions from diplomatic student to minister. However, the bourgeois Vandeul and Derville-Maléchard were also promoted. Portalis *fils* passed from diplomatic student to minister in two years. The ministerial corps was dominated by nobles by 1812, but in that year some of the most important positions were held by non-nobles. What might be concluded from all this is that the diplomatic service was still, to a certain extent, a career open to talents, but one of the more useful talents was the name and social graces which went with noble birth and made a noble more acceptable to foreign courts.

The place of origin varies considerably among the different sections of the service.[15] With one exception, all of the members of the Ministry came from within the 1789 frontiers of France, the exception being born in the colony of St. Domingo. Of the forty-four whose birthplaces are known, fifteen came from Paris; thirty-nine from the north of France.[16] The fact that they were all French could have been the result of deliberate policy. Unlike the members of the external service, the bureaucrats in Paris were in a position to know all the secrets of foreign policy. Several factors explain the concentration in Paris and northern France. The bureaucracy was, to a certain extent, a family business, and any bureaucrat following in his father's footsteps would come from Paris or Versailles. Recruitment was bound to be localized—it would be very expensive to travel from Marseilles to Paris in the hope of obtaining a position, possibly unpaid at first, in the Ministry.

The secretaries were recruited from a wider background than were the bureaucrats, and while the majority still came from northern France, the proportion was smaller. Twenty-two of thirty-seven came from Paris. Two of the secretaries were born outside France, both of French parentage. There was no correlation between the place of birth and the location of their diplomatic missions. Of the thirteen born in southern France, four served in southern Europe, seven in northern Europe, and two in both spheres; of the twenty-four born in northern France and western Germany, ten served in northern Europe, eleven in southern Europe, and three in both areas. This fact reflects the professional nature of the secretarial corps: a secretary was expected to serve anywhere in the French embassy network without any apparent consideration of the climate, culture, or geography of his background.

The geographical importance of the north as a factor in recruitment declines even more with the ministerial corps. Thirty-seven of the sixty-six known, or about half, came from the north, only thirteen from Paris. Thus the north provided 89% of the bureaucrats, 60% of the secretaries, and 56% of the ministers. Paris provided 34% of the bureaucrats, 19% of the secretaries, and 20% of the ministers. This is roughly what one would expect—the lower levels of the service were recruited locally, the highest level from a far broader geographical background.

But whereas there was no relationship between the geographical location of the secretary's appointment and his background, there is a very close relationship in the ministerial corps. Of the twenty-six ministers born in southern France or Europe, fourteen served exclusively in southern Europe; of the forty ministers born in northern France or Europe, twenty-nine served in northern Europe. This suggests a strong geographical consideration in the appointment of ambassadors. The climate seems to have been a factor. For example, Gouvion St. Cyr, from the north, was recalled from Spain because of his complaints about the climate, and an effort was made to find him a post in northern Europe.[17] Salicetti and Fesch, born in Genoa, served in Italy. In fact, all but two of the ministers who served in Italy came from southern France. Bacher, Ney, and Helflinger were born and served within 200 miles of the Rhine, and Otto and Reinhard served in Germany, where they had been born. In short, the ministers, unlike the secretaries, were often selected for specific posts where their specialized knowledge of the country or culture would be valuable—they were not expected or required to serve in various areas of Europe. They might be transferred from embassy to embassy within Germany or Italy, but rarely between northern and southern Europe.

The ministerial corps, in contrast to the bureaucrats or the secretaries, contained a number of foreigners. Salicetti and Fesch were born in Corsica before it became a French province in 1768. Otto, born in Baden, was educated in Strasbourg and was naturalized before the Revolution. Reinhard, born and educated in Württemberg, entered France during the Old Regime and joined the Ministry during the Revolution. The absorption of satellite states placed a great deal of diplomatic material at France's disposal, but only two of the satellite diplomats, Serra from Genoa and Saint Marsan (Asinari di San Marsano) from Piedmont, joined the French service. The absorption of Belgium brought the Mercy d'Argenteau family into the French Empire: François Mercy d'Argenteau, Napoleon's minister in Bavaria, was the nephew of Florimand, Austrian ambassador to France on the outbreak of the Revolution.

Thus Horn's suggestion that the French diplomatic service was devoid of foreigners by 1800 is not quite accurate,[18] although during the Napoleonic period it was an Imperial rather than a national service, as Corsica, Genoa, Piedmont, and Belgium were part of the Empire. The presence of foreigners is even more striking for as the crucial year 1813 opened, one Napoleonic minister in four was foreign. They represented France in Berlin, Vienna, Munich, Dresden, and Cassel, the first legations to be affected by the Russian advance. The foreigners seemed to have served as loyally as their French counterparts, though Napoleon suspected in 1813 that Serra's "position as a foreigner doesn't give him the zeal desired in these moments of crisis."[19] This was not Napoleon's first complaint against Serra, but, significantly, he was never removed. Although foreigners could represent France, it was impossible for a Frenchman to represent foreign countries. Holland was refused permission to appoint a Frenchman to Naples, even though Holland and Naples were both satellites ruled by Napoleon's relatives. The reason given was that the Frenchman might have to act against France, which would present difficulties of dual loyalty. It was forgotten that the converse might be true for the foreigners in French service.[20] After 1815 Mercy d'Argenteau went back to Belgium; Reinhard continued in French service, and Saint Marsan represented Piedmont at the Congress of Vienna.

Some diplomats began their diplomatic career as students at the age of seventeen. The average age of the diplomatic students was slightly over twenty-one, and the oldest was twenty-nine. The average age of those recruited into the Ministry was twenty-three, but some had been students for several years. They could expect to work up to a position of first or second *commis* by their early forties, and some *commis* served past the age of seventy-five. Years of experience alone would carry a bureaucrat to the position of first *commis*; but ability seemed to play a part in the appointment to the two highest categories, *chef* and *sous chef*. Thus the *sous chefs* were appointed at an earlier age (thirty-eight on average) than were the first and second *commis*; and the *chefs*, having served an apprenticeship as *sous chefs*, were appointed on average at the age of forty-five. There were exceptional cases, of course. Roux was first *commis* at thirty-one, *sous chef* at thirty-two, and *chef* at thirty-nine. At the time of Napoleon's coup, the average age of the bureaucrats was forty-three. It rose slowly—to forty-four (1803–5), forty-five (1806–8), forty-six (1809–10), and then remained even at forty-eight after 1810. This gradual aging of the bureaucracy reflects a slow return to the normal within the administration. At the time of retirement or at the end of the Napoleonic period, twelve employees were in their fifties, seven in their sixties, three in their seventies, and Goffinet, the *doyen* of the employees, was eighty-one!

On the whole the secretaries were a remarkably young group of men. Usually they were appointed in their early twenties, and only six of the thirty whose ages are known served past the age of forty. Their average age rose from twenty-eight in 1800 to thirty-one in 1803, remained stable, then rose from thirty-two in 1808 to thirty-four by 1811. These changes are readily explained. The external service was being reestablished in 1800 and 1801, and the newly appointed secretaries tended to remain in office. This youthfulness placed a considerable burden on the service as the secretaries often became chargé d'affaires *ad interim* during the absence of their minister. Latour-Maubourg, for example, was in charge of the important Constantinople embassy in 1808 when he was only twenty-six.

The ministers and ambassadors were almost twenty years older than the secretaries. Their average age changed in roughly the same pattern: it remained about forty-four from 1800 to 1806, then rose steadily during the peace of Tilsit, declining sharply in 1812. This decline was caused by the massive turnover on the eve of the Russian invasion, when many diplomats inherited from the Revolution were replaced by younger men. Average figures are perhaps misleading. A better picture of the youthfulness of the service is provided by the fact that five of the ministers were appointed in their twenties, twenty-seven in their thirties, and twenty-one in their forties, while only twenty served after the age of fifty. Only one diplomat seems to have complained that he was too young for his position, a complaint motivated by a desire for a recall.[21] The others, in spite of their youthfulness, were continuously asking for promotions to more important missions.

The information about the education of the diplomatic agents is far too fragmentary to produce any real conclusions as to the educational qualifications required to enter the career. This information does, however, give some idea as to the type of education received by some of the diplomats, and there appear to have been differences between the educational backgrounds of the three major levels of the service. For most of the diplomats, including many of the ministers, the type of education is completely unknown. Then in some cases, the education will be defined as *éducation distinguée* or *bonne éducation* or *très instruit*, phrases which suggest that the subject was sufficiently educated for the career, but tell us nothing about that education. The administration at that time was not concerned with the paper qualifications of the diplomats. A diplomat would not be appointed unless he was sufficiently educated, and after his appointment no record of the education was required.

A common background for the ministers was the military schools which produced several of the generals as well as civilians such as Bourgoing and Larochefoucauld. France contained a number of secondary educational institutions known as *collèges*—the *Collège de la Flèche, de Lisieux, des Grassins, de Châtillon-sur-Seine*, to name but a few. At least nine ministers had been to such *collèges*, and Hédouville, Champagny, and Clarke had attended both a military school and the *Collège de la Flèche*. Universities were more rare: Bourgoing and Otto were trained for diplomacy in the University of Strasbourg, Reinhard studied literature under Goethe in the University of Tübingen, and Saint Marsan was a

student at the University of Pisa. With the decline of recruitment from
the Church, the seminary was a less common background. Only Cardinal
Fesch appears to have been trained in a seminary. Finally, some ministers
were educated at the more important *écoles*, such as the École de Brunswick, where Lezai-Marnesia was trained for diplomacy.

With the secretaries, the military school was a less common background, the *collèges* more popular, and none of the secretaries had been
to a university. Malartic was a product of the new *Polytechnic*. Of the employees of the Ministry, at least eleven had been to a *collège*. Only one of
the employees, Tessier, had been to a military school, and only one,
Rosenstiel, had been to a university. Seven of the employees are known to
have studied public law, which was a kind of liberal arts course involving
history and politics as well as law.

The identification of the institutions does not really tell us much about
the education received by the diplomats. Some specific examples should
help. The graduates of the University of Strasbourg—Otto, Bourgoing,
Rosenstiel—had studied public, international, and feudal law, history,
and languages. The graduates of the *collèges* seem to have studied history,
geography, modern languages, and a few other courses such as philosophy,
classics, chemistry, physics, or mathematics, and possibly public law. The
rule that all secretaries would be recruited from among the *auditeurs* of
the Council of State would have standardized and improved this education, for the *auditeurs* had to have a degree in public law. One has the
general impression, then, that the French diplomats were fairly well educated by the standards of the day, that the lower ranks had studied history
and foreign languages, that the higher ranks had been to a *collège* or a
university or military school and had a fairly good basis in history, languages, literature, and public or international law.

The language proficiency of the diplomats is also difficult to estimate
because of the lack of information. One finds general comments: Desaugiers knew the "languages of the north," someone else "knew several
languages." Much of the evidence comes from application forms where
the applicant tended to exaggerate his abilities. The foreign languages
were not always relevant: Massias, who spoke English, Italian, and Spanish, was appointed to Germany.[22] Still, at least seven secretaries knew
more than four languages and some of the employees of the Ministry were
excellent linguists. These languages were always European. For Oriental
languages, translators known as drogomen were employed, and the Minis-

try contained a School of Oriental Languages. In terms of language proficiency, one has the impression that the employees of the Ministry could read several languages, the secretaries could read, write, and speak one or more foreign languages, with the ministers having poorer language proficiency than the professional secretaries. Perhaps the language proficiency is best illustrated by the fact that only three embassies, Warsaw, Madrid, and Constantinople, employed interpreters. The language qualifications improved as one moved towards the lower levels of the service—a minor minister in Germany probably knew more languages that did a full ambassador.

The lists of French diplomats from different periods and different sections of the service document the recurrence of family names. The diplomatic service was, to a certain extent, a family career, and it would be useful to establish the degree and importance of family connections. There were several families of diplomats during the Napoleonic period. Auguste Talleyrand, minister to Switzerland, was the nephew of the Foreign Minister, and son of one of Louis XVI's ambassadors. Salignac-Fénélon, secretary in Germany 1802–13, claimed a relationship to Talleyrand,[23] and Salignac's son became a diplomat. In the administration, a prefect or administrator could not have his relative serve as secretary. This rule had applied to diplomats during the Revolution,[24] but was not enforced by Napoleon. Antoine Caillard was the head of the Archives Division, his son was *commis* in the same division, and his nephew was a secretary throughout the period. The Durant brothers, Joseph and André, served throughout the period in various positions in both the internal and external service, and were for a while *chef* and *sous chef* of the South Division. Théodore Hédouville, minister at Ratisbon and Frankfort, was the younger brother of General Hédouville, minister to Russia, who had another relative with him in Russia as a diplomatic student.

Naturally there was a considerable degree of intermarriage within the diplomatic service. Laforest began his career under a Demoustier. Demoustier's son later became Laforest's secretary and married Laforest's daughter. At least two other diplomats, Helflinger and Ligueville, married their ambassador's daughters.[25] Hué de Groisbois was Champagny's brother-in-law,[26] a significant factor in Hué's diplomatic career as his appointment to Naples coincided perfectly with Champagny's term at the Foreign Office. Didelot had married Sophie Gérard de Rayneval and felt it necessary to thank Talleyrand when Maximilien Rayneval was appointed secretary in Russia in 1802.[27] But the closest Rayneval connection was with the Bourgoings. Gérard de Rayneval had supervised Bourgoing's debut in diplomacy during the Old Regime. In 1800 Bourgoing trained Gérard's son, Maximilien de Rayneval, in Copenhagen and Stockholm, and Maximilien in turn trained Paul Bourgoing in Prussia during the Restoration.[28]

In the external service a minister could often have his relative placed as diplomatic student in his legation, a situation taken advantage of by at least seven ministers. This may have been a device to appease the ministers rather than to train diplomats; only two relatives of Champagny were promoted from diplomatic student to secretary. The bureaucracy tended to be a family business—Cornillot and Butet followed their fathers in the Ministry, the sons of Rosenstiel and Barbie entered the Ministry, and Brulé's brother helped him in the passports section. In 1792 there were two members of the Lebartz family in the Ministry, both related to Beuscher, and we have already mentioned the Durants, Caillards, Raynevals, and Talleyrands. In all there were thirty-four relationships involving fifty-three members of the service at all levels. These relationships were responsible for appointments in several cases, but it should be noted that it was fairly common for a son to follow in his father's career, as happened frequently in the army and consular service.

Finally, it is important to understand what happened to the diplomats after their diplomatic service or after the Napoleonic period. The bureaucracy was a career for most of the persons employed in the Ministry. Their future after their service during the Napoleonic period proves this fact. Of the fifty-seven whose future is known, thirty stayed in the Ministry into the Restoration. Four retired during the Napoleonic period and seven died in office. Ten more continued in the diplomatic service, eight in the external service, two as consuls. The remaining six had more interesting futures. D'Asnières fought in the 1812 campaign, then became a writer and translator during the Restoration. Roederer left the Ministry in 1805 to become one of the youngest prefects in the Empire. Posuel, who had served Champagny as secretary in Austria and at the Ministries of the Interior and Foreign Affairs, followed him in 1811 to the *Ordre de la Réunion* which Champagny then administered.[29] Monnier broke completely with the tradition of the French bureaucracy by going into business.[30]

The future of the secretaries indicated the professional nature of the secretarial corps. Half of them continued in the diplomatic career, ten as ministers during the Napoleonic period, a further six as ministers during the Restoration, and twelve secretaries were retained by the Restoration. Bogne de Faye retired in 1815;[31] and Lablanche was retired in spite of repeated applications for a new appointment.[32] Six secretaries entered the consular service, possibly because the pay was better. Hué de Groisbois was promoted from secretary to resident in November 1810. He returned to Paris from Naples, but was never given permission to go to his new post and was replaced without ever holding the position.[33] Siméon and Jacob entered the diplomatic services of the satellite states, Siméon as Westphalia's minister to Berlin, Jacob as *chef* of a division in the service of the Kingdom of Italy. Marivault, secretary in Holland, became Commissioner of Police in Holland when it was absorbed into the Empire. Thus Napoleon used the diplomatic service as a source of recruitment for administrators for annexed lands. Two secretaries in the Austrian embassy, who had been recruited from the army as diplomatic spies, returned to the army on their own request.[34] Posuel followed his ambassador to the Ministry of the Interior, and one secretary, Gandolphe, died in office.[35] Five secretaries entered other branches of the administration, two of them becoming prefects. After 1815 several of the secretaries achieved political positions of some importance, nine as peers, three as deputies, and Portalis, Demoustier, and Latour-Maubourg as cabinet ministers. Lefebvre spent the years after 1815 in the archives writing a history of diplomacy from 1763 to 1805, which was finally published by his son.

The military character of the appointments of the generals is proved by the fact that seventeen of them returned to the army after their brief diplomatic careers. Eight of Napoleon's ministers continued in diplomacy after the Restoration, and Saint Aignan returned to the service under the July Monarchy. In Italy, Derville, Jourdan, and Moreau St. Mery became administrators of the states in which they had been ministers, and Salicetti, who had been a minister in northern Italy for several years, was ordered to join Joseph Bonaparte's administration in Naples.[36] Moreau, as administrator of Parma, refused to discipline the people and was dismissed from the administration and from the Council of State. He then returned to the United States, where he had been during the Revolution, and wrote about the colonies. Three other ministers retired from active service. Beauharnais, Verninac, Rivals, and Nicolai were retired in spite of numerous applications for employment from the latter three.[37] Saint Marsan and Mercy d'Argenteau served their own governments in Piedmont and Holland after the abdication. Four of the ministers were exiled —Eschasseriaux and Alquier as regicides by the Restoration, Lucien Bonaparte by Napoleon because of his independence, and de Pradt by Napoleon because of his incompetence. Cardinal Fesch went back to the Church; Raymond was the only minister to enter the consular service. Sémonville, Cacault, Champagny, Beurnonville, d'Aguesseau, Hédouville, and St. Marsan received senatorships as rewards for their service.

To a certain extent the ministerial corps was an apprenticeship for higher political office, though it was not pursued as such by the diplomats. Champagny and Caulaincourt went to the Foreign Ministry from ambassadorships, Portalis and Dejean passed directly from diplomacy to ministerial positions, and Clarke became Minister of War in 1807. La Valette, one of Napoleon's closest collaborators from the armies of Italy, Egypt, and the coup, returned from Dresden to become Director-General of Posts. He was instrumental in Napoleon's return from Elba, for which he was tried and condemned to death during the Second Restoration. He avoided Ney's fate with the help of his wife, a Beauharnais, who took his place in the prison cell so that his absence and escape would not be noticed. Then Baudus took him to the Ministry of Foreign Affairs and hid him in Bresson's suite, where he remained while the police checked the roads out of Paris. After the search ended, La Valette escaped to Bavaria. He was pardoned in 1820.[38] Many ministers had to wait until the Restoration to enter the highest offices of government when Clarke, Gouvion St. Cyr, Victor, Portalis, Lauriston, and Demoustier became cabinet Ministers. Beurnonville, Bourrienne, and de Pradt were active in the First Restoration, and Didelot continued to serve as prefect. Nine Napoleonic diplomats were elected deputies during the Restoration; an equal number were appointed peers. But many of the diplomats who had been more closely identified with Napoleon had to wait for the July Monarchy to achieve their political goals. After 1830, Sébastiani, Bignon, and Latour-Maubourg became ministers, Derville reentered the prefectoral corps after fifteen years of unemployment. After 1830 the upper house included ten more Napoleonic diplomats, seven of whom were career diplomats. One can conclude then, that some of those diplomats most closely identified with Napoleon were ignored by the Restoration, but almost all of the professional diplomats were retained in the service after 1815, and many were promoted to higher office.

A typical employee of the Ministry of Foreign Affairs in 1807 could be expected to come from a petit bourgeois family in northern France or Paris. After completing his education he would enter the Ministry in his early twenties, possibly as a diplomatic student. For him, the Ministry would be a career—gradually he would work up to first *commis*, or, if particularly able, to *chef* or *sous chef*, and he would remain in the Ministry until he died. A secretary in the external service of 1807 would probably be twenty-five years old, of noble or petite bourgeois origin, born in northern France, and educated in a *collège*. He would have entered the diplomatic service at the age of twenty, and by the age of thirty would probably have been promoted to a minor legation. The ministers were recruited almost equally from noble and bourgeois and petit bourgeois backgrounds. Before becoming ministers, they were army generals, secretaries, or members of the Imperial Court. If they came from the north of France, they tended to serve in northern Europe, if from the south, in southern Europe. Unlike the secretaries and the employees, several ministers were born outside France and five were foreigners. The ministers were considerably older than the secretaries, often better educated, but not as professional. After their diplomatic service, many of the ministers returned to the army or were promoted to important political positions in the Napoleonic or Restoration governments. Throughout the period, at all three levels, there was a steady increase in the level of diplomatic experience and in the average ages, and, in the external service, there was a marked change in the social origin of the ministers and secretaries as the nobles came to dominate while the bourgeois were gradually eliminated.

Chapter 4

Appointments and Dismissals

In theory the three Consuls had the power to appoint the heads of diplomatic missions.[1] The Constitution was silent on how this was to be done, on whether anyone's advice had to be considered, or on who appointed the subordinate external personnel or the employees of the Ministry in Paris. Although we can assume that two of the Consuls, Lebrun and Cambacérès, exerted little influence, the extent of Napoleon's influence remains to be estimated.

Several persons at the time commented on the system of appointments. Chaptal, an embittered former minister, stated that cabinet ministers drew up lists for the vacancies, but that these recommendations were usually passed over for the protégé of some influential general.[2] Another minister claimed that in civilian appointments the merits of the individuals were canvassed by a great number of persons.[3] Paul Bourgoing, a Restoration diplomat and son of an Old Regime and Napoleonic one, states that attachés and secretaries were appointed without examination by the Foreign Minister, the members of the Ministry, or the ambassadors.[4] Historians, if they have looked at the question at all, have usually attributed appointments to court intrigue.[5] The one thing that all of these commentaries have in common is that they are not based on any detailed or thorough study of appointments.[6] Appointments to the Ministry will not be discussed in detail as there is not enough evidence to warrant any conclusions in this respect. The evidence, if available, would probably suggest that the Foreign Minister and heads of the divisions made most of the appointments, that family connections were quite important, that unemployed external secretaries were sometimes given positions in the Ministry, and that promotion was on the grounds of experience and seniority.

Napoleon's influence over the selection of ministers is most obvious in the appointments of generals. Often Napoleon merely wrote to the Foreign Minister informing him of his choice, as in the case of Gouvion St. Cyr, Gardane, Vial, and Andréossy.[7] Similarly, Narbonne, Lannes, Junot, Victor, and Hédouville were appointed directly by Napoleon. It is probably safe to conclude that sixteen other appointments of generals were made by Napoleon. There is no specific documentary evidence on these appointments. Talleyrand or others could have influenced them, but the nature and purpose of these appointments, and the relationship of the generals to Napoleon, suggests strongly Napoleon's own influence. These nominations would include the early appointments in northern Italy of Clarke, Dejean, Jourdan, and Petiet, the appointment of Napoleon's personal friends Sébastiani, Caulaincourt, Andréossy to Constantinople and Vienna, and the other generals Macdonald, Ney, Turreau, and Beurnonville to Berlin and Madrid.

The motives for the selection of these generals are fairly easy to detect. In several cases the appointments were purely military. Gouvion St. Cyr commanded the French army in Spain. His appointment as ambassador simply combined military and political control.[8] When the English navy threatened France's allies, it was logical to send a general to instill confidence and to assist the defense. Hence Macdonald and Victor were sent to Denmark in 1802 and 1805, and Sébastiani to Turkey in 1806. During the War of the Third Coalition, Larochefoucauld was replaced in Austria by Andréossy because: "In this situation, it is necessary to give the embassy to an officer."[9] Fifteen of the generals had served with Napoleon in Italy, had assisted at the coup d'état of Brumaire, or were his aides-de-camp. They were used extensively, especially during the early period, because they were the only persons Napoleon knew or could trust. Also, by 1800 the only persons in France who had the prestige to impress or influence foreign governments were the successful generals, and the practice of using them dated from the Directory.[10] In informing Beurnonville of his appointment, Talleyrand explained that it would help remind foreigners of French victories.[11]

A further motive may have been the fear of a counter-coup. It is well known that the generals, especially those from the Army of the Rhine, were distressed with the course of events. While the generals from the Army of Italy were appointed because of their reliability, Ney, Macdonald, Brune, Jourdan, and Beurnonville were appointed both to appease them and to remove them from Paris. The employment of generals reached its highest point during the Peace of Amiens, when they occupied thirteen of the thirty missions, including all the main ones except Austria and Rome. At least nine other military appointments were mooted. Bernadotte was supposed to go to Philadelphia, but was too clever to accept this obvious exile. Lannes incurred Napoleon's displeasure by mishandling some funds and by addressing Josephine in a manner too familiar for the new court etiquette,[12] and Clarke, according to Bourienne, was exiled to Florence because he sat in Napoleon's place at the *Théâtre Français* and failed to rise when Napoleon arrived.[13]

Napoleon appointed his uncle, Cardinal Fesch, to Rome, partly because he was a cardinal. It can be assumed that he appointed his other relatives, Lucien and Josephine's brother-in-law François Beauharnais. Lucien's appointment was a diplomatic exile resulting from the publication of a *Parallèle de César, Cromwell et Bonaparte* by the Ministry of the Interior, of which Lucien was in charge. Napoleon's displeasure with his impetuous brother may have been augmented by Lucien's administrative incompetence and hostility to the centralizing tendencies of the regime.[14]

The Emperor exerted his influence over a great number of nonmilitary appointments to the ministerial corps. In rallying the old aristocracy, he appointed Larochefoucauld to "a court in Germany" which turned out to be Saxony, and later to Holland.[15] A similar motive may account for the stillborn nomination of Chateaubriand to the Valais.[16] In Italy Napoleon met three of the men he was later to employ as ministers: Cacault, whom he appointed to Rome, Saint Marsan, and Salicetti, a fellow Corsican. As Poland was extremely important to the Imperial foreign policy, Napoleon controlled the appointments of the diplomatic agents in Warsaw: Serra, Bignon, de Pradt, and Bignon again in 1813.[17] Napoleon also supervised the promotion of professional diplomats. Serurier, promised a promotion from secretary in 1805, was appointed minister to the United States in 1810.[18] As could be expected, his influence reached down to the lower levels of the corps with the selection of diplomats for Baden, Ratisbon, and even the tiny Valais.

But while Napoleon made a great number of appointments, there was also a definite system of appointments operating at the ministerial level. With or without Napoleon's request, the Foreign Minister would draw up lists of vacancies plus lists of those persons deemed most suited to fill them. By examining all such cases one should be able to determine the relative influence of Napoleon and the Foreign Minister and the degree of professionalization in ministerial appointments. It must be stated that apart from these recommendations, the Foreign Minister exerted little or no influence on the selections.

A host of appointments were made directly on the recommendation of the Foreign Minister. They included some extremely important ones, such as Otto and Larochefoucauld to Austria, as well as Demoustier to Karlsruhe and Latour-Maubourg to Stuttgart.[19] Napoleon asked for a proposal for Switzerland in 1802; the appointment of an experienced diplomat, Verninac, suggests Talleyrand's influence. Nor did Napoleon accept all the recommendations made by the Foreign Ministers. He regarded one of Talleyrand's proposals as "a bad joke" and told Talleyrand to present someone more suitable.[20] A group recommendation was made in September 1808, when three embassies, Berlin, Karlsruhe, and Cassel were vacant. But of the ten names put forward, only one, Bignon, was accepted.[21] Two of the remaining nine, however, received subsequent appointments.

The largest group of nominations was made on 5 December 1811. As early as August Napoleon had informed Maret that the service was in chaos, and had requested proposals for all vacancies. The report arrived in November. Three embassies, Stuttgart, Würzburg, and Hesse-Darmstadt, were vacant, and a fourth, attached to the Saxon Princes, had been created. Maret drew up a list of fourteen candidates. He proposed three senior diplomats, one general, four secretaries, and six members of the Imperial Court. The transfer of one diplomat created a fifth vacancy. The five diplomats appointed were all on Maret's list, and four of the five had received his particular attention.[22]

In almost all of these appointments the motives mentioned were experience and ability, a word which was never defined. In each recommendation the diplomatic services were recorded, and it was noted if Napoleon had read their reports or commented favorably on them. Thus Bignon would be a good choice for Karlsruhe as he had ten years experience; Serurier had been in the service for seven years and "Your Majesty has been very satisfied with his conduct."[23] Naturally the opinions of the ambassadors under whom these diplomats had served were important in determining the Foreign Minister's decision to recommend and Napoleon's decision to appoint. Maret said of Vandeul that: "All the ambassadors under whom he has served have expressed their appreciation for his knowledge of affairs and his zeal and devotion."[24] He was appointed within a month. Being known personally to Napoleon was a further reason, as the selection of the chamberlains from the Imperial Court suggests.

In theory a foreign government should be consulted about the choice of minister to be accredited to it. In practice, at least in Napoleonic practice, this was seldom the case. Napoleon exercised considerable control over the choice of foreign diplomats for Paris, but the custom was seldom reciprocated. For example, Napoleon refused to accept Cardinal Letta from Rome, or Cobenzl from Austria.[25] He told Sardinia that he wanted Saint Marsan as its envoy, and suggested to Spain that Frias would be acceptable.[26] French ministers in Vienna and Florence approved the choice of Austrian and Tuscan diplomats.[27]

There was some consultation over the choice of French ministers. Stockholm was asked if it wished to receive Massena; and Portalis *fils* was appointed to Ratisbon on the request of the German Archchancellor.[28] A foreign government could influence appointments by its attitude towards French diplomats. Serra was accredited to Saxony because he had been favorably regarded by the King of Saxony while in Warsaw. (The King of Saxony was nominal head of Poland.)[29] Joseph, as King of Naples, requested and received Aubusson, but was unable to have Roederer appointed to Spain. In Holland Louis asked for Dupont-Chaumont, but Larochefoucauld was appointed.[30] The one monarch whose advice was sought and accepted was Alexander I of Russia, because he was the only monarch Napoleon regarded as even a near-equal, and because Napoleon wanted the Russian alliance to succeed. In 1802 Napoleon decided to send "a general who would be acceptable personally to His Imperial Majesty."[31] In 1807 Alexander was asked if Laforest was acceptable, and in 1811 was given a choice between Lauriston, Larochefoucauld, and Narbonne.[32]

In general it appears that diplomats were rarely consulted about their own appointments. Lauriston complained that he had been appointed during his absence, as had Macdonald.[33] Lannes thought he had been consulted, but when he wrote to refuse the offer, he found that the appointment was an order. He had been offered Constantinople, but had refused it to his regret.[34] Some diplomats were not even informed of their nominations: Victor heard of his from Duroc, and Aubusson from the Princess of Lucca.[35] Several persons were offered the Russian legation in 1802; Macdonald refused to go, and Beurnonville excused himself on the grounds of poor health.[36] In 1807 Laforest accepted the post, but did not want to go, while Caulaincourt refused it but finally had to accept.[37] Two professional diplomats were consulted about appointments. Cacault, recalled from Rome, was offered any other legation in Italy, and Bignon was offered Karlsruhe in 1808 and Poland in 1810, both of which he accepted.[38]

There is very little evidence to suggest that persons other than Napoleon and the Foreign Minister had any influence on the appointments of ministers. The one possible exception is Lezai-Marnesia's appointment to Salzburg. Roederer had recommended him to Napoleon early in 1802, but his appointment in December 1803 more likely was due to his successful mission to Switzerland in 1802, and according to his brother, to the intervention of Josephine, who was related to him.[39] Paul Bourgoing, speaking of his father's disgrace, says that Josephine, Maret, and Talleyrand tried to have him reappointed and failed, but Ernouf claims that Maret's efforts were later successful.[40] Ernouf also argues that de Pradt was a protégé of Duroc's, and was appointed in spite of Maret's objections. [41] Without providing proof, various dictionaries speculate on outside influence, such as Fouché's over Bourienne's nomination or Laforest's over Demoustier's. This evidence, or lack of it, suggests strongly that appointments at the ministerial level were made almost exclusively by Napoleon and his Foreign Minister.

When one passes from the ministerial level to that of the external secretaries, one finds a striking decrease in Napoleon's influence over nominations. Chateaubriand claimed that Napoleon appointed him to Rome. Napoleon, he stated, was a great discoverer of men who knew that a talent such as Chateaubriand's required no apprenticeship. He was soon promoted because Napoleon knew that "I was one of those people who is good only in the highest offices."[42] Napoleon may have appointed four other secretaries, which would account for five of the hundred nominations of secretaries, not an excessive attention to administrative detail.

The degree of influence of the Foreign Minister on secretarial appointments is seen in the recommendations he made and in the number of these that were accepted. Many were accepted outright, such as Hermand,

Jacob, and Durant for Spain.[43] The appointment of the three secretaries for the Austrian embassy was the result of consultation between the Foreign Minister and Napoleon. In 1806 Napoleon accepted Talleyrand's proposed first secretary, but rejected the other two; while in 1809 he rejected Champagny's first slate of nominations and accepted the second completely, possibly after consultation.[44] Napoleon told Maret to send a good secretary to Berlin in 1811 to complement the minister, who "doesn't see enough": Lefebvre, a secretary with eleven years' experience, was sent.[45] There are other examples to document the Foreign Minister's influence, but the system of selecting secretaries from lists drawn up by the Foreign Minister obviously was not used extensively, as it accounted for only twelve appointments.

The greatest number of appointments at the secretarial level were professional ones, that is, promotions or transfers made by Napoleon and the Foreign Minister, sometimes on the recommendation of the ambassadors and ministers. Of the appointments not already accounted for, eleven were promotions from the rank of diplomatic student or attaché, twenty were transfers from other secretarial positions, seven were the reappointments of secretaries who had served under the Revolution, and a further seven represented the promotion of *auditeurs* of the Council of State. This latter movement had been initiated in 1806 and effected largely in 1811–12. It was a policy of selection and training, and was supervised by the Foreign Minister and the head of the Archives Division. Together with the appointments made by Napoleon on the recommendation of the Foreign Minister, this represents a total of fifty-eight of the hundred secretaries appointed during the period.

A few ministers were able to select their own secretaries. Sémonville, Durant, and Brune had their protégés appointed, and Otto secured the promotion of two of the persons working under him.[46] At least eight recommendations, however, were rejected, so the influence of ministers was not very considerable. Few other people had any influence over secretarial appointments. In fact, one of the few documented examples is Duroc, whom Napoleon allowed to select a second secretary for Austria because Napoleon wanted a military spy.[47] This secretary and another one in the same embassy were the only ones appointed for purely military reasons, and the third secretary even received his orders from the Minister of War. Barthélemy, Senator and former diplomat, recommended Marandet, who was appointed, and Lamarre's application carried supporting letters from Clément de Ris, Démeuniers, and Rochambeau, as well as General Brune, whose secretary he became.[48]

Napoleon exerted practically no influence over the selection of diplomatic students. He placed three students in the Ministry in the Year IX,[49] and asked if there were places for several others. Similarly, the influence of the Foreign Minister declines sharply as one reaches the lower levels of the service. Latour-Maubourg and Rayneval entered the service under Talleyrand's guidance.[50] A possible four other appointments suggest that the Foreign Minister was mainly concerned with the appointment of secretaries.

The ministers and ambassadors had a preponderant influence over the choice of students and attachés. They often selected their relatives, as in the case of Alquier *fils*, Rivals *fils*, St. Marsan *fils* and Didelot Ferté. Sémonville's two attachés were related to him, as were Champagny's two attachés in Austria. Clarke, minister to Florence, selected his two students,[51] as did at least a dozen ministers. At least nine other attachés were selected by ministers. Also, a minister could often select the interpreters for his embassy.

It is only when one reaches the level of the nonsalaried external personnel that persons outside the diplomatic service had any real influence over appointments. It is here that the court intrigue and the favored generals can be detected. The main source of information on this aspect is a single list of diplomatic students for 1802, indicating who made the recommendations.[52] The students were sponsored by three Councillors of State, three generals, three Senators, two by the third Consul Lebrun, two by members of the Ministry, a Tribune, the Minister of the Interior, and three by other persons. Evidence from other sources augments this list as one finds successful recommendations from Lebrun, Josephine, Maret (as Secretary of State), and the former Director, Barras. Delavau owed his appointment to recommendations from Hauterive, Count Lacepède, Champeunze, and Defernon.[53] In all, twenty-three students were appointed in this way.

The evidence of these minor appointments is far too scanty to permit detailed and accurate conclusions, but it does appear as if Napoleon and the Foreign Minister were little concerned with the selection of students, that ambassadors could select their attachés, and that influential members of the government and army were able to obtain places at the lowest level of the service for their protégés.

While dealing with the appointments at each level, we have discussed the reasons for them. Several other motives may be mentioned here. In some cases a specific experience was partly responsible. Bourgoing, sent to Denmark, had spent years in Hamburg; Bourrienne had traveled extensively in Germany though his appointment was an exile caused by his implication in a financial scandal.[54] Bignon was selected for Warsaw in 1811 because he was reliable, intelligent, and active, because Napoleon wanted someone more intelligent than Serra, and because of his administrative experience in Berlin and Vienna.[55] Competence in foreign languages was of obvious importance. Champagny successfully recommended Desaugiers for Stockholm because he knew the languages of the North. In 1806 Napoleon insisted that a secretary in Vienna be a German-speaking officer.[56] Lecoulteulx, as well as being recommended by his family and Bourgoing, had studied German for three years.[57] The influence of family connections was unquestionably important, but it is difficult to estimate. General Gardane asked for the Persian embassy because his grandfather had negotiated the Franco-Persian treaty of 1715.[58] Some of the motives were unique. Bourgoing was brought back from exile only after his eldest son had distinguished himself in battle, while it was argued that Bourgoing's monarchist past had influenced his first appointment.[59] Narbonne's appointment to Vienna was influenced by his name, manners, and intelligence, as well as by his friendship with Schwartzenburg and Metternich.[60] De Pradt's appointment to Warsaw is the most difficult to explain. Apparently Napoleon wanted a new man with sufficient influence to dominate all the Polish factions. De Pradt was certainly new, and, as a Cardinal, had the necessary rank and followed in a long tradition of French Cardinal-ambassadors to Poland.[61]

A brief study of resignations and recalls helps to reveal the reasons why diplomats were replaced, the possibilities of promotions, the conditions under which the diplomats worked, and the number who resigned from the service. Ten ministers asked for and were granted recalls. They included, not unnaturally, Lucien Bonaparte and Lannes, who had been exiled,[62] several generals such as Sébastiani, Victor, St. Cyr, and Macdonald, whose missions had been military, and four other generals. The threat of recall was used to pressure foreign governments, and several ministers had to return to France because of the deterioration of relations. Since Russia, Austria, and Turkey refused to recognize Napoleon as Emperor, the ministers there were recalled. Champagny, Dejean, and La Vallette were promoted directly from the service to the government in Paris. Cacault was recalled from Rome because Napoleon wanted a Cardinal; his replacement, Cardinal Fesch, was recalled because: "It is no longer acceptable for you to remain in a court so poorly disposed towards us," as was Fesch's replacement, Alquier, because it was soon beneath Napoleon's dignity even to have an ambassador at Rome.[63]

Several ministers were dismissed for incompetence or poor conduct. De Pradt was replaced because "it appears that he lacks the qualifications for the position he holds,"[64] an accusation which would be difficult indeed to refute. Didelot was recalled because "he knows nothing" and Napoleon wanted someone "more intelligent and more active." An indication of the treatment of France's diplomats comes from the letter informing Didelot of his fate: according to Maret, it was necessary to give the post to Alquier, there was nothing personal in this, and Napoleon was perfectly satisfied with Didelot's conduct and would soon reappoint him. It was the second time Didelot had been dismissed: the first time Napoleon had commented that "he doesn't know the A B C's of his trade," and his only notification was the appointment of someone else to his post.[65] Reinhard intervened openly and, what was worse, unsuccessfully in the Swiss elections and had to be replaced; Beauharnais had the misfortune to intrigue against the Prince of Peace in Spain.[66] Montholon was dismissed "for having made a marriage that was contrary to customs and honor," the woman in question being twice divorced.[67] Pichon, charge d'affaires in the United States, became involved in some financial complications in relation to the supplying of the expedition to Saint-Domingo. His case was investigated and he was dismissed, an event which accounts for his extremely hostile attitude to the Napoleonic government.[68] Only two ministers left their posts without being recalled. The first, Lannes, was sent back after being severely reprimanded by Talleyrand.[69] Gardane's unexpected departure from Teheran prompted Napoleon to state that his return was a crime, that his letters indicated "that something was wrong in his head," and that Napoleon could see only "little zeal . . . and a clear violation of his duties." He was disgraced.[70]

But these individual cases explain only a few of the circumstances under which missions ended. The fate of almost all of the diplomats is known, so it is possible to analyze accurately their recalls. Of the 108 appointments made at the ministerial level, twenty-two ended in promotion within the service, and nine in promotion or transfer outside the service. Twenty-six were driven from their posts by war or the deterioration of relations, and twelve ministers became redundant with the disappearance of their legation or the resident country. Eleven retired, one died in office, eight were dismissed. Larochefoucauld was replaced by an officer, Gardane left without a recall, five requested their recalls, and three remained in office after the abdication.

Secretaries were recalled for much the same reasons as ministers. Political relations with Sweden and Portugal deteriorated, so Caillard and Rayneval had to return to France, though Caillard was ordered to use ill health as a pretext.[71] Several secretaries, including Desportes, Hermand, and Vandeul asked to be recalled.[72] Napoleon ordered the Foreign Minister to replace Sabartier de Cabre because "One says that he has the habits and taste of an Englishman."[73]

In the law of 3 Floréal, Year VIII on the organization of the service, diplomats could be dismissed only after a committee of five had investigated the complaint and heard evidence on both sides. Only one such case arose during the period. Aubusson complained to Napoleon that his "detestable secretary of legation," Artaud, had intrigued against him, interfered with his official correspondence, and was acting as though he, and not Aubusson, were the ambassador. A specific complaint was that Artaud had visited the Queen of Tuscany without Aubusson's authorization and against his better judgment. A committee was appointed, including the senior *commis* Hauterive, the retired diplomat Rayneval, and Mornard. This committee read all the relevant correspondence and listened to Artaud's defence. The committee made a fair and thorough investigation of the case. Aubusson was criticized for his ignorance of diplomatic regulations, and for his inability to handle his subordinates. In defence of Artaud, it was pointed out that other superiors had thought highly of him. But the facts remained: Artaud had knowingly approached a foreign government without his superior's permission, and had proved himself incapable of working for Aubusson since flexibility was one of the essential qualities in a secretary. The committee recommended that Artaud be dismissed and that copies of the report be sent to all French diplomats. Napoleon accepted the report; Artaud was dismissed.[74]

As with the ministers, it is possible to make a more detailed examination of the reasons why secretarial missions ended. Of the hundred secretarial appointments, forty-two ended in promotion or transfer, twenty-six were ended by war, fifteen ended when the state was absorbed or the ambassador replaced. Four secretaries left the service, three were dismissed, one died in office, and two remained after Napoleon's abdication. Little is known about the other seven. This evidence indicates that the secretaries had a more stable career than the ministers under whom they served.

There were a total of 111 appointments to the ministerial corps during the Napoleonic period.[75] Of these, Napoleon is known to have made twenty-three, and twenty-one more can be assumed from the fact that the appointees were generals, his friends, or his relatives. Twelve appointments resulted from a system whereby Napoleon selected the ministers from a list of candidates prepared by the Foreign Minister. Of the remaining appointments, five were professional diplomats retained from the Directory, four came from the Imperial Household, and twenty-five were promoted from the ranks, that is, they were selected by Napoleon and the Foreign Minister. With these nominations, the influence of foreign governments was minimal, and the diplomats themselves were rarely consulted. The main motives for selection were ability, experience, reliability, and prestige, though the desire to rally hostile factions or to remove specific persons from Paris played a part. Napoleon's influence was most pronounced during the early years of the regime when the insecurity of his position was reflected in the appointments of his military friends to most of France's embassies. By 1810 the generals had been replaced by experienced diplomats, and the influence of the Foreign Minister was being increasingly felt.

At the secretarial level there were a hundred appointments, of which five were reappointments following a war or a mission, four were secretaries inherited from the Directory. There were sixteen about whom too little is known. Napoleon made five selections, ambassadors made ten, and persons outside the service made one or two. Eighteen of these forty-two had diplomatic experience. In addition, fifty-eight of the hundred were professional appointments in that they were made on the Foreign Minister's recommendation, were transfers or promotions, and the motive was experience or ability. At the subordinate level, ambassadors and persons outside the service had more influence than did Napoleon or the Foreign Minister; but not enough is known about the attachés and students to estimate relative influence over the selection or to identify the dominant motives involved in their appointments.

As mentioned earlier, some historians have stated that appointments to the Napoleonic administration were a result of court intrigue. This may have been true of the administration in general; it was certainly not true of the diplomatic service. This study has revealed that at the ministerial level the appointments were made by Napoleon and the Foreign Minister; at the secretarial level by Napoleon, the Foreign Minister, and the ministers or ambassadors. There is practically no reliable evidence whatsoever of persons outside the diplomatic service influencing appointments of ministers or secretaries. For the Ministry in Paris there is also no evidence of outside influence, and the nature of the appointments and promotions there suggests that they were based on experience rather than favoritism. Practically the only persons appointed through the influence of generals, politicians, or members of the court were the diplomatic students, and only a fraction of them were appointed this way. Moreover, they received no salary, they could be promoted only on the recommendation of a salaried member of the diplomatic service, and, in fact, few of them were ever promoted. Promotions in the diplomatic service were professional in the sense that they were made by members of the diplomatic service and for reasons relevant to diplomacy.

Chapter 5

Diplomatic Training

Under the Old Regime and the Revolution there was no regular system of diplomatic training, and most ministers and secretaries were appointed without benefit of any specific preparation for diplomacy. At the time of Louis XIV, a program of diplomatic training was instituted with students attached to the Archives Division of the Ministry and to the large legations. By 1710, however, the state was bankrupt and the position of diplomatic student became a venal office. In the eighteenth century the policy of promoting diplomatic students to secretaries ended, and the secretaries came to be selected by the ambassadors. This meant that the secretaries were often inexperienced, the Minister of Foreign Affairs did not know them, and the secretarial corps was unstable. In 1771 the position of councillor of embassy was reestablished, and fourteen councillors were nominated, but the position was again suppressed in 1774.[1]

In the 1770s Foreign Minister Choiseul devised a new program. He decided to recruit promising students from the military schools, send them to the University of Strasbourg, then have them apprentice for several years as diplomatic students before being appointed as secretaries. The director of the military school, Pâris-Duvernay, was instructed to select several students and direct their studies towards diplomatic subjects. Jean François Bourgoing was selected and he first studied German. Then, after an examination by Gérard de Rayneval, *premier commis* in the Ministry of Foreign Affairs, Bourgoing was sent to the University of Strasbourg to study public law under Schoepflin. Such famous diplomats as Metternich, Pfeffel, Reinhard, and Hardenberg were products of this school. After two years in Strasbourg, Bourgoing was attached as diplomatic student to the French mission at the Diet of Ratisbon. Unfortunately the young Bourgoing disobeyed an instruction and was sent back to the army.[2] The policy was then discontinued. The Revolution, while releasing a tremendous flood of creative energy, produced nothing constructive in the way of diplomatic training, possibly because its foreign policy virtually destroyed the diplomatic service.

The absence of a formal program or system of training did not mean that diplomats were appointed without any preparation whatsoever. Often secretaries had apprenticed as attachés, some of the *commis* in the Ministry were recruited from the supernumeraries who worked there, and, from time to time, secretaries were promoted to minister, and ministers to ambassador. This was training in the sense of apprenticeship, but it should not be confused with a formal, regulated training system or program. Some degree of apprenticeship had always existed in the French Ministry of Foreign Affairs. Many of the diplomats Napoleon inherited from the Old Regime and the Revolution had reached the position of minister or ambassador only after years of service at the more junior ranks of chargé d'affaires or secretary. Cacault, for example, had entered the Old Regime service as secretary in Naples. During the Revolution he had worked up from chargé d'affaires to minister in a minor legation, and served Napoleon as minister to the Papacy. Bacher had been trained in the Ministry, served as secretary for eleven years, and was chargé d'affaires when Napoleon came to power. Others such as Laforest had worked upwards through the consular service.

Naturally Napoleon continued to recruit many of his senior diplomats from the junior levels of the service. He selected several of his first ministers from the Ministry in Paris, including such career diplomats as Reinhard and Durant. Many of the professional diplomats of the Old Regime who had begun as secretaries or attachés were retained and promoted by Napoleon. Laforest began his service to Napoleon as secretary to the general peace negotiations of 1802, became minister in a minor German post, minister plenipotentiary in Berlin, then ambassador to Madrid. Many of the better secretaries such as Serurier, Latour-Maubourg, Hédouville, or Demoustier were promoted to ministerial positions. Similarly, beneath the rank of minister, a successful attaché could become secretary, the better secretaries moved from second to first class or to more important and prestigous embassies. Within the Ministry, the better qualified personnel moved slowly but steadily up the ladder of authority. Sufficient examples of such apprenticeship and promotion can be found to establish the diplomatic service as a professional and hierarchical bureaucracy; but such apprenticeship did not constitute formal diplomatic training. It was too haphazard, too irregular, too subject to abuse to satisfy either Napoleon or the professional instincts of the Ministry of Foreign Affairs.

The necessity for a method of training diplomats was recognized by the new Napoleonic government. By article two of the Law of 3 Floréal, Year VIII (23 April 1800) on the organization of the personnel, a class of aspirants was established in the diplomatic service. They were to serve alternately in the Ministry and the legations, and were to be trained and examined. Those aspirants who exhibited sufficient aptitude for diplomacy were to be promoted to the rank of *élève*, and the successful *élèves* would later become *commis* in the Ministry or secretaries in the legations. The position of aspirant would be temporary, but the *élèves* would definitely be attached to the career and they would have an annual salary of 600 francs. The method of examination and the plan of instruction were to be determined later.[3] The form letter which all aspirants received did not indicate a very elaborate system of training. Talleyrand, the Minister of Foreign Affairs, was appointing them on the basis of a report on their studies and aptitude. The head of the legation to which the aspirant was attached would decide whether the aspirant should be promoted to *élève*.[4] It was, in short, a simple method of apprenticeship with the original selection undetermined and promotion in the hands of the ambassadors and ministers.

The first evidence of the application of the law is a letter from Talleyrand to Napoleon, dated in the Year VIII (1800), stating that Talleyrand was selecting a number of *élèves* from among the young men in the Ministry—the rest would remain aspirants.[5] At least six persons received the form letter stating that they had been appointed aspirants and could be promoted to *élève*.[6] A document in the archives lists approximately fifty aspirants, and the total number appointed was over sixty.[7] They assisted at various negotiations, and were found in the Ministry and in almost every legation and embassy.

A plan of study was devised in Germinal of the Year X. It assumed that the aspirants knew French, Latin, one or two modern languages, geography, and history. The program included the study of public law, maps, history, genealogies, and constitutions. For this study, the correspondence and memoirs in the Ministry could be used, and the students might make indexes of the volumes in the archives.[8] Several aspirants were attached to the Archives Division. La Tour du Pin, after two years in Russia, worked in the Archives for five years under Tessier, director of diplomatic students.[9] Adolphe Merinville spent two years in the archives researching, classifying, and indexing the political correspondence with England for 1764.[10] The other aspirants in the Ministry did various types of work in the archives and the political divisions, familiarizing themselves with the methods of work and of negotiations and with France's relations with various states.

Part of the training consisted of supplementing the regular courier service in times of emergency or of carrying special packages such as treaties. It was an excellent practice. A student on his way to St. Petersburg would, at each French legation along the way, deliver instructions from Paris, meet the minister and his secretaries, dine or stay overnight. On occasion students were even introduced at court. In the conversations at the table, in private conversations with the young secretaries and attachés, in interviews with the minister, the student would come to appreciate aspects of diplomacy which could never be imparted by formal instruction. In traveling back and forth across Europe the student would acquire a vast knowledge of topography, of conditions, of the economies, of peoples and governments, and of public opinion. Upon returning, he would be interviewed by the Foreign Minister and possibly by Napoleon himself. By the time of appointment as secretary, some students had traveled throughout Europe and knew dozens of French diplomats. It was an exciting and stimulating experience, pregnant with opportunity for the eager and inquisitive student. It was one of many exciting adventures of a preindustrial age, destroyed forever by modern technology.

Several secretaries were recruited from among these diplomatic students. In some cases the training was highly relevant—Portalis *fils*, attaché at the negotiation of the Treaty of Amiens, became secretary in London. St. Genèst, Garonne, Lablanche, and Bogne de Faye were all appointed secretaries in the legations in which they had served their apprenticeship. Before his appointment as secretary in Russia, Prévost had been aspirant in Russia for two years, in the Archives Division for one year, in Constantinople for one year, and had written a memoir on the murder of Paul I of Russia, a subject of considerable importance at the time. Serurier's career indicates the most consistent attempt at training.

He became secretary in Cassel after serving a short apprenticeship in the Ministry. After he left Cassel, his supervisor, Bignon, recommended him by stating that he had studied diligently all aspects of diplomacy and had executed successfully all the missions entrusted to him. Then, before taking up a new position as chargé d'affaires in Holland, he returned to the Ministry, studied all the correspondence with Holland from 1795 to 1805, and wrote a twenty-three page report on Franco-Dutch relations and all the developments in Holland in the ten-year period. Even his position as chargé d'affaires and first secretary in Holland was a matter of training for higher office, which he achieved in 1811 with his appointment as minister in the United States.[11]

In all, fifteen aspirants were promoted to secretary and five were promoted to *commis* in the Ministry. But in spite of these twenty cases of promotion, the program envisaged in the Law of 3 Floréal, Year VIII was only a partial success. Apart from Talleyrand's initial division of the existing apprentices into *élèves* and aspirants, there are no examples of aspirants being promoted to *élève*, and after a while the distinction between the two grades became blurred in the official correspondence. While a plan of study was designed and followed in some cases, the method of examination was never adopted. Rivals, whose son had been appointed aspirant in his legation, asked if his son's promotion could be based on an examination rather than a personal recommendation, which would naturally be biased by the family connection, but the letter went unanswered.[12]

There were other faults in the program. As with any system of apprenticeship, the training could be only as good as the minister directing it. Hédouville, a general inexperienced in diplomacy, was given eight students to train while Cacault, a diplomat of twenty-five years' experience, was given only one. The eight attachés in Russia were in the worst possible location for training: St. Petersburg was at the far end of the diplomatic system, no other diplomats or heads of state passed through Russia, and it was difficult to communicate with the Russians. Bavaria was a far better location in terms of diplomatic activity, but only one student was trained there. The wastage rate among the students was high, and many of those who wanted to stay in the career and were even recommended, had to find other jobs. Some of these were inexcusably treated. By 1811 Didelot-Ferté had spent ten years as an attaché, four of them in Denmark. He was in Denmark at the time, the position of second secretary was vacant, and he was recommended for it by his brother, the former minister to Denmark; by Alquier, the new minister; and by Desaugieres *ainé*, the chargé d'affaires and first secretary. His application was ignored; the position remained vacant.[13] The appointment of an aspirant was often a convenience rather than a serious attempt to train diplomats. Any minister could have his son or relative attached to his mission, but when it came to promoting the attaché to a paid position, it became obvious that the Ministry had little intention of treating the position seriously.

This formal program of apprenticeship was never canceled—years later attachés were still being promoted to secretaries, and secretaries trained in the system were becoming ministers. But Napoleon was not at all satisfied with the way the diplomatic service handled its training program. In fact, he was not satisfied with any of the methods of training used by the various branches of the French administration.

In his general concepts of bureaucracy, Napoleon was decades ahead of his time. This is especially true of his ideas about administrative training. He firmly believed that a modern bureaucracy must be staffed by qualified persons trained specifically in the ways of administrative procedure. What he wanted was a single training program from which all branches of the administration would receive their chief functionaries. Those in the program must form a group and have a title which carried prestige and influence. They would be recruited from the governing class of the French state, for those were the families with whom they would have to work. But entrance would also have to be sufficiently flexible to allow gifted young men to advance. Thus, the young men would come from the ancient families with the tradition of public service, from the families that had risen during the Revolution, from the families of Napoleonic officialdom, and from those who lacked such connections but exhibited outstanding ability. The whole system operated under the Council of State, the chief legislative body in France. The program was known as the auditoriat of the Council of State; the young men were the *auditeurs*.

The system began with the Law of 19 Germinal, Year XI (April 9, 1803) by which sixteen *auditeurs* were attached to the five sections of the Council of State and to the six ministries represented on the Council, Justice (Legislative Section), Finances and Public Treasury (Finances Section), Interior, War, and Marine. After several years of training in the Council, the *auditeurs* were to be attached to the administrative and judicial careers. A decree of 26 December 1809 determined the qualifications for becoming an *auditeur*. The candidate had to be under the age of twenty-one, have satisfied the conscription laws, and have a guaranteed income of 6,000 francs. After two or three years at the Council, the *auditeur* would be examined by three Councillors of State. This law confirmed the division between the 40 *auditeurs* attached to the various ministries and the Council, the *service ordinaire*, and the 120 *auditeurs* in the *service extraordinaire*, and confirmed their salaries of from 500 to 2,000 francs. The Law of 7 April 1811 divided the auditoriat into eighty first, ninety second, and 180 third class *auditeurs*. This law also established a system of promotion, with one year as third class necessary before promotion to second class, and two years as second class before promotion to first class.[14]

Originally the system did not include the training of diplomats, partly because the Ministry had its own program, partly because the Ministry was too jealous to allow any other body to interfere with its personnel. Then, in 1806, Napoleon decided to bring diplomatic training under the auditoriat. The debate in the Council of State was introduced by Hauterive, senior employee in the Ministry and its representative in the Council.[15] Hauterive proposed the decree stating that all the secretarial positions vacant or coming vacant would be given to *auditeurs* of the Council of State, who had first spent a period of study and attendance at the Council. According to Hauterive, the most important advantages would be that Napoleon would know the *auditeurs* personally and that they would be motivated by personal devotion to him. The secondary advantages were the training, seriousness, maturity of judgment, and knowledge they would gain at the Council of State. The *auditeurs* could not become secretaries until they had completed one year at the Council, and the existing personnel, internal and external, would not be affected in the present or in the future by the decree. The new system, then, was an extension of the auditoriat of the Council of State to include the Ministry of Foreign Affairs. Two months later Napoleon asked Talleyrand to recommend the most capable *auditeurs* to the vacancies.[16] Apart from one appointment, the decree was, for reasons unknown, forgotten for the next four years.

The policy of training secretaries in the auditoriat was inaugurated in 1810 with the appointment of eight *auditeurs* to the Ministry of Foreign Affairs. The Council of State was then asked to determine the salaries, functions, and training of these eight *auditeurs*, a function that was initiated by the Councillor of State St. Jean d'Angély, who referred to the auditoriat as "a nursery of diplomatic agents who would be reliable, educated, and capable." The *auditeurs*, according to St. Jean, should be trained in the Ministry, for secrecy was essential in diplomacy and the external secretaries had to be highly trusted. The young *auditeurs* should have nothing to do with the secretaries in the legations. (This idea was applied: in the early years there were dozens of diplomatic students in the external service. After 1810 almost all the students were trained in the Ministry in Paris). Secondly, St. Jean assumed that Napoleon wanted the *auditeurs* instructed and had drawn up a plan of studies. There were several things the *auditeurs* could do by way of apprenticeship: they could do the preparatory work for any matters of foreign affairs which the Council of State debated, and they might participate in the debate; they could assist at conferences; they could receive foreign princes and diplomats at the frontiers and accompany them to Paris; and they could deliver Napoleon's letters to foreign sovereigns.[17]

St. Jean proceeded to describe the plan of studies that would be developed for the *auditeurs*. It was assumed that they had a general education and an excellent knowledge of modern history. They would have to take a course in public law. The actual diplomatic training would take place in the Archives Division of the Ministry. There they would study the strengths and weaknesses of the various countries and the changes in relative power, the methods used in negotiations, and the methods of maintaining peace and the honor and dignity of the sovereign. The specific project would be a study of the Seven Years' War. Each of the eight *auditeurs* would study the correspondence with one country, would examine the general situation before and after the Treaty of Aix-la-Chapelle and during the eight years of peace before the war, and all the memoirs drawn up for the period. They would analyze the documents chronologically and write a résumé of the events and diplomacy leading up to the war. To assist the study, the Ministry drew up a detailed bibliography of the best books, a catalogue of maps and prints which could be used, and a list of the best histories of the modern states. The project would be supervised, and the *auditeurs* would be advised and examined by Hauterive. They would learn of the key developments in diplomacy, mistakes that had been made, and the way in which the mistakes had combined with the situation to produce disasters. They would also learn to appreciate "The importance of credit, of character, and especially of a good reputation."[18]

The examination of the *auditeurs* before the committee of three Councillors of State provided a sophisticated method of evaluating the candidates. The examination results stated the candidate's age, wealth, family background, education, experience, preference for employment, the supporter of his application, plus the opinion of the three examiners. Chasteau, one of the *auditeurs* promoted secretary, belonged to "one of the most distinguished families of Bordeaux. He had received an excellent education, and knew languages and history." Brunet de Panat had studied Latin, mathematics, Italian, English, history, public law and, in the opinion of the examiners, was so well prepared that he could be employed almost anywhere. Marquet de Montbreton had studied Latin and German, but needed further instruction. He was attached to the Ministry but was not promoted to secretary.[19] The secretaries who were nominated for the position of *auditeur* were also examined by the committee. The quality and quantity of the information in these examination reports is so superior to that in the personnel dossiers of the diplomats that one must conclude that this was the first time the government had accurate documentary evidence on the education, background, experience, and quality of its external agents.

The system of *auditeurs* marked a tremendous advance in technique over the previous system of training or the general system of apprenticeship. In contrast to the system of *auditeurs*, that of apprenticeship required no minimum standards of education or languages, no administrative training, no archival research, no family or financial support, no regular promotion, and no examination. The wastage rate among the diplomatic students was high, making the career uncertain; the system was haphazard and uneven in the quality and length of the training. Almost all these defects were overcome by recruiting the secretaries from the auditoriat. The only advantage of apprenticeship was that the old diplomatic students often had several years of experience in the external service which the *auditeurs* lacked at the time of their appointments as secretaries. The auditoriat was, in short, an advanced and modern method of diplomatic training, one on which it would be difficult to improve.

The eight *auditeurs*—de Chasteau, de Gabriac, de Marcieu, de Maussion, Marquet de Montbreton, Prévost, Jordan, and D'Asnières—were appointed to the Office of External Relations of the Council of State on 21 June 1810. Of these eight, Jordan, Prévost, and D'Asnières were already in the external service, where they remained. The other five went to the Ministry to be trained by Tessier and Hauterive. Chasteau and Marcieu wrote historical memoirs on the diplomatic correspondence for the period from the Treaty of Aix-la-Chapelle to the Treaty of Paris of 1763. The reports, completed under the direction of Tessier, were checked very carefully by Hauterive.[20] After several years in the Ministry, Chasteau was appointed secretary in Stuttgart, Marcieu became secretary in Dresden, and Gabriac was appointed secretary in Naples. Marquet and Maussion remained at the Ministry until 1813, Maussion assisting at the sittings of the Council of State presided over by Napoleon. In January 1812 two more *auditeurs*, Laubepin and Brunet de Panat, were attached to the Ministry, though Laubepin had been a *commis* for eight years. Six months later Brunet was appointed attaché in the Warsaw embassy.

It is necessary to establish the degree to which the program of March 1806 and the plan of September 1810 were applied. The whole matter became greatly confused, for many secretaries received the title of *auditeur* without ever training in the Council of State. In determining the effectiveness of the program, one must exclude these secretaries from the survey. Durand, in his study of the *auditeurs*, mentions the decree and the fact that there were five *auditeurs* in the secretarial corps in 1813. He does not, however, state whether they were *auditeurs* appointed as secretaries or secretaries given the honorary title of *auditeur*, and he confuses the question by mentioning the *auditeurs* in other positions in the service.[21] Masson mentions the decree and lists the *auditeurs* by name, drawing no distinction between those who were *auditeurs* first and those who were secretaries.[22] Bruun states unequivocally that after 1807 all the secretaries of legation were chosen from the auditoriat, assuming that if Napoleon willed it, then it must have been so.[23] By 1812–13 nine of the twenty secretaries were *auditeurs*, but only three of them had actually been trained as *auditeurs*. However, the program did not come into operation until 1810, and of the seven secretaries appointed after 1810, three were *auditeurs*, three others being students from the previous system of training. In spite of this apparent success and application, the auditoriat, as a method of training diplomats, was in serious trouble by 1813.

The attempt to impose the training system of the auditoriat on the diplomatic service involved Napoleon in a direct confrontation with the Ministry, a confrontation in which Napoleon was the loser. This was the only major issue of administrative reorganization in which Napoleon and the Ministry were at odds. Napoleon's failure to impose his will casts an interesting light on the inherent strengths of an entrenched bureaucracy or, alternately, on the weaknesses of a new government, however dictatorial and determined, which has ideas unacceptable to the civil service. In the auditoriat, Napoleon desired a common training program from which all branches of the administration could be staffed. But the Ministry of Foreign Affairs wanted a program which would be essentially under its own control. There could be no compromise between two such programs. The Ministry was willing to accept the auditoriat on condition that existing members of the diplomatic service be appointed and trained as *auditeurs* and then returned to diplomacy. In other words, the selection and promotion and part of the training of the candidates were to be in the hands of the Ministry. This point was made abundantly clear by Hauterive in 1806 when he introduced the debate on the *auditeurs* in the Council of State, for in that debate Hauterive argued strongly that existing secretaries should be appointed and trained as *auditeurs*.[24] In fact, the Ministry had already prepared a draft decree listing sixteen secretaries and five *commis* whom they wanted appointed as *auditeurs*.[25]

However, such ministerial interference in the auditoriat would completely thwart Napoleon's plan for a common program independent of all the individual ministries. Napoleon had explained this clearly to Talleyrand and Hauterive before the debate in the Council of State. The fact that Hauterive persisted in his argument before the whole Council of State is an important indication of the degree of opposition Napoleon tolerated in that body. Hauterive had his say, but Napoleon's will was dominant. Secretaries were not to become *auditeurs*, the Ministry was not to select the *auditeurs*, and the draft decree appointing secretaries and *commis* as *auditeurs* was ignored.

Napoleon had won the debate in the Council of State. He had triumphed over the civil service in theory, but had he won in practice? The answer is no. Within the year a number of secretaries were appointed *auditeurs* without ever experiencing the training of the auditoriat and without ever losing their identification with the diplomatic service. Napoleon could draft his own laws word-for-word and force them through the assemblies without change, but he could not supervise the detailed application of those laws. There were dozens of secretaries and hundreds of *auditeurs*. Napoleon could not check personally every application to keep secretaries out of the auditoriat. His intentions were therefore betrayed by the bureaucracy through the simple nonapplication of the decree or by ignoring the decree and recommending whomever they wanted as *auditeurs*. And they recommended secretaries for the title of *auditeur* in spite of Napoleon's repeated objections, both oral and written.

The appointment of many diplomats as *auditeurs* was not the only violation of Napoleon's will. Ultimately it mattered little that many secretaries acquired the title of *auditeur*. What did matter was whether new diplomats were trained in the auditoriat. Here the Ministry substantially modified Napoleon's intentions. As explained, some *auditeurs* were attached to the Ministry to complete their training, and some of these were promoted to secretary. As they left, vacancies occurred for new *auditeurs* who had completed their education and common training in the Council of State. Hauterive attempted to have these vacancies filled by diplomatic students selected by the Ministry. This, of course, was refused, as it would have destroyed the common features of the auditoriat program. The refusal, in turn, made Hauterive increasingly determined to oppose and frustrate a program which he and the Ministry could not control.[26]

In 1813 the Secretary of State, Maret, asked the Minister of Foreign Affairs which of the first-class *auditeurs* he wanted to appoint to the four vacancies in the Ministry. In a long letter to the Minister, Hauterive recommended that the Minister ignore the request and not fill the vacancies at all. In Hauterive's opinion, only certain people had the natural qualities for diplomacy and these qualities would have to be verified before intensive training, naturally by several years of apprenticeship at the Ministry, preferably under Hauterive's supervision. If suitable, the Ministry could then send them to the auditoriat for administrative training, then reappoint them to diplomacy. The Ministry would control their careers throughout. Maret was asking the Ministry to recruit its students from a group of *auditeurs* already selected, supervised, trained, and examined by persons outside the Ministry. Hauterive, ever jealous of the prerogatives of the Ministry, regarded this as a humiliation, as placing diplomacy in a subordinate position to the Secretary of State. Such jealousy was traditional for Foreign Affairs—Hauterive spent his entire life arguing that Foreign Affairs should enjoy a special relationship with Napoleon and all sorts of privileges (like separate archives) not bestowed on other ministries. At any rate, if Foreign Affairs could not send its own personnel to the auditoriat for training, then it did not want *auditeurs* at all, regardless of their qualities. Caulaincourt accepted Hauterive's advice

—the four vacancies were never filled.[27] Napoleon, of course, was completely absorbed with the campaign in Germany and could not possibly take the time and effort to force his will on the Ministry.

By 1813 there were only three *auditeurs* left in the Ministry; in effect, the program had been abandoned. Had Napoleon won in 1813–14 the plan doubtlessly would have been revived. In the appointment of secretaries as *auditeurs*, in the refusal to recruit diplomatic students from among the trained *auditeurs*, the Ministry openly and successfully obstructed the will of the "dictator." When Napoleon's opinions clashed with the deeply rooted prejudices of the bureaucracy, Napoleon's decrees got no further than the third level of the administrative pyramid (the top three levels being Napoleon, the Cabinet Ministers, and the *chefs de division* like Hauterive). When he could, Napoleon controlled every detail of administration, or appointed trusted friends to execute his will. But he and his friends could not control everything. Hauterive was in the Ministry eleven years before Napoleon's coup d'état and was still there fifteen years after Napoleon's abdication. In France governments come and go; the bureaucracy goes on forever.

Beginning with the traditional system of apprenticeship, the Napoleonic government made two attempts to impose a formal method of training on the diplomatic service. The system of apprenticeship had long been in existence, with some secretaries and *commis* being recruited from the miscellaneous personnel in the Ministry and the legations. It was essential to an established bureaucracy, for it meant that diplomats moved up a regular pyramid of positions, being promoted to higher office only after the fulfillment of lesser duties. But it did not include supervised training, and it was haphazard in its application. Far superior was the plan of 1800 whereby young diplomatic students would receive specific training in the Ministry or the legations, and move by fixed stages into the lower levels of the administration.

While this marked a vast improvement over simple apprenticeship, it did not satisfy Napoleon's lust for rationality, uniformity, and central control. In 1806 he decided to extend the training program of the auditoriat of the Council of State to the diplomatic service. This plan provided a thorough method of selecting, training, and examining young administrators, some of whom could then receive intensive training in the Ministry before becoming secretaries in the legations. It was a modern and sophisticated system. It was also the only major administrative reform at-

tempted within the diplomatic service by Napoleon. Unfortunately, the
Ministry wanted complete control of its training program, and eventually
was able to avoid selecting as diplomatic students *auditeurs* who had been
trained for general administration in the Council of State. The success of
the Ministry in thwarting Napoleon's intentions provides an excellent
illustration of the bureaucratic limitations on Napoleon's power, and of
the traditional jealousy of the Ministry of Foreign Affairs. But before
the program was stifled, several young diplomats succeeded in obtaining
a preparation for administration and diplomacy vastly superior to anything that had existed before or was to exist until well into the twentieth
century.

Taken together, these three systems produced a highly skilled and
trained service, the vast majority of whose members had been profes-
sionally trained or prepared for the positions they held. In the Ministry
itself, many of the *commis* had begun as attachés, almost all of the senior
commis had previously served in junior positions. Under Napoleon six
men were appointed *sous chef*. All of them had previously been *commis*.
Five others became *chef*, four of them being promoted from the lower
ranks. Twenty-eight students or *auditeurs* were promoted to the position
of secretary, accounting for 60% of all new secretaries appointed by Napoleon. In the first five years, 45% of the secretaries had been students;
between 1805 and 1809, 55% had been students; and after 1809, 70%
of secretaries had been trained for their positions. The trend towards
formal diplomatic training was unmistakable. Twenty-six of Napoleon's
ambassadors and ministers had previously occupied inferior ranks in the
service or been trained specifically for their positions. Many others were
promoted from minister to ambassador or from minor to major legations. Within the service this trend towards better training was continuous. There was a steady increase in the number of appointments of
those trained for the service with the result that every year there was a
higher proportion of *commis*, secretaries, and ministers who had previously been trained for their positions. Although this trend towards professionalization came partly from within the service, it came mainly from
Napoleon.

Chapter 6

The Diplomatic Career

Napoleon, it is commonly believed, established or consolidated the "career open to talent." Hiring, promotion, and reward were supposedly based on merit rather than on birth or connections as in the Old Regime. Like many generalizations about Napoleon, this one has never really been proved, certainly not for the diplomatic service. In many aspects the Napoleonic administration returned to pre-Revolutionary practices. Was this true of hiring, promotion, and reward as well? Why exactly did Frenchmen enter the diplomatic service? Were they attracted by the salary, the prestige, the emoluments, and if so, were their expectations fulfilled? We will never really know what life was like for a Napoleonic diplomat. We cannot recreate his life, but we can read his complaints and learn about the conditions under which he labored. We can discover many of the rewards and vexations of the diplomatic career.[1]

The salaries of ministers were fixed according to the post. In general there were three categories of posts and hence of ranks—embassies (ambassadors), legations (ministers), and residences (residents and chargés d'affaires *en titre*). If a specific mission were upgraded or downgraded, the rank and hence the salary of the diplomat would be changed. The diplomats in different posts within this general framework received different salaries depending on the importance of the post and on the cost of living. Ambassadors in the large states received between 150,000 and 250,000 francs; those in Naples and Holland received 80,000. The most notable exception was Caulaincourt, who received 480,000 francs as ambassador to Russia. At the other end of the scale, the diplomats in the residences in Parma, Frankfort, or Ratisbon received salaries of less than 30,000. The ministers in eleven of the legations received salaries of 40,000 francs. A number of legations carried salaries of 40,000 to 60,000 francs. These included the minor powers of Bavaria, Denmark, and Florence. Only the most important legations—Berlin, Philadelphia, Naples—carried salaries of over 80,000 francs. Throughout the period there was a gradual inflation in the salaries as the minor residences were eliminated and the other missions such as those in Germany were upgraded.

It was established in the chapter on personnel that the most important positions in the diplomatic service went to Napoleon's closest friends—his relatives, generals from the Armies of Italy or Egypt, or his aides-de-camp. Naturally, these people received the highest salaries. Twenty of the seventy-one diplomats received salaries of over 100,000. They included three of Napoleon's relatives, five of his aides-de-camp, four officers from the Army of Italy, two other generals, and the Abbé de Pradt from the Imperial Household. Of the remaining five, three held large salaries only briefly. Only two professional diplomats, Otto and Laforest, worked their way to a high salary: both had over thirty years' experience before becoming ambassadors.

Eighteen ministers earned salaries of 80,000 francs. They included seven generals, six professional diplomats, and four diplomats who spent a large part of the Napoleonic period in diplomacy. Of the twenty-nine ministers who received salaries of 40,000 to 60,000 francs, six were generals. The noticeable difference at this level is that twelve of the twenty-nine were professional diplomats and five others were diplomats through most of the period. This trend is further accentuated at the lowest level of the pay scale. Of the fourteen diplomats who earned less than 40,000 francs, eight were professional diplomats and four spent most of the period in diplomacy. Often the salary paid in a specific post would be increased if the new diplomat were one of Napoleon's friends. Cardinal Fesch succeeded Cacault and obtained two and one half times Cacault's salary. Cacault had twenty-five years' experience, but Fesch was Napoleon's uncle. Not only did the generals receive the best-paid positions in the service, but many of them were allowed to retain their military pay as well, a privilege doubtless resented by the professional diplomats.

Since the salary depended on the post, a promotion usually consisted of transfer to a more important position carrying greater prestige and salary. Six ministers were promoted after less than four years of service. Included in this group were Josephine's uncle Beauharnais, Josephine's chamberlain Aubusson, Generals Hédouville and Narbonne, and Councillor of State Champagny. Only one, Cacault, was a career diplomat. Of the five who received promotions while serving four to eight years, Beurnonville and Vial were generals, Eschasseriaux and Sémonville were Revolutionary politicians, and Auguste Talleyrand was one of Napoleon's chamberlains. Such career diplomats as Bacher, Durant, Helflinger, Hirsinger, and Massias received only one promotion in approximately ten years, and some of these were insignificant. Besides this Alquier, Andréossy, Derville-Maléchard, and Bourgoing, with an average of eight years' service, actually received less in their last post than in their first.

However, as Talleyrand proved, a diplomat's salary could sometimes be augmented by graft. In this respect, the most successful diplomat, next to Talleyrand, was Bourrienne. As minister to Hamburg, his salary was only 40,000 francs. However, Hamburg was a chief port of entry for British goods, and it remained so in spite of the Continental System. This system was designed to exclude English goods, but to distinguish between these and non-English goods it was necessary to have a certificate of origin. The easiest way to evade the system was to obtain false certificates of origin which various people, such as Bourrienne, were willing to issue—for a price. Actually Bourrienne's corruption should not have surprised anyone, for his original appointment to Hamburg, resulting from his involvement in a financial scandal, was intended as a disgrace. Thus Napoleon does not seem to have been surprised to learn that Bourrienne had accumulated seven to eight million francs from violations of the Continental System. This astronomical figure was the equivalent of the annual costs of the Ministry.

Napoleon's attitude toward the situation clarifies his policy on corruption. In letters to Davout, who commanded the French forces in northern Germany, and to Champagny, Napoleon stated that Bourrienne had received this sum and that it would be relinquished and used for public works. To begin with, Bourrienne would contribute two million francs towards the construction of the new Ministry of Foreign Affairs. Six months later Napoleon decided that the situation would have to be investigated and that Bourrienne would have to give three-quarters of the money to the new Ministry building.[2] It is interesting that Bourrienne was not punished and that he could keep one-quarter, which was two million francs. In the official history of Napoleon's foreign policy, Bignon states that Napoleon sent Bourrienne the bill for the new Ministry. The anti-Napoleonic bias of Bourrienne's memoirs[3] is therefore not surprising.

Few salaries are ever "adequate," and Napoleon's ministers were not slow in complaining about their "poverty" and "hardships." Hirsinger thought his salary was inadequate; Helflinger wanted help with his debts; Massias's personnel dossier is filled with complaints about his low salary, his expenses, the tardiness with which his expenses were paid, and of his resulting debts. Beurnonville, who always found his salary meager, was the only diplomat to complain about his salary and travel grant as well as establishment costs.[4] Some complaints could not be justified. The avaricious Abbé de Pradt complained that his salary and establishment expenses were too low, although his salary was three times that of his predecessor, and according to Bignon, he had in addition to 150,000 francs as diplomat, 30,000 as bishop, expenses of establishment of 50,000, and nevertheless had asked Warsaw to provide an embassy for him.[5]

Several specific cases of inadequate salaries can be identified. During the Napoleonic period, Saxony became an important French satellite, an outpost on the flank of both Austria and Prussia, and an advance post with regard to Russia. It was an important communications center for the French system, and the King of Saxony became Duke of Warsaw. In spite of this, the salary of the minister, 40,000 francs, had not changed for forty years, and Bourgoing complained that if the salary were not increased, he and his family would be ruined. Champagny enumerated all of the reasons in a report to Napoleon: Bourgoing's pay was smaller than that of other ministers in Germany, the expenses of Dresden were increasing daily, the legation was a stopover for dozens of travelers, and Saxony's political importance had increased greatly in the previous fifteen years so the minister had to entertain on a higher level. Besides all this, Bourgoing was an old and able diplomat with a large family. As a result the salary was increased to 50,000 francs. This satisfied Bourgoing, but his successor found that sum inadequate.[6]

Although such justified complaints were sometimes acted upon, more often, the salary was left unchanged. If a salary were inadequate because of peculiar circumstances, then Napoleon preferred to make a special reimbursement to the minister rather than to increase the formal salary, which would tend to be a permanent change. These special reimbursements could come from the secret budget. Caulaincourt received 100,000 francs per year in this way. A more common method was to grant a *gratification.* In normal times the French minister in Austria would be treated much like the French minister in England or Russia. In the Napoleonic period, however, Austria was particularly important, so the French ambassador to Austria received annually a *gratification* of 40,000 to 50,000 francs. Sometimes ministers were given extraordinary grants to cover special expenses, although some of these, such as 100,000 francs for Fesch and 180,000 for Beauharnais, could better be classified as corruption.

The salaries of the secretaries were fixed according to the posts. In the embassies, the first secretaries had salaries of 12,000 francs, the second secretaries usually had 8,000 to 9,000, the third secretaries received 4,000 to 5,000 francs. In the legations, most first secretaries received 6,000 to 8,000, the second paid only 4,000 to 6,000. The legations with only one secretary paid only 4,000 francs. Private secretaries were paid by their ministers; attachés or diplomatic students received no salary. These secretarial salaries were almost completely stable. Of the forty-six secretarial positions, the salaries in thirty-nine remained unchanged throughout the period. Most of the secretaries, however, received rapid increases in salary as they were promoted from the lower ranks or transferred from smaller legations. Promotion could, in fact, be very rapid, and many secretaries doubled their salaries after only five years' service.

The employees of the Ministry received lower salaries than the diplomats in the external service, but since they had no expenses to pay out of their salaries, their real income may have been equal to or greater than that of the members of the external service. In 1800 the *chefs* were paid 10,000 francs. After one year, this was raised to 12,000, then to 18,000 in 1802. Similarly, the salaries of the *sous chefs* were raised in the first few years from 6,000 to 9,000 francs. This brought the salaries of the chief employees into line with the importance of their functions and the inflation of the Revolution. They remained fixed at 18,000 and 9,000 for the rest of the period and into the Restoration. For the *commis* and miscellaneous staff, there was a gradual inflation of salaries throughout the period. For example, a first *commis* received about 3,500 francs in 1800. By 1802 this had increased to 4,000 and was 6,000 by 1805.

Promotion in the Ministry itself was made essentially on the basis of seniority. Twenty-three employees received no salary increases at all—eighteen of these served less than four years, only two served over eight years. On average the employees were promoted every four years, promotion being in proportion to seniority, the reverse of the situation in the ministerial corps. The size of these salary increases is also relevant. For those serving less than four years, the increase amounted to less than 50% of the original salary. Of those serving four to eight years, eight received increases between 50% to 100% and two had their salaries doubled. But of those serving over twelve years, ten received increases of less than 50%, eleven had increases between 50% to 100%, and seven had their salaries doubled. None of the diplomatic students in the Ministry received salaries, though they could receive reimbursements or gifts for special services or missions.

Besides financial rewards, there were a number of emoluments for diplomatic service, such as titles in the nobility.[7] The Napoleonic nobility was created primarily for three reasons: to stabilize the Empire; to fuse the ruling elements of the Old Regime, the Revolution, and the Napoleonic regime; and to serve as a system of reward. The greatest reward went to the first Minister of Foreign Affairs when Talleyrand became a Prince. Talleyrand's successors all held the title of Duke. Seventeen ministers were given titles of nobility as a reward for diplomatic service, or to enhance the prestige of their office. The list includes practically all of Napoleon's major professional diplomats who attained the rank of minister. The obvious rewards were prestige and increased salary. Alquier requested the title of baron as a reward for his eleven years service; but a comment by Napoleon made it obvious that the title would also enhance his prestige in his new position at the Swedish court.[8] There was some correlation between the service and the rank of the title. Of the five counts, four were members of distinguished Old Regime nobility or held high rank and appointments in major states such as Spain. In six cases the title of baron went to diplomats of the rank of minister plenipotentiary. Lower ranking professional diplomats were often appointed as chevaliers.

A number of titles were given to persons who had distinguished themselves in both diplomacy and some other field. Among them were nine generals, including Caulaincourt, who became Duke of Vicence while serving as ambassador to St. Petersburg. Cardinal Fesch accumulated a number of titles, probably because he was Napoleon's uncle. A number of other titles were bestowed upon ministers that had little or nothing to do with their diplomatic careers. Only three secretaries, Bogne de Faye, Dodun, and LaBlanche, received titles for diplomatic service. Within the Ministry, Hauterive, the senior employee, became chevalier in 1808 and later count; three other *chefs* became chevaliers. It can be concluded that the titles of the Napoleonic nobility were used freely as a reward for diplomatic service, to enhance the prestige of the diplomats, to supplement their salaries, and as an important motivation for entering or remaining in the service.

The Revolution had abolished titles, distinctions, and awards on the assumption that these were unjust symbols of inequality, privilege, favoritism, or corruption, and that an honest republican would work hard and serve loyally simply out of duty and patriotism. Napoleon had a much more realistic appreciation of human nature, of man's natural desire for prestige and honors. "It is with 'baubles' that mankind is governed," Napoleon stated as the proposal to create the Legion of Honour was being debated.[9] The Legion was created in 1802 as a reward for military and nonmilitary service and achievement.[10] Those appointed to the Legion received a decoration, a salary or pension, and the social advantage of belonging to one of the units or cohorts into which the Legion was divided. Let us see how the Legion was used to reward diplomatic achievement and whether the diplomats appreciated these "baubles."

At its creation, the positions in the Legion were divided among the different branches of the administration and the other fields which needed recognition, the army receiving the overwhelming number of appointments. In the initial appointments of Grand Officers only one diplomat, Talleyrand, entered the Legion. On 14 June 1804 (25 Prairial, Year XIII) an enormous number of commanders were appointed, twelve of whom were diplomats. They all received the same letter of congratulations stating that the appointments were an "expression of Napoleon's satisfaction." Lacepède, director of the Legion, later stated that it had been Napoleon's intention to appoint all the ministers as commanders.[11] At roughly the same time the Grand Eagles of the Legion were appointed, only one diplomat, Talleyrand, receiving this title. The *Almanach National* also lists ten diplomats entering the Legion before the Year XIII at the rank of Legionnaire, including three ministers and five *chefs de division* of the Ministry. In all of these cases the Legion was granted for professional reasons. Thus, at the time of its creation, six members of the Ministry and four ministers or secretaries were appointed Legionnaires, twelve ministers were appointed commanders, and Talleyrand was appointed Grand Officer and later Grand Eagle.

After this initial staffing of the Legion, appointments could be made only when a vacancy occurred, or when the entire organization was being expanded. Like other Napoleonic institutions, the Legion soon suffered from neglect because Napoleon refused to delegate the power of appointment to anyone else and did not have the time to supervise all appointments himself. The well organized pattern of the Years XII and XIII soon broke down in practice, and it became very difficult to find any logic or organization in the subsequent appointments. Most, but not all, of the ministers were later appointed, but these appointments were not automatic. Some secretaries entered the Legion, but not necessarily those with the most important functions or the longest service. More important diplomats tended to receive the highest decorations; but only the generals could really count on appointment at the highest level. For the personnel of the Ministry, the first organization suggested that the five main *chefs* would hold membership; but in 1813 Maret argued that since 1804 most of the employees who were members had died or retired, and in nine years the Ministry had not received any new favors.[12] In 1810 Champagny submitted a list of the principal members of the service who had not been nominated: three ministers and three secretaries were soon appointed, three other secretaries were not.[13] This was a haphazard method.

Membership in the Legion was much sought after by the diplomats. Bacher applied for it in the Year X and again in the Year XII, finally receiving the appointment in the Year XIII as a recognition of his forty years' service.[14] Secretaries, such as Dodun, Lefebvre, Latour-Maubourg, and Lajard, all applied directly to the Foreign Minister. Several ministers asked for appointments for their secretaries.[15] Ney, for example, recommended his secretary, Rouyer, arguing that the appointment would be infinitely good for the service by enhancing Rouyer's prestige. The recommendation was passed on to Napoleon by the Foreign Minister, Champagny, and by Lacepède, director of the Legion, but their requests went unheeded.[16] It was not unnatural for persons outside the service to make recommendations. General Hédouville recommended his brother, Théodore. The recommendation was seconded by Lacepède, and Théodore was finally appointed in 1809.[17] The recommendations of the Foreign Minister were often, but not always, decisive. Appointments were much appreciated. Of the first twelve diplomats appointed commanders, at least six replied immediately with expressions of gratitude ranging from simple thanks to Reinhard's boundless gratitude and offer of lifelong devotion to Napoleon.[18]

The Legion of Honour proved the truth of Napoleon's maxim, for indeed it is with "baubles" that men are led. By failing to make membership an automatic reward for appointment or promotion, Napoleon ensured that everyone understood that the fountain of all privilege was Napoleon and Napoleon alone. There was sufficient regularity to make the system work, and sufficient favoritism to make everything ultimately dependent on Napoleon. In its application, the Legion reflected that fine balance between logical administration and personal politics that was the hallmark of Napoleon's political genius.

A further incentive for joining the diplomatic service was the prestige embodied in a foreign decoration. Naturally the Foreign Ministers tended to accumulate the greatest number of foreign decorations, as it was customary for Foreign Ministers to exchange medals in a "mutual admiration society." Ministers sometimes received decorations from the states in which they served, as happened in at least a dozen cases. There was no apparent reason for the presentation: they were given to diplomats of varying quality and length of service and under different circumstances. Sometimes, in the same state, one diplomat would receive a decoration and his successor would not. Only three secretaries obtained foreign decorations, two of them given by Persia, which tended to decorate every member of the French mission, possibly because Persia had not seen a French diplomat since 1715! Before accepting a foreign decoration the diplomat had to have the permission of the French government. Only one French diplomat, the indefatigable Laforest, appears to have asked for a foreign decoration.[19] With his coat glittering and tinkling with assorted decorations, many a French diplomat stood proudly among his compatriots of lesser distinction.

In addition to titles and decorations, there were other rewards to which diplomats aspired and were appointed. Several of the diplomats were promoted directly to ministerial office. Others retired to the Senate, that prestigious and remunerative Valhalla for exhausted diplomats, generals, and politicians. Otto and Laforest received honorary appointments to the Council of State, and in 1813 Otto became a Minister of State, a position of cabinet rank but without responsibilities. Many of the secretaries obtained appointments as *auditeurs* of the Council of State without ever being attached to the Council. Barbie de Bocage, the great geographer of the Ministry, was appointed to the Institute in 1806. Other positions were sought after—Demoustier, for example, wanted to become Napoleon's chamberlain.[20] Diplomats also received medals— all the heads of missions received medals commemorating Napoleon's coronation and later his marriage. Fesch, Napoleon's uncle, obtained a unique reward for his mission. He was allowed to keep the embassy in Rome as his private residence.

The frequency and length of leaves were important factors in the working conditions of the members of the external service. There was little exchange between the internal and external services, and certainly no policy of spending time in the Ministry between missions. Thus a leave was often the only time a professional diplomat returned to France and to Paris. There was no fixed policy for leaves. General Clarke, when requesting a leave, stated that it had always been customary to grant one year's leave after eighteen months' residence,[21] but the evidence suggests that this was far from the truth in practice or in theory. Clarke received only two months' leave.

Available evidence indicates that very few professional diplomats obtained leaves. After four years in one post, Hirsinger received a fortnight's leave to regain his health; after only two months in Sweden, Bourgoing was given three weeks for reasons of health.[22] Durant obtained permission to attend his daughter's wedding. While home he became ill, then his wife became mortally ill, and the leave stretched into ten months.[23] Serra's negotiation for a leave was typical. He first applied in January 1811 because he had been away for three years and private affairs demanded his attention. He reapplied in May, but the request was refused. By the end of May he had developed four excuses for a leave: the desire to give a personal account to Napoleon, three years' absence from France, thirty years' service, and a desperately ill father. A further request in November finally brought success—a brief leave was granted between missions to Württemberg and Saxony.[24]

Secretaries received leaves as infrequently as did the ministers. Only eight examples have been discovered in a secretarial corps of sixty who served on average five years each. The leaves granted were far from automatic—Siméon asked five times in a period of fifteen months before he received a leave, his second in six years.[25] Various reasons for requesting leaves were advanced, but they generally had little effect. After almost six years in the admittedly dangerous climate of Constantinople, Latour-Maubourg began asking for a leave to reestablish his health, but it was granted only when supported by a long medical statement signed by two doctors whose signatures were verified by an independent witness.[26] Demoustier had trouble discovering an effective reason. His first request, based on the death of his grandmother, fell on deaf ears. The second request, based on his desire to marry, was favorably received.[27] Even the rigidities of Napoleonic administration could not extinguish the Frenchman's sympathy with *l'amour*.

One of the hazards of diplomacy was that social responsibilities made it important that the diplomat's wife be suitable. If a person married an unacceptable wife, then he would not be appointed or his wife would not be allowed to accompany him. Unmarried diplomats had to have the permission of the government before they married, a regulation that was spelled out clearly to at least one diplomat.[28] The policy was logical and necessary. Rayneval, the secretary in Russia, applied for permission to marry a woman who was related to the Russian Foreign Minister and whose brother was Alexander's aide-de-camp. Caulaincourt, Champagny, and Alexander supported the application. Napoleon made the decision which he considered to be best for the service: they could marry, but Rayneval could not serve in Russia.[29] One diplomat married without Napoleon's permission. In 1812 Montholon, newly appointed minister to Würzburg, married Mme de Vassal, divorcée of his fellow diplomat Bignon, as well as of M. de Vassal. Montholon was immediately recalled and dismissed from the service as it would be an intolerable affront to the Elector of Würzburg to have a divorcée at his court.

Bignon, while never achieving the diplomatic rank to which he aspired, managed to find compensation in other fields. Besides being one of the discarded husbands of Mme de Vassal, Bignon was involved in a marital controversy in 1808. He had just been appointed minister in Baden when Napoleon heard that he had married a certain Mlle Chevalier who, apparently, had been his "companion" while he was administrator in Berlin in 1806 and 1807. Napoleon believed her too dishonorable to be a French diplomat's wife, and it might prove embarrassing for Bignon to keep her there secretly. If the marriage had taken place, then Bignon would be recalled and given a position within France. With perfect French logic Bignon replied that he knew he needed permission to marry; he had never sought that permission, there-fore he obviously was not married. Besides, nothing could interfere with the pleasure of serving Napoleon. Mlle Chevalier would not accompany him to Baden, and he would break off all contacts with her.[30] Mlle Chevalier seems to have had an affinity for French diplomats, for Hédou-ville mentioned her while he was minister in Russia, and Caulaincourt knew of her. The rule seems to reflect the morality of the age—the mar-riages of diplomats were controlled but it was acceptable to have a mistress. Caulaincourt, whose marriage to the divorced Mme de Canisy Napoleon consistently postponed, took a mistress in Russia, apparently with Napoleon's approval.

In several cases wives were not permitted to join their husbands abroad. Neither Clarke nor Beauharnais could take their wives to Tus-cany; and Beauharnais was even told that he had a choice between his wife and the appointment.[31] He took the appointment. The separation in some cases was dictated by the military situation. Laforest could not have his wife in Spain during the Peninsular War. Larochefoucauld did not have his wife in Austria in 1806,[32] and Lauriston's wife was not per-mitted to accompany him to Russia in 1811, much to Lauriston's regret.

One of the administrative malpractices which was most annoying to diplomats was that they were sometimes appointed or recalled without being properly or quickly informed. Champigny, one of the diplomats inherited in 1799, learned of his recall in the local paper. Aubusson learned of his appointment from the Princess of Lucca, and had to write to Paris for confirmation. Didelot was one of several diplomats who was dismissed or even disgraced without any explanation.[33] The most em-barrassing situation occurred when a successor appeared in the resident capital before the current minister had heard of any change. When Andréossy arrived in Vienna in 1806 the ambassador, Larochefoucauld, had to write to Paris for an explanation and for instructions.[34] One of Talleyrand's unenlightened habits was to promise appointments or re-wards during a conversation which were later forgotten. In one conver-sation with Bacher, both Bacher and his private secretary, Schwebel, were promised appointments. Bacher had to write for confirmation, and Schwebel's appointment never materialized.[35]

The best example of the mistreatment of the diplomats and the uncertainties of the career is the fate of Marivault. In 1805 he heard a rumour that Serurier had been appointed to his position, which was first secretary in Holland. On 19 April 1805 he wrote to Talleyrand, stating that he had heard of Serurier's appointment and that he hoped he would receive a new appointment in Germany or in the prefectoral corps. Eleven days later (he still had not heard officially of Serurier's appointment) he stated that his position was becoming extremely embarrassing and he hoped that Serurier would soon arrive. This time he merely added that he would like to take the waters at Aix. On May 24 Talleyrand wrote to Van de Goes, a member of the Dutch government, stating that Serurier had been appointed since Marivault wanted to take the waters! Three days after that Talleyrand told Marivault that he could take the waters, adding that he would recommend him for a new appointment. Then Talleyrand wrote to Serurier stating that Napoleon had accepted Marivault's request to take the waters, so Serurier was being appointed to the vacancy.[36] No doubt Serurier was an excellent diplomat and was being trained and promoted through the ranks, but Marivault, who was thirty-three years old and had spent thirteen years in diplomacy, was inexcusably treated. Later on he did obtain a position in the administration of the Dutch satellite, but his diplomatic career was in ruins.

Diplomacy could not be regarded as a particularly dangerous or unhealthy profession. Still, some details of the fate of several diplomats illustrate the conditions under which they labored. It was the posts in southern Europe that caused concern. Lamare, former secretary in Constantinople, died in the Middle East of an "acute sickness"; Gandolphe, secretary in Rome, died of a contagion which ravaged Rome in 1804. The climate of Constantinople played havoc with Sébastiani's wounds,[37] though it must be admitted that military wounds tended to become more serious after a diplomatic mission had failed. Persia was the most dangerous post. Rousseau was appointed second secretary, but as Napoleon told Talleyrand, Rousseau's brother could accompany the mission to replace him if he should die. This was no unnecessary precaution. On a mission to Persia in 1806, Romieu had died, English poison being the suspected cause.[38]

Normally the diplomatic service would be one of the safest employments, but the violence of the wars affected diplomatic immunity. All of the known cases of violation of immunity were perpetrated by Russia, the last country to enter the European diplomatic system and hence the one with the least respect for the practices of European diplomacy. In 1812 the Russians captured Édouard Lefebvre, secretary in Berlin. He was classified as a prisoner of war, taken back to Russia, and imprisoned until the peace treaties were signed in 1815. Rayneval was the last member of the French embassy to leave Russia in 1812. On his way from St. Petersburg, he was mistreated, his papers were seized and searched, and he was placed in a slow and leaky boat for the trip to Germany. Napoleon's reply to this provocation was typical: the Russian secretary in Paris was to be treated in exactly the same manner.

Opinions on how hard the diplomats were forced to work must remain largely speculative. Naturally there was great diversity in the workloads in different posts and under different circumstances. Still, one forms the opinion that the Napoleonic diplomats were hard-working administrators. There are three reasons for this impression. First, the dispatches contained a considerable amount of information which would require some effort to obtain and arrange, and the dispatches document some of the activities of the diplomats themselves, such as the number of conversations with Foreign Ministers and heads of state. Second, the diplomats' correspondence includes a considerable number of complaints about the workloads and requests for additional staff. In fact, the workload of the diplomats must have increased steadily, because the amount of information demanded by Paris increased while the size of the external missions was gradually reduced. Finally, such literature as was produced by the diplomats came after and not during the diplomatic missions, which suggests that the diplomats did not have much leisure time. This was not always true for the subordinate personnel. Desaugiers wrote patriotic poetry; Chateaubriand was bored in Rome; and de Ségur wrote frivolous comments on the margins of the legation archives in Copenhagen. But on the whole, one is left with the impression that most of Napoleon's diplomats were hard-working administrators.

Apart from the generals who accepted their diplomatic appointments because they were ordered to do so, there is little specific documentary evidence indicating why diplomats served. From the evidence uncovered, however, a number of reasons can easily be deduced. In the first place, there were the salaries, with most ministers earning about 40,000 francs, secretaries receiving about 6,000, and the employees of the Ministry perhaps 6,000. Officially the government regarded the external salaries as compensation for expenses rather than as pure salaries,[39] but the analysis of salaries paid to the different diplomats suggests that they were rewards as well as repayments. In addition to the salaries, there were numerous fringe benefits. Ministers received expenses for establishment and for service costs, and both ministers and secretaries were reimbursed for travel costs. Often diplomats received *gratifications* to reimburse them for extraordinary expenses or as rewards for their services. In addition, diplomats and negotiators often received a valuable gift at the end of each mission, such as a diamond-studded portrait of the sovereign. When the Treaty of Amiens was signed, each employee of the Ministry received an extra month's pay. The diplomats in the external service traveled considerably, enjoyed excellent food and entertainment, and mixed freely with the highest and most important circles of society. Their position was one of enormous prestige—Caulaincourt, for example, became the personal friend of Alexander I of Russia. The external service was quite unstable during this period, but employment in the Ministry provided a safe and stable career. During his career, or at its completion, a successful minister might expect an appointment to the Legion of Honour, a title in the Napoleonic nobility, a senatorship or appointment to the Council of State. For the employees there was sometimes a small retirement pension.

On the other hand, there were several disadvantages to the career. Salaries were not always adequate, and several diplomats were almost ruined financially by their appointments. For the external service, leaves were rarely granted. Appointments could result in years of virtual exile from France; in fact, diplomatic appointments were sometimes used as a method of exile. In the internal service the most serious drawback would be boredom caused by the failure to transfer people to the external service or even between the divisions, and the slowness of promotion, the inevitable result of the high degree of stability. In the external service the most serious disadvantage was the instability of the career, caused mainly by the wars and international confusion but partly by poor administration. Another serious disadvantage to the external career was that Napoleon's friends were often given the most important missions and the largest salaries. This mistreatment of the regular diplomatic service occurred all too frequently.

Chapter 7

Duties and Functions

Existing studies of European diplomatic institutions tend to ascribe to diplomats a limited variety of activities. For Louis XIV's diplomats, Roosen identified only five duties—negotiating, informing their government regularly, influencing other governments, protecting various people, and defending the King's prestige.[1] Similarly, for the English diplomatic service, two recent studies identify and examine only four or five functions of the ambassador.[2] However, research into the subject of the Napoleonic diplomatic service has revealed that the Napoleonic diplomats were engaged in at least thirteen activities, a substantial difference in functions from the four or five identified by Roosen, Horn, and Lachs. Napoleon, exceptional ruler, demanded more activity from his bureaucrats than did most leaders. It is therefore necessary to distinguish between normal diplomatic functions and those especially relevant to the Napoleonic service. In the former category are the basic duties such as representing France, informing the French government, writing regularly, negotiating treaties, supervising the consular service, and maintaining peace. Other diplomatic duties that were especially important to Napoleonic diplomats included influencing other governments, spreading the Revolution, assisting the army, supervising trade, collecting "contributions," influencing public opinion, and protecting French-owned lands. In all these aspects of the diplomat's work, examples have been drawn from the political correspondence and memoirs of the diplomats themselves, as well as the diplomatic instructions.

The first duty of the Napoleonic diplomat was to represent his country and his sovereign at foreign courts. This duty consisted of being a member of its diplomatic corps, of having a legation and maintaining a *bonne table*, of acting as liaison between the two governments, of keeping the foreign country informed of French policy, or of what Napoleon wanted them to believe was French policy, and of protecting Frenchmen in the foreign state. The formal instructions invariably stated that the diplomat would cultivate good relations between the two states. At other times the diplomats would be instructed to maintain the influence of the French government, to attract the other government to the French system, to gain supremacy over the other members of the diplomatic corps, or to maintain enthusiasm for Napoleon.

Relations between the two countries were coordinated by both the French ambassador abroad and the foreign ambassador in Paris. The degree to which these two channels were used depended on the quality of the two diplomats and on how much they were trusted by the two governments. Franco-Russian relations were coordinated through the French ambassador in Russia, as both Napoleon and Alexander preferred the French ambassador to the Russian ambassador in Paris. On the other hand, Franco-Portuguese relations were maintained largely by Talleyrand and the Portuguese ambassador in Paris, with the French minister, Lannes, fulfilling a secondary role in Lisbon. In fact, Talleyrand was supposed to have told the Portuguese minister that all negotiations would be handled in Paris, and that the Portuguese government could regard Lannes's mission as absolutely meaningless. This story came to Lannes directly from the Portuguese Regent, which indicated a considerable lack of discretion on his part, and which, needless to say, provoked a violent reaction from Lannes.[3]

One of the methods of representing France was the maintenance of a *bonne table* and the holding of various celebrations. These celebrations marked the great French events such as July 14, Napoleon's birthday, important victories, the birth of Napoleon's son, and successful peace negotiations. The celebrations could take various forms, from an illumination to celebrate a victory to the lavish banquets held by the French ambassador to win over the Russian nobility. Lavish entertainment seems to have characterized especially the legations in St. Petersburg, Warsaw, and Dresden. The resident in Warsaw had a special fund of 60,000 francs a year to maintain an "open" table so that everyone interested might be well received. Dresden was the eastern outpost of French domination and an important point of communications—in 1811 the minister's wine cellar contained 1,349 bottles of wine of twenty different types, the most popular ones being Graves, Bordeaux, and "vin blanc de Würzburg."[4]

Representing France was the first responsibility of the Napoleonic diplomat; informing his government was the most important, and it was as an information service that Napoleon made the greatest use of his diplomats. In instructions to both Eugène de Beauharnais, Viceroy of the Kingdom of Italy, and Murat, King of Naples, Napoleon made it clear that he regarded foreign diplomats as legitimate spies,[5] and it is as spies that he used his own diplomats. The general written instructions issued at the beginning of each mission invariably told the diplomat to keep his government informed of everything that happened in the resident country—in the government, court, and administration, in industry, agriculture, and commerce, in public opinion, in all military and social affairs, in every village and every canton. Also the diplomats were to find out as much as possible about neighboring states. Keeping the government informed was the object of more special instructions than almost any other duty. In time of war, for example, all the diplomats in and near the area concerned would be instructed to send whatever military information they could obtain, and if this information were insufficient, then more detailed instructions would be sent from Paris, possibly with funds for secret agents.

The information came from a variety of sources—conversations, the observations of members of the French and satellite missions, the local press, friendly government officials, and members of the pro-French factions. French couriers were expected to be observant. Secretaries and diplomatic students were sometimes sent on fact-finding missions. The French diplomats could employ secret agents to provide information, and funds were always available for this purpose. The Ministry in Paris also employed agents for special espionage missions. The difficulty of obtaining information varied with the degree of French influence. In the satellites information was simply demanded from the local government; in allied states information could be requested, but it was wise to check it; and in less friendly states agents had to be used.

A detailed study of the informative aspects of the diplomatic service can be made through the example of the legation in Warsaw. This legation was one of the most important in terms of espionage for several reasons. In the first place, information on practically all of Europe west of Poland could be obtained easily from the satellite governments or French armies of occupation. Second, very little was known about Russia. Third, Russia was relatively inaccessible—there was little trade and few travelers, and the French embassy in Russia had difficulties in obtaining information because of the distance, the language barrier, and the hostility of the ruling classes to France. Finally, the invasion of Russia proved to be the largest military operation of the Napoleonic period, and information on Russia was essential to this invasion. It is also a good legation to study because its espionage activities were well organized and well documented, whereas information on spies in other legations is more fragmentary.

Between 1802 and 1807 a number of French agents visited Poland and sent back massive reports on most aspects of the country. A regular channel of communications was established only with the appointment of Serra as resident in 1807. Although he reported regularly on the situation within the Grand Duchy of Warsaw, he neglected military affairs and made little effort to obtain information on the Russian or Austrian parts of Poland or on Russia itself.

The collection of military information was a secondary duty for Serra because his appointment had coincided with the honeymoon period of the Tilsit Alliance, when Napoleon's main attention had been devoted to the consolidation of French power from Portugal to Poland. The deterioration in Franco-Russian relations, however, dictated a change in Poland. As Foreign Minister Champagny said, Napoleon wanted in Poland an agent who would be "reliable, intelligent, quick and active, the advanced sentinel of the French Empire," who would know everything that happened in the Duchy and in the rest of Poland, who would provide reliable military information.[6] The new minister, Bignon, was instructed to obtain complete information from within Russia on everything that was relevant to a military operation.[7]

Bignon immediately began sending all the military information on Russia that he could assemble; but he qualified it by stating that he did not have the means to check its veracity. He outlined several of the problems involved in spying on Russia. Serra's organization had consisted of one French officer who had never reported. As always, many were willing to offer information for money, but as the Russian border was strictly closed, they usually travelled only to the border to report all the gossip they had heard. Bignon found it incredible that in the previous years when the Russian police had been less active, no one in the government of the Duchy had established regular contacts with the Russian parts of Poland, and Polish military headquarters had not even verified the military information it had received. Now that the border was closed, the Poles in Russia were afraid to cooperate. Bignon had just employed three men whom he trusted and was trying to build up a network, but this was difficult: agents who worked exclusively for money could not be trusted. Until new agents began reporting, his information would not be accurate, as he had no way of discounting rumors.[8]

It took almost a month for Bignon to get his spy network in operation. The first military report based on the reports of the spies came on 8 May, a long detailed report denying the rumors of the Poles.[9] Then Bignon began sending military intelligence on Russia, nine reports in May, four in June, two in July 1811. This information was not sufficient. In August Foreign Minister Maret ordered Bignon to redouble his efforts to obtain information, and specifically to establish a more comprehensive system of observation for which he would have a special fund of 3,000 francs a month.[10] By September the system was operating. This revitalized espionage network began to report to Bignon, who passed the information on to Paris. Reports which were mainly intelligence numbered seven in September, five in October, eight in November, and two in December. This meant that roughly one-third of Bignon's reports and the largest amount of his reporting in terms of length consisted of military and other information on Russia.

The French government was still not satisfied. At the end of 1811 Foreign Minister Maret wrote to Bignon saying that the information provided was quite useful and that he had done excellent work, but did not have enough reliable agents. If war began, the organization would not be sufficient. Bignon was to expand his spy network into a wartime secret police headed by three men, each having twelve agents under his orders. The three men were to be Polish soldiers who had fought in the previous campaigns, who were intelligent and trusted, spoke German and Russian, and were experts on three different areas of Russia bordering on Poland. Agents were to be sent over the different routes into Russia and there were to be agents in the different Russian cities such as Riga and Pinsk. For good information Napoleon would pay 12,000 francs per month, and all of Bignon's expenses would be paid. Bignon was sceptical of whether the results would justify the efforts. He set about selecting the three men, and the Ministry in Paris recruited at least one agent who was placed as his disposal.[11] In the first half of 1812 correspondence from Warsaw consisted overwhelmingly of military and other information on Russia. Bignon wrote up to eight reports per month, and also sent the entire reports of some agents plus many extracts from other reports.

It would be difficult to evaluate the quality of the information that Bignon obtained on Russia, since the evaluation would necessitate a comparison with the other French sources of information and with Russian documents. Nevertheless, some evaluation of France's espionage organization in Poland can be made. In the first place, it was incredible, as Bignon said, that neither France nor Poland had seized the opportunity of the first years of Tilsit to establish contacts in the Russian parts of Poland. Napoleon demanded masses of information from his ambassador in Russia, who, because of his isolation at St. Petersburg, was in a very poor position to provide it; but Napoleon never attempted to establish an accurate picture of western Russia or to develop a spy network which could produce the information when required. Bignon was appointed in December 1810 to obtain information on Russia. It was not until August 1811 that he was given 3,000 francs per month for espionage, and not until December 1811 that he was specifically instructed to establish a hierarchy or cell system and allocated 12,000 francs per month. By that time Bignon could report that he doubted the success of the operation, mainly because the Russian border was firmly closed. More important was the fact that the agents did not penetrate very deeply into Russia so that by 6 July, only thirteen days after the invasion of Russia, the Grand Army had passed the agents. In the final analysis, there is little reason to believe that a better espionage system would have made any difference. The decision to invade Russia was made against the recommendations of some of Napoleon's chief advisors, including the two ambassadors to Russia, Caulaincourt and Lauriston. Napoleon consistently refused to accept much of the excellent advice he did receive.

The diplomats were required not only to send information, but also to correspond regularly and frequently, even if there was nothing to report. Thus reporting frequently became a duty in itself. Throughout the period, especially after 1808, this frequency increased in response to constant demands from Napoleon for more information. In February 1809

Foreign Minister Champagny was instructed to order all the diplomats to add to their dispatches a regular bulletin listing all important events for the period covered and giving an account of the present state of the government. On 2 March 1809 Napoleon told Champagny to ask all the diplomats to send frequently a chronicle on the members of the governing family.[12] One year later Napoleon complained that he knew nothing of several states, and that only three ministers were reporting often enough; all diplomats and consuls were to write daily informing France of what was happening in their countries.[13] Six months later the ministers were ordered to send a monthly report on the state of the local military forces.[14] By 1811 the French ambassador in Russia was ordered to write daily so that his letters would form a sort of journal giving the events at the time they happened rather than as they appeared to him several days later when he came to write his dispatches. This ambassador was the first to be so instructed, but other diplomats were to receive the same order subsequently.[15] In 1812 the ministers were told to send fortnightly bulletins summarizing all that had happened during the previous two weeks.[16] Then, in 1813, the summary of the state of the armed forces was to be sent once a week instead of once per month.[17]

This constant demand for more information had several effects. A few diplomats reacted by questioning the utility of the new types of correspondence, pointing out that the bulletins would only repeat information already given.[18] Most diplomats reported everything of importance, and some of them stated realistically that there was nothing to report. General Victor, minister to Denmark, thought he had solved his problem quite easily by double spacing his next report so that it covered twice as many pages.[19] But such methods did not satisfy Paris: the diplomats were forced to increase the frequency of their reports. They could do this only by including details they really thought unimportant, or by including everything they heard about neighboring states. Both methods were harmful. The one submerged the important facts in a mass of unimportant detail; the other swamped the Ministry with a mass of unverified rumors. It can be argued that the Ministry became overinformed, that the constant demand for quantities of information finally reduced the overall quality of the information available. In volume, Napoleon had more information on Russia than on any other state; it was with Russia that he made his greatest mistake.[20]

The negotiation of treaties was, of course, an important function of the diplomatic agents. At the major negotiations, the French team was headed by Joseph Bonaparte or the Minister of Foreign Affairs or, in the case of Tilsit, by Napoleon himself. The real work of these negotiations, however, was done essentially by the professional diplomats like Otto (Treaty of Amiens) or Laforest (Treaty of Lunéville), plus the secretaries. Negotiations of secondary importance were often initiated by the regular external agents, then completed by a political agent personally loyal to Napoleon. For example, in 1805–6, the French minister in Berlin began negotiating a treaty with Prussia, but the negotiations were soon dominated by Duroc, Napoleon's aide-de-camp. All minor negotiations, such as trade treaties or alliances with smaller countries, were conducted by the regular external agents.

Another of the functions of the diplomatic agents was the maintenance of peace. As Napoleon said, the diplomats were his "officiers pour la paix," in contrast to the generals, who were his "officiers pour la guerre."[21] Maintaining peace was rarely mentioned in the instructions, except in specific cases when Napoleon regarded peace as a particular goal of a diplomatic mission. The ambassador to Austria in 1806 was to regard his mission as one of peace, to avoid any provocation, to talk of peace and to maintain good relations.[22] The problem at that time was that Napoleon was still at war with Prussia and Russia, and an Austrian declaration of war would have placed the French armies in an extremely precarious position. The maintenance of peace was the greatest single problem facing the diplomatic service. In attempting to fulfill this duty, the diplomats offered Napoleon advice which, if accepted, could have postponed or prevented the wars with England and Russia and the final disaster of 1813–14.[23]

Although Napoleon drew a sharp distinction between his diplomatic and consular agents, the former being concerned with political affairs, the latter with economic matters, in practice the distinction was less clear. The diplomatic agents had to encourage French trade and enforce the Continental System; the consular agents reported political developments as well as economic opportunities. Besides this, the two networks were united in the individual countries in that the resident diplomat was in charge of all consular agents in his country. The diplomatic agents exercised a nominal control over the consuls, informing Paris when a consul came or left, giving the consuls instructions, making recommendations, making provisional appointments, acting as consuls when necessary, handling and sometimes summarizing the consular correspondence, collecting their votes on various referendums, and mediating the problems arising between consuls. The diplomats also involved themselves in some consular affairs, sending information on the prices of various commodities and on tariffs, handling complaints against French merchants, reporting on commercial shipping, on import and export figures, and controlling and issuing certificates of origin.[24] These activities, not mentioned in the official instructions or in the political correspondence, were merely part of the routine work of the French diplomats.

Normally a diplomat will try to influence the government to which he is accredited. In Napoleonic times influence gave way to domination. The French diplomats who wielded the greatest power were those appointed to northern Italy, where their powers equaled those of a governor. The powers of General Petiet, French minister in Milan, were ennumerated in an *arrêté* of 17 June 1800 which was dictated by Napoleon: Petiet would handle all relations between the Cisalpine Republic and all other parties; all finances would be under his control; no money could be spent without his orders; and he alone could convoke the General Assembly.[25] The power of General Dejean, minister in Genoa, was even greater. Like Petiet, he handled all relations with the government, controlled all finances, and convoked the Assembly, but he also presided over the Assembly and was especially responsible for looking after the interests of the Republic. The Assembly was convoked to draft a constitution: in fact, France provided the constitution and Dejean ensured that the Assembly, which he had appointed, accepted the constitution with only minor modifications.[26] Similarly, in Lucca, the French minister had the mission of selecting a government and imposing a constitution which had been drafted in Paris.[27] It was through these constitutions, and later the Napoleonic Codes, that French diplomats continued to spread the French Revolution to the rest of Europe, for although the Napoleonic government became increasingly conservative within France, it remained highly revolutionary in terms of the rest of Europe.

The satellites in central Europe enjoyed a greater degree of independence, and apart from the supervision of the Continental System and military affairs, the French diplomats only intervened on specific occasions. In Switzerland, Verninac was ordered to encourage the liberal elements so that liberal ministers could dominate without recourse to French military assistance. With the outbreak of war against Austria in

1809, the French minister in Dresden told the Saxon government to expel the Austrian diplomats. And, in one of the few examples of personal initiative, General Victor told the Danish government not to allow a Russian fleet to anchor at Copenhagen, but he was quick to ask for further instructions in the matter.[28]

The situation in the Grand Duchy of Warsaw offers an excellent example of the influence exerted by French diplomats in different circumstances. Napoleon had wrested the area around Warsaw from Prussia, had dictated its laws and institutions, and had given sovereignty over the Grand Duchy to the King of Saxony. The Duchy was then ruled by a number of Polish ministers, each responsible to the King of Saxony. The first French minister, Serra, was instructed to observe the effects of the new institutions, to identify the obstacles and problems in the establishment of the new system, and to help in rallying all shades of opinion to the new government.[29] In his relations with the government of the Duchy, Serra's successor, Bignon, followed the strict limits imposed by diplomacy: he told the ministers what Napoleon wanted and in private conversations he gave his advice. One of the problems was that he had no instructions as to how he was to influence the government. Because of this, he never interfered in the affairs of the Duchy except in matters of fortifications, which he interpreted as a vital French affair.[30]

The decision to invade Russia resulted in a significant change in the position of the Grand Duchy of Warsaw, which became the center of French operations rather than an outpost of the French Empire. This in turn led to a vast change in the powers of the French agent in Warsaw. The velvet glove employed by Bignon in his relations with the government of the Duchy was discarded with the appointment of de Pradt as full ambassador. De Pradt's detailed instructions made it clear that the Duchy would be governed from the French embassy, for de Pradt was ordered to direct and advise the government and the administration and to supervise a reorganization of this government. Former minister Bignon, with a certain degree of jealousy, noted that de Pradt was acting like a viceroy.[31]

In general, then, the degree of influence or domination of French diplomats was related directly to the degree of independence of the state involved. In northern Italy the military satellites were governed by the French ministers; in central Europe the ministers rarely intervened except in military and trade matters. But, as the example of the Grand

Duchy of Warsaw indicated, in some satellites the degree of French domination could vary from noninterference to almost total domination, depending on the situation and on the degree of attention given by Napoleon to any problem that might develop there.

In spite of the fact that Napoleon drew a sharp distinction between his military and diplomatic agents and severely criticized several diplomats for interfering in military policy without specific orders, constant warfare necessitated some degree of involvement of the diplomatic service in military matters. Macdonald and Victor went to Denmark to help with the defense of Copenhagen; Ney's diplomatic appointment to Switzerland at the time of the Act of Mediation masked his role as military and political leader; and Gouvion St. Cyr was to negotiate with Portugal or lead a Spanish-French army into Portugal. These cases all involved the appointment of army generals for specific missions. Besides these missions, the regular diplomats were sometimes engaged in military affairs.

In several cases the diplomats had to ensure that the satellite forces were up to strength or that recruitment of Imperial troops in the satellites was adequate. Auguste Talleyrand was told in 1813 that this was his most important function, as there were hardly any Swiss troops left in Napoleon's service. In Baden Nicolai was instructed to speed up the supply of reinforcements. The main content of Vandeul's correspondence from neighboring Hesse-Darmstadt was in reference to recruitment, which was the main subject of his relations with the local government.[32]

The diplomats fulfilled a variety of other tasks that were essentially military. The ministers in Spain and Genoa organized the supply of the Army of Egypt and the garrison in Malta; Reinhard told the Swiss government to send troops to guard the St. Bernard; Otto told the Bavarian government how its forces would be organized once it had joined the Confederation of the Rhine; and Reinhard, as minister to Westphalia, even had to tell the King of Westphalia what was wrong with his military position.[33] Bignon, resident in Warsaw, reports in his memoirs that his most important functions were supervising the work on Polish defenses and spying on Russia. In one instruction he was ordered to fortify two cities, arm the Polish lancers with rifles and increase their number, organize military transport and a transportation service, and check the resources of the Duchy, instructions he fulfilled in the following months.[34] In these military activities the diplomats acted on specific instructions from Paris. The military role was not a general duty and was rarely mentioned in the general instructions issued at the beginning of each mission.

French diplomats were invariably ordered to encourage French trade. This duty was usually prescribed in the written instructions, though the wording and the emphasis might be changed. For Napoleonic diplomats, however, the encouragement of trade took on a special significance with the development of the Continental System.

The enforcement of the Continental System was, from the very beginning of the period, an important function of the French diplomatic agent, even though the Continental System is usually dated from 1806. Before the signing of the Treaty of Amiens, Lannes was instructed to have the Portuguese government confiscate all English goods and property and to keep English ships out of the harbors; and in Naples Alquier was to try to persuade the government to exclude English goods.[35] The Treaty of Amiens made no provision for the reestablishment of normal economic relations between England and France or the French satellites, and during the peace French diplomats continued to concern themselves with the Continental System.[36] As soon as relations with England deteriorated, the restrictions on English trade were intensified. On 20 May 1803, Napoleon wrote to Clarke that since war seemed probable, Tuscany should begin preparing a general embargo against English ships.[37] Throughout the period the general instructions to French diplomats included the enforcement of the Continental System. Even in distant Persia, General Gardane was told: "The most important object of your mission is to prevent all commerce between Persia and England, and to exclude all English agents and traders from the Persian ports."[38]

The enforcement of the Continental System was also one of the few duties which were repeatedly and specifically indicated in Napoleon's letters to his Foreign Ministers. The details varied: Larochefoucauld and Andréossy were to ensure that American ships with colonial goods did not stop at Trieste; Prussia was to be criticized for admitting ships refused at Stralsund; a diplomat in Baden was to apply a certain tariff within twenty-four hours; and other diplomats were to be criticized for not enforcing the system vigorously.[39]

French diplomats, expecially in northern Italy, were concerned with the collection of "contributions" from the occupied countries. Napoleon invaded northern Italy in 1800 because it could provide the two things he most desperately needed—a victory against Austria which would lead to peace, and financial resources which would prevent the bankruptcy of the new government and finance the army. The French diplomats in Genoa (Dejean and Salicetti), Piedmont (Jourdan), and Tuscany (Clarke, Siméon, and Beauharnais) were all ordered to collect money for the French army. In Genoa General Massena, commander of the occupying army, demanded 2,000,000 francs immediately, plus 500,000 francs per month. The French minister, Dejean, explained to Talleyrand that it was impossible to provide these sums as Genoa's wealth depended on her commerce, which had been destroyed in the wars. Massena repeated his demand, prompting Dejean to state that Massena was dreaming if he thought Genoa could provide the money. Dejean would raise as much money as possible, but 500,000 francs per month was an impossible sum.[40] Other satellites such as Holland and the Duchy of Warsaw had to pay for French armies, and one of Lannes's duties in Portugal was the collection of a 20,000,000 franc indemnity negotiated in the Franco-Portuguese Treaty of 1801.[41]

Propaganda, as Holtman has shown,[42] was one of Napoleon's main weapons in the struggle for Europe, and one with which the Ministry of Foreign Affairs was deeply concerned. Often the Napoleonic diplomats, especially those in Germany, were ordered to suppress newspapers which were not pro-French. These orders were specific, and often came directly from Napoleon. He wanted the *Gazette Générale* in Ratisbon suppressed because the editor had insulted France. The *Gazette de Munich* annoyed him because it was not animated "d'un bon esprit" and, more specifically, had said that Russia had won the Battle of Eylau. Some papers were criticized for excessive zeal: the *Journal de Francfort* had fabricated a ridiculous letter from Napoleon to Prince Charles of Austria, but Napoleon wanted a letter published which would not insult Austria and which would contain only the truth, "truth" being whatever Napoleon thought it should be. For Prussia, both the French minister in Berlin and the Prussian minister in Paris heard Napoleon's complaints: they were ordered to suppress all newspapers which were "bad."[43]

This aspect of propaganda, the suppression of hostile newspapers, was essentially negative. On the positive side, French ministers distributed bulletins of the Grand Army, had satellite governments insert specific information in their papers, established a newspaper in Poland, placed reliable men in charge of the papers in Westphalia, and ensured that the papers in Germany rebutted the arguments and articles in the Austrian press.[44] It is impossible to evaluate the effectiveness of these propaganda activities; but in general, Germany between 1806 and 1813 did not doubt France's capacity to defeat her enemies, and the suppression of hostile papers and general control over information undoubtedly contributed to this feeling.

The establishment of the Napoleonic nobility required the creation of a vast number of estates for those ennobled. Often the estates came from lands in the satellite states that were confiscated from France's enemies and were given to Napoleonic officials as a reward and to give them a vested interest in the preservation of the Empire. Besides these, Napoleon retained a great number of estates for his own revenue, particularly in Poland. The protection of these estates then became a special responsibility for the Napoleonic diplomat. Durant, for example, was instructed to defend Talleyrand's rights in his estate of Benevento in Naples. In Poland Serra was instructed to ensure that the government of the Duchy treated the French landholders the same as the Polish ones, the fear being that the French estates would be overtaxed.[45]

Most Napoleonic officials, including the diplomatic agents, were involved in the security or policing of the Empire. Both foreigners and Frenchmen entering France had to have passports, and these could be obtained only from a diplomatic or consular agent. In fact, one of the main occupations of the legation in Frankfort was the issuing of passports, which, according to Hédouville, occupied much of the time of the minister, the secretary, and a private secretary.[46] The general rules for the control of passports were issued by Fouché, the Minister of Police,[47] but individual decisions as to who should have passports were made by the diplomats. In Austria, Larochefoucauld was criticized for issuing passports to everyone, including Austrian army officers. In future he was to issue passports to persons who had a specific reason for traveling to France, but in other cases he was to wait for Napoleon's decision.[48] Similarly, persons could not enter Russia without passports, so Fouché asked the ambassador in Russia to obtain blank passports for the use of spies.[49] On the other hand French diplomats also helped the Police Ministry with the surveillance of French *émigrés*.[50]

At the time of Napoleon the first duty of the diplomat was to represent his country; his most important duty was to inform his government. Other regular duties included writing frequently, supervising the consular service, and negotiating treaties. The maintenance of peace was the only normal diplomatic activity in which the Napoleonic diplomats failed, the fault resting with Napoleon and not with the diplomats. These six duties constituted the basic activities of European diplomats. Besides these, the peculiarities of the period and of Napoleon dictated that other relatively minor duties should take on outstanding importance for Napoleon's diplomats. These included dominating satellites, collecting money, enforcing the Continental System, participating in propaganda activities, and supervising military affairs. Other miscellaneous duties were policing the Napoleonic Empire and protecting French-owned lands throughout Europe. The relative importance of these duties varied with the time and place, the provision of information being the only one that was consistently important throughout Europe and throughout the period.

Chapter 8

The Functioning of the Diplomatic Service

Diplomatic relations were established or reestablished between two states by the successful negotiation of a peace treaty. This treaty would regulate all the relations between the two states, and would identify the names and titles of the two sovereigns and their territories. Any change in this relationship would then be established through further negotiations. One treaty would establish peace and normal relations, a second treaty might provide for a special commercial or trade relationship, a third treaty might guarantee the second state's neutrality and still another might bring the two states into alliance. In this period of perpetual change, negotiating these treaties became a very important part of the diplomat's work.

Napoleon's first concern in 1799 and 1800 was the establishment of external peace, for without peace he could not attempt to solve the internal problems of France. The victories of Marengo and especially Hohenlinden opened the way to peace with Austria, France's most immediate and important enemy. The suspension of hostilities called for negotiations, to take place at Lunéville in northeastern France. The negotiating team was selected in much the same way as all of the important negotiating teams of the period. It was a professional team consisting of experienced diplomats as well as a few attachés, and was headed by someone known to and trusted by Napoleon himself. The team at Lunéville consisted of Joseph Bonaparte as head of the mission; Antoine Laforest, an experienced and able diplomat as secretary; and Roederer *fils* and Demoustier as attachés.

Joseph received his orders either directly from Napoleon or from Napoleon through Talleyrand.[1] The main items of the treaty—the extent of Austrian losses and the main outline of the settlement in Germany—were decided by Napoleon through his personal negotiator, Joseph; and the details of the settlement were worked out by the regular diplomatic service. Laforest went on from Lunéville to negotiate the reorganization of Germany implied in the Treaty. In this he was assisted by Mathieu, the Ministry expert on Germany, and by Marandet and St. Genèst as attachés. Then, in another move typical of Napoleonic diplomacy, Laforest and Marandet were appointed minister and secretary to one of the states (Bavaria) with which they had negotiated. They would thus be in the area where the treaty was being applied, could report on the situation, and could advise the Ministry on any problems arising from the treaty. In this way Napoleon accepted the advice and services of the regular diplomatic service; but he kept control of the negotiations through the appointment of his own agent, who reaped most of the fruits of the successful negotiations.

Joseph Bonaparte headed three other negotiating teams during the early years of the regime. At Amiens Joseph was assisted by Dupuy as secretary, and Portalis *fils* and Roederer *fils* as attachés. But Joseph was ordered, in effect, to retain the preliminary treaty which had been negotiated in England by the professional diplomat Otto. So, although Joseph received the acclaim, the real work of negotiating was done by a regular diplomat, and Amiens really amounted to a renegotiation of the same treaty with Napoleon firmly controlling the negotiations through Joseph. One of the secretaries, Portalis *fils*, became secretary of embassy in London.

The settlement with the United States was negotiated at Mortefontaine by Joseph Bonaparte; de Fleurieu, the former Minister of Marine; and Roederer, a constitutional and legal expert. The secretary of this commission was Pichon, a former diplomat and consul, who became secretary in the new legation in Philadelphia. The attaché, again, was Roederer *fils* from the Ministry. Joseph also presided over the negotiating of the Concordat with the Papacy, this time with the help of the Abbé Bernier and the Councillor of State, Cretet.

At the same time as these major negotiations were being conducted, normal diplomatic relations were also being restored with the other states of Europe. A treaty with Naples was negotiated by Alquier and

André Durant, who then became minister and secretary in Naples. The minister in Denmark, Bourgoing, negotiated the reestablishment of relations with Sweden and became minister in Stockholm. The minister in Prussia, Beurnonville, helped negotiate peace with Russia and was offered the St. Petersburg legation. The important peace negotiations with England and Austria and Rome were conducted by Joseph Bonaparte; the less important one with Naples, Sweden, and Russia were handled by more regular members of the diplomatic service.

Once negotiations had been completed, normal diplomatic relations would be established through the exchange of missions. However, before sending a regular minister, Napoleon on rare occasions sent one of his aides-de-camp on a preliminary mission. In Russia Caulaincourt visited Alexander in 1801 before Hédouville arrived as minister. Six years later Savary visited Alexander before Caulaincourt arrived as full ambassador. These preliminary missions were designed to inform Napoleon of the situation and to improve relations between the two states.

Before leaving for a mission, a newly appointed diplomat might spend some time in the archives in Paris studying the correspondence and the treaties with the state to which he had been accredited. Didelot read all the relevant documents before taking up his position in Stuttgart, and Serurier read the correspondence with Holland for the period 1795 to 1805 and wrote a résumé of it before leaving for Amsterdam.[2] After some research or reading, the diplomat would obtain his letter of credit, a single document stating his name and rank and his position as Napoleon's representative to the foreign head of state, signed by Napoleon, the Secretary of State, and the Foreign Minister.[3] When he obtained his letter of credit, the newly appointed diplomat would take an oral oath of loyalty to the constitution and to Napoleon. He would also receive his instructions. Several diplomats received oral instructions from Napoleon or the Foreign Minister, and most diplomats received written instructions. This administrative process did not always function smoothly: Serra was held up for twenty days awaiting such a letter, although Napoleon was impatient for him to leave.[4]

The basic form of these instructions was a summary of the recent history and relations between France and the relevant state identifying that state's importance to France as ally, satellite, potential enemy, or observation post. The instructions then mentioned the diplomat's general duties such as maintaining good relations, maintaining the dignity and prestige of France, keeping the French government informed of all developments, and encouraging trade. Any specific instructions, such as sending military intelligence, would be mentioned. This form was not always followed. Sometimes there would be no mention of the historical background; sometimes the diplomat would be told to consult his predecessor's instructions; and the number of prescribed duties varied from time to time. For the diplomats proceeding directly from one legation to another, the instructions would usually be sent to the new position.

On several occasions embarrassment arose when a diplomat arrived before his letter of credit, for he could have no legal status until he presented his letter. Serurier arrived in Holland in 1805, but Marivault, the chargé d'affaires, refused to turn over the legation or to present him at court until his letter arrived. In fact, Marivault had never been informed that a successor had been appointed, although Serurier had known this for at least four months. Cases of diplomats arriving before their letters occurred much too frequently, a reflection of administrative incompetence in the Division of Finances, which handled the legal documents. Another problem was created by a complete break in relations. When this was caused by war, the problem was minimized because the entire legation and all the papers would go to Paris, to return after the war. But too often breaks were caused by simple administrative blunders. One secretary was granted an extended leave; the minister then had to leave the post, so relations were broken simply because there was no one to appoint as chargé d'affaires. In these cases all the papers of the legation would be locked and sealed and given to a friendly member of the diplomatic corps, usually the Spanish minister. The next French minister would then have to obtain the papers from him on presentation of suitable letters of authorization. At any rate, armed with instructions, letters of credit, copies of treaties, and a cipher, and assisted by a secretary and other personnel, the new minister would be ready to begin his mission.

The French legation would be lodged in, if possible, the best residence available in the capital city. Then as now, it was assumed that the quality of the diplomat's lodging was a reflection of the prestige, power, and influence of his sovereign. Suitably housed, the diplomat would then have to be presented at court. The ceremony for this was standardized. The French minister met the Foreign Minister or was introduced to him by the representative of one of France's allies. The letter of credit was shown and a general exchange of views took place. The next day the French minister was presented at court by the Foreign Minister. This ceremony usually involved his presentation to the head of state and his wife, and polite conversation was exchanged. The French minister sometimes made a speech explaining how the interests of the two states coincided, mentioning the problems or situations they had in common, or how much both sovereigns were devoted to peace. This ceremony was very important, for the manner in which the diplomat was received illustrated the nature of the resident country's attitude towards France. The procedure, atmosphere, and the words exchanged at this meeting constituted the substance of the minister's first dispatch.

The main function of the diplomatic agent was to inform his government; so the main content of the political correspondence was information as to what was happening in the resident country and what the diplomat was doing. The frequency of the correspondence varied in proportion to the importance of the country and its status at the time. A minor residence might report twice a month; a minor legation once a week; an embassy three or four times a week; and the ambassador to Russia was expected to write daily. The information was sent in the regular dispatches which were numbered consecutively from the diplomat's first in that mission or from the first of the year. Besides these dispatches, there were three other types of communication. Instructions were answered in letters which were not numbered, the letter usually stating that the instruction had been received and acted upon. There would be one letter per item in the instructions. Private letters were sent when the diplomat had a complaint or request to make. The fourth type of communication was the bulletin. These were used to give summaries of dispatches, reports on the military strength of satellite armies, or on the state of commerce. This division was not established in the instructions, but was a tradition in the Ministry, one followed by the experienced diplomats and often confused by the nonprofessional ministers.

This correspondence was usually carried to Paris by courier, though sometimes it was sent by the normal postal service. France had several couriers who worked over different routes such as the Paris-Berlin route.[5] For Italy, a courier left Paris for Naples four times a week. Later two couriers a day were dispatched, one for Milan, one for Naples. This service was organized by La Valette, Director-General of the Postal Service, and carried the correspondence for all branches of government.[6]

Sometimes the couriers of other states would be used—the Prussian courier often carried the correspondence for both the Prussian legation in Paris and the French legation in Berlin, but important documents were always sent by French couriers.[7] Sometimes officers were deliberately used as couriers. Dispatches for Copenhagen and Stockholm went to Hamburg, where Davout, commander of French forces in northern Germany, gave them to "very intelligent" officers who reported on events in Denmark and Sweden. Couriers were also used for important and immediate communications. In this case, a courier would leave Paris with special instructions for a diplomat, and would then deliver the diplomat's reply directly to Paris. This was how communications were handled when Laforest and Duroc were trying to negotiate a Franco-Prussian alliance in Berlin in 1805. Diplomats were always to send special couriers if they obtained important information and, in the absence of a courier, a subordinate member of the legation would be sent. Except for Spain after 1808, the communications system appears to have worked quite well, possibly because Napoleon threatened any tardy courier with an immediate prison sentence.[8]

When the regular postal service was used or when it was feared that couriers might be intercepted, it was sometimes necessary to put the dispatches in cipher. The diplomats might encode all or part of a dispatch, and some diplomats began using the cipher in mid-sentence. Ciphers were always used if the contents were such that he did not wish the local government to know and if he had the slightest fear that his couriers might be intercepted and the message read. In Paris these ciphered dispatches were sent directly to the Codes Division, where they were deciphered apparently by the *chef*, Campy, as he invariably signed all deciphered dispatches.

The cipher consisted of a number system, with the numbers representing each word or letter. In one cipher, common names and nouns were represented by the numbers 1 to 164. Thus 1 was Bonaparte, 2 Cambacérès, 3 Lebrun, 4 Maret, 10 Ministry of Finance, 87 Prussia, 88 King of Prussia, and so forth. This might appear too simple, so the base number could be raised by up to 10. If the number 7 were identified, then the system would be based on 7, each number would be raised by 6, so that Bonaparte would become 7, Cambacérès 8, and so on. The letters of the alphabet were represented by successive numbers rising irregularly by an increasing progression beginning with 501. So A to D were 501 to 507 (rising by 2), E to H were 510 to 519 (rising by 3), I to K were

523 to 530 (rising by 4), L was 546 (rising by 5), M to O were 543 to 554 (rising by 6), and so on.[9]

Each legation had a number of separate ciphers. A small legation such as that in Munich had three, two ordinary and one reserve.[10] The St. Petersburg embassy had two ordinary ciphers, one reserve, plus separate ciphers for correspondence with Stockholm, Copenhagen, Riga, Vienna, and Constantinople. Each of these ordinary and reserve ciphers contained two parts, for ciphering and deciphering, so for each legation the Ministry and the diplomat used different ciphers.[11] Thus the Ministry would have had for the twenty legations, 120 separate ciphers, each of which could be readily changed. This would present France's enemies with a formidable task of deciphering. Cracking these ciphers would probably be a matter of time—the French Codes Division did try to decipher intercepted correspondence. In 1810 the French obtained the key to the Prussian cipher, which Napoleon sent to the Foreign Minister "for his eyes alone," and with a comment about how useful it would be.[12] This proves that the French had not previously cracked the Prussian cipher, though they had obtained the Prussian archives in 1806 and controlled the country after 1806. The ciphers in the Ministry were obviously bulky, for when Talleyrand went to Milan with Napoleon in 1805, he ordered the diplomats to send their ciphered dispatches via Paris as all the deciphering apparatus was there.

Normally the ciphering and deciphering proceeded smoothly; at least there were few complaints about it in the correspondence. The most important problem was that some diplomats arrived at their posts without copies of the cipher so they could not send ciphered messages. The greatest exception to the normal pattern occurred in 1812. Foreign policy and the diplomatic service were being directed by Maret from Lithuania while Napoleon advanced into Russia. As the couriers were frequently attacked by Cossacks, Maret sent his correspondence, which included abstracts of the diplomatic correspondence from all over Europe, to Napoleon in cipher. Unfortunately, Napoleon did not have a copy of the cipher, which prompted this rebuke to Maret: "You have written to me in cipher. I do not have a cipher. That displeases me as I do not know if what you have said is important."[13] Such a muddle is far from the picture of Napoleon as an administrative genius.

None of the documents describes the functioning of the Ministry, but research would suggest the following administrative processes. The correspondence arrived at the two political divisions of the Ministry. Given the frequency of the correspondence, the estimated weekly inflow would be as follows. The North Division received two or three dispatches from the more important states such as Russia or England, and one or two per week from the minor courts. The South Division received two or three from Madrid or Rome, one or two from the minor legations. The North Division, then, received twenty dispatches per week, the South Division twelve, with these numbers being doubled during the wars of 1805 to 1807 and during the later period 1811 to 1813.

At the political divisions the correspondence was separated—that pertaining to financial affairs went to the Finances Division, newspapers and statistics to the Archives, and that pertaining to instructions was filed with those instructions. The expert or specialist in each Division assembled, presumably, the dispatches with the instructions to which they pertained, then discussed the situation or the information with the *chef* or *sous chef*, who in turn discussed the matter with the Foreign Minister. He, or one of the *chefs* acting on his directions, then assembled the correspondence into a portfolio for Napoleon's attention.

The executive branch of the Napoleonic government consisted of Napoleon; the Secretary of State, who was the chief executive officer and the key man in the government; the cabinet Ministers; and the Ministries. It was not a cabinet government, as the Ministers rarely met together. Instead, they dealt with Napoleon through the Secretary of State. The one exception to this rule was the Minister of Foreign Affairs, Talleyrand, who had the privilege of meeting directly with Napoleon and met with him daily. Napoleon outlined his work schedule in a letter to Talleyrand in 1806. Every day Talleyrand would read the incoming dispatches from the ministers and would send them, together with translations of significant foreign newspapers to Napoleon.[14] Because Talleyrand had a special relationship with Napoleon and met him directly, we have no way of knowing if this schedule were followed.

Fortunately for the historian, Champagny did not have any special relationship with Napoleon, but dealt with him through the Secretary of State, and the process is therefore documented in the Secretary of State's archives.[15] The archives in question contain cover letters from Champagny which prove that the diplomatic correspondence was sent to Napoleon daily. These cover letters state what dispatches had come in, which of them were important, whether the Foreign Minister had met any members of the diplomatic corps or had received any notes from them. The letter might contain advice on any of these points. This letter accompanied the departmental portfolio which included the entire incoming dispatches or extracts from them if Napoleon were busy or if the Foreign Minister thought them unimportant, reports or memoirs or documents that Napoleon had requested, and copies of letters, decrees, conventions, and other documents for Napoleon to check before the Foreign Minister dispatched them.

After reading all the documents, Napoleon met with the Foreign Minister. Napoleon may have made a few decisions orally at these meetings, but in general his decisions were dictated to his secretaries and delivered by the Secretary of State's office in the late afternoon. Occassionally the decision took the form of a single word, *approuvé*, written at the bottom of a report, but usually the decision was incorporated into a formal letter. One such letter to Talleyrand referred to seventeen separate subjects and was thirteen paragraphs long.[16] In one day alone Champagny received nineteen letters from Napoleon.[17]

When given a problem, Napoleon might take advice from any number of sources. He had the diplomat's dispatches in which information and advice were mixed together; and he knew the opinion of the Foreign Minister. Sometimes he asked for advice from the senior members of the Ministry. Before making major foreign-policy decisions, such as that of the absorption of Rome in 1810, Napoleon had the Ministry draft reports for his information. According to Driault, it took all the *commis* and eight translators fifteen days to draft this particular report. Napoleon had an insatiable curiosity. From 1799 to 1814 the Foreign Ministers constantly received demands for reports on every conceivable topic affecting Europe. Reports could also be demanded from persons outside the Ministry. Before deciding on a Polish policy in 1807, Napoleon asked for reports from a former employee of the Polish Foreign Ministry, from the French agent and propagandist Montgaillard, and from the Swiss Jomini.[18] We also know that persons outside the Ministry advised on foreign policy. Talleyrand was a consultant long after he had left the Ministry, even in the autumn of 1813. It is likely that Napoleon discussed policy with the other two consuls, with Maret, and with his favorite generals such as Duroc and Berthier. There is a curious document in the archives which suggests that all the cabinet Ministers met together to debate the question of a declaration of war against England. The marginal notes are unclear, but they suggest that the issue was debated, the declaration of war was approved by five votes to two, and the decision to arrest all Englishmen in France was then passed by seven votes to none.[19] This, apparently, was the only time the cabinet ministers met together to debate foreign policy.

A decision, once made by Napoleon, was given either orally or in writing to the Foreign Minister. As Godechot says, the ministers were simply *agents d'exécution* or *commis.* This opinion was actually shared by the ambassadors themselves. When asked if Maret's appointment as Minister of Foreign Affairs would change foreign policy, Ambassador Lauriston replied: "No. The Emperor governs so much by himself that a minister is nothing more than a pen, and not the hand that guides it."[20] Napoleon personally drafted the formal instructions for important missions. The Napoleonic correspondence contains many examples of instructions given to the Foreign Minister stating exactly what he would say to the French diplomats.[21] Contrary to accepted opinion there was no difference in the way Napoleon treated Talleyrand and his successors in this matter. Napoleon exercised strict control over the instructions drafted by all of his Foreign Ministers. In less important cases, he gave the Foreign Minister his instructions in general terms. Then the employees of the Ministry prepared drafts of the instructions, and a final copy was written and signed by the Foreign Minister. Sometimes Napoleon even checked this copy before it was sent. These instructions were usually very short. The first paragraph acknowledged receipt of the minister's dispatches and mentioned that Napoleon had seen them and made a decision. The second paragraph stated the decision or gave the instruction. The ministers seldom heard from the Foreign Minister. On average a minister received perhaps one letter from Paris for every five or ten dispatches he sent. They were informed by the *Moniteur,* the official government newspaper, and by an occasional circular from the Ministry.

After delivery to the diplomat by courier or post, the instructions would be executed as quickly as possible. If the diplomat were to meet the Foreign Minister, he would do so and report the conversation in his next dispatch. Most of the instructions, in fact, took this form; the diplomat's role being that of liaison between the two governments. If the instruction was in relation to a person—to obtain information or assist him—then the diplomat would do what he could and report by letter. Unless the matter was settled by this instruction and the diplomat's action, the diplomat's reply would go to the Foreign Minister, presumably with the preceding correspondence and instructions. Napoleon would then decide whether further action was necessary or whether the diplomat should be congratulated for the successful execution of policy.

The basic length of time for this administrative process, that is, from the receipt of the diplomat's dispatch to the reply by the Ministry, was approximately two to five days. The time required depended on the importance of the decision. Some couriers came directly to Napoleon. He read the report, dictated a reply, and the courier was dispatched within the same hour. Other decisions, such as what to do with Rome in 1810, were debated for months. While Napoleon was on tour or on campaign, the Minister of Foreign Affairs and several secretaries accompanied him. Then dispatches, if unciphered, came directly to headquarters and were acted upon. If Napoleon was separated from the Foreign Minister, he might intercept the courier and take immediate action without even consulting the Foreign Minister, sometimes without even informing him. There is a possibility that Napoleon made some decisions too hastily, for he ordered Champagny to keep letters for three or four days before sending them because foreign policy should seem the result of careful development.[22]

At the beginning of the period Napoleon appointed generals whom he knew to many of the important posts. These generals on occasion wrote directly to him. This practice was naturally frowned upon by Talleyrand, who ordered General Dejean, minister to Genoa, to communicate with him and not Napoleon. Dejean's reply, and the tone of his reply, revealed the attitude of these generals to the Foreign Minister. In somewhat blunt language, Dejean said that he had not written to Napoleon, but that he certainly reserved the right to do so if he felt the issue were important or outside the scope of foreign affairs.[23] The degree of independence exhibited in this reply suggests that in the first years Napoleon could not trust the foreign ministry and that he appointed diplomats who were responsible and loyal to himself. After Tilsit, the French ambassador in Russia wrote to both Napoleon and the Foreign Minister, but since both read these letters, the purpose of this double correspondence is unclear.[24] Examples of such direct communication between Napoleon and the French diplomats are very rare; normally all communications went through the Ministry.

The basic weakness in this administrative structure and, one suspects, in the entire Napoleonic administration, was Napoleon's inability to delegate responsibility or authority. The only real authority possessed by the Minister of Foreign Affairs was the authority to manage the Ministry in Paris. The decisions with regard to foreign policy, the execution of policy, instructions to diplomats, appointments, salaries, leaves, and emoluments were made by Napoleon. There was no apparent reason for this near-total concentration of power in his hands. Policy could have been formulated and the Foreign Minister could have executed that policy, but Napoleon insisted on making all the decisions. Naturally, no one man could remember all the details of administration.

This degree of domination tended to destroy the initiative of the Ministers of Foreign Affairs. By December 1810 Champagny was reduced to bringing the smallest details to Napoleon for his decision, and Napoleon had to tell him to take more initiative.[25] Similarly, by the summer of 1813, Maret had lost all initiative. Napoleon became increasingly critical of him as Foreign Minister. He accused Maret of leaving missions vacant; in fact, it was Napoleon who made all decisions on leaves and appointments. Maret's degree of helplessness is indicated by Napoleon's remark: "I know perfectly well that you have made a report, but I can't concern myself forty times with the same thing."[26]

It was possible for Napoleon to dominate the Foreign Ministers completely because they worked directly with him. The Foreign Minister was the *premier commis* of the Ministry. Napoleon dictated the most important of his letters, checked the rest, and made all the major decisions. In this situation the Foreign Minister could have little initiative. But it was different for the members of the external service. In terms of time, they were weeks if not months away from Paris. They had to have sufficient initiative to respond to emergencies and to interpret their instructions in the light of local circumstances. Still, it is difficult to determine how much initiative the diplomats were allowed in the fulfillment of their duties. It was impossible, of course, for the Foreign Minister to state in formal instructions how much initiative a diplomat should have, so his flexibility was determined by circumstances, by the personalities of the participants, especially Napoleon, and, in the final analysis, by a feeling of the members of the service of what they could and could not do.

The reason for the limitation of a diplomat's freedom of action was stated clearly by Napoleon in a letter to Lannes, minister in Portugal and one of Napoleon's closest friends from the days of the Army of Italy.

In diplomatic matters it is necessary to move carefully and with reserve, and to do nothing which is not covered by instructions because it is impossible for a single agent to appreciate the effects of his actions on the overall situation. Europe constitutes a system. Whatever happens in one place affects the rest. It is therefore necessary to act in concert.[27]

One matter on which the initiative was definitely limited was the freedom to communicate in writing with foreign governments without specific instructions. In 1806 Napoleon criticized the chargé d'affaires in Switzerland for writing to the Swiss government without instructions.[28] Later, in May 1808, a general instruction was sent to all the diplomatic agents telling them that they could correspond with foreign governments only if they had received specific instructions to do so. Serra wrote an eight-page reply to this order which is interesting because Serra was a professional diplomat trained in the Italian school and because he was in a particular situation which demanded a great number of communications with the local government. It is also an exact and detailed statement of the amount of freedom that had to be left to the diplomat's discretion.

Serra began by admitting the advantages of the instruction to the diplomats, for the less responsibility they had, the less likely they were to make mistakes. In ordinary diplomatic missions the ministers could usually wait for instructions for everything they did; but the situation in Napoleonic Europe was different, especially with the French armies camped in the allied states, for the Napoleonic diplomats had a special relationship with these armies. In fact, Serra's instructions stated that he would be the intermediary between the French army and the government of the Duchy. There were an excessive number of contacts between the French and local authorities because of military movements, policing, guarding the frontiers, and helping with the customs, and because of the coordination between the military chiefs of Warsaw, Berlin, Stettin, and Breslau. The *Intendant Général* of the Grand Army had many contacts with the Duchy over matters of military administration, finances, and French claims. Serra handled the hundreds of problems arising from the French domains in the Duchy. He said he did not mind referring all these problems to Paris, but clearly he thought it impossible. It would take a month, many communications involved unimportant details, and many, such as the problems of policing and food supply, had to be decided immediately. Naturally questions would be referred to Paris if it were possible to do so; but Serra argued that the matters mentioned had to be dealt with by himself, that this was what he had always done and it had always been acceptable.[29] The reply to this letter is missing, but we know that Serra continued to act as he had in the past.

The amount of freedom Napoleon allowed his diplomats is best illustrated by his own criticisms of diplomats who had exceeded their instructions. Cardinal Fesch was "an old woman" because he had criticized another cardinal and told him to go to Paris. Napoleon added: "Don't interfere in things you don't understand."[30] Diplomats were severely rebuked for interfering in military affairs. Didelot had the misfortune to exceed his instructions in dealing with Marshal Ney, and was told by Napoleon: "You have concerned yourself with military affairs, for which you are not competent. My military officers and my diplomatic officers have distinct functions. There is nothing in common between them; they don't even speak the same language."[31] The rebuke did not have a lasting effect, for several years later Didelot was again criticized for involving himself in military affairs.[32] French diplomats were expected to obey precisely all French laws. When Lezai-Marnesia dated a letter according to the Gregorian rather than the Republican calendar, Napoleon criticized him with the comment: "As long as a law exists, it must be obeyed. My ministers should set an example of respect for the law."[33]

Some French diplomats dominated the governments to which they were accredited, but always on specific orders from Paris. When diplomats exerted pressure without orders they were severely criticized. General Clarke went further than instructed in trying to influence Tuscan religious policy, referred to the inability of either the King or the Queen to govern, recommended that Napoleon prepare to replace the Queen as soon as the King died, and even discussed these problems with foreign diplomats in Florence. Clarke was also indiscreet and disrespectful in discussing the illness of the King, suggesting that he was a mad paranoid subject to epileptic fits. In another dispatch Clarke even suggested that the fits were brought on by excessive sexual activity! Upon receiving these dispatches, Napoleon wrote to Talleyrand expressing his disapproval. After commenting that a diplomat must inform his government and obey instructions, Napoleon pointed out that Louis I was King of Tuscany, and that as such he could do what he liked with the laws of his country, that he was as independent as the King of England or the Emperor of Austria. "Our minister must gain influence by his advice, never by threats." Finally Napoleon ordered Talleyrand to write to Clarke, making him "understand that he is ambassador in Florence, not governor of Tuscany." [34]

An example of a diplomat who disobeyed an instruction will also help to indicate the kind of circumstances under which a degree of initiative was allowed. Taylor, English minister in Cassel, was one of three English diplomats involved in plots on Napoleon's life. Napoleon decided that it was incompatible with the dignity of France and of her sovereign that a French diplomat be in the same diplomatic corps as an English "conspirator." The government of Cassel was informed that either the English or the French diplomat must leave the court and the city. Two weeks later Taylor returned, and Bignon was again told that either he or Taylor would have to leave. Taylor left, but returned seven weeks later, at which time Cassel recognized him as official English minister. Bignon then returned to Paris, leaving St. Genèst as chargé d'affaires.

Napoleon decided that it was an insult for even a chargé d'affaires to be at the same court as Taylor and, to end the matter, St. Genèst was ordered to leave Cassel within twenty-four hours. If Cassel wished to resume relations, negotiations could take place in Paris. While these instructions were in transit, however, the Elector of Cassel finally decided in favor of France. Taylor would not be recognized and was ordered to leave. Given this situation, St. Genèst decided to disobey instructions and remain in Cassel, explaining that he was torn between the duty to obey and his certainty that Napoleon would approve his remaining. He fully realized that he was disobeying a specific instruction, but he felt that the execution of that order would be harmful to France's interests as the Elector's decision had assured some degree of French ascendency. Talleyrand made no comment on the action or the motive, but St. Genèst was told to stay in Cassel, and it was implied that he had made the correct decision. [35]

In general, however, Napoleonic diplomats were not permitted to take any major steps without having specific instructions. Except for minor details and specific situations, they could not communicate in writing with the resident government without orders from Paris. They could not assist other French agents without orders. Their instructions told them what they were to do and how to do it. When they exceeded these instructions they were criticized, often by Napoleon himself. The strict discipline imposed by Napoleon does not seem to have destroyed all initiative—in 1810 and even in 1813 it was still necessary to criticize diplomats for exceeding their instructions, and the control exercised over the diplomat's actions and methods did not prevent the diplomats from advising or attempting to advise their government. There was, therefore, a relatively good balance between overall control from Paris and a certain degree of initiative for the detailed application of policy and for emergencies. Nor is this discipline an example of "authoritarianism" of the regime. As Napoleon pointed out to Lannes, successful diplomacy dictates that the system be directed from the Ministry as only the Ministry could know the overall situation.

A common misconception is that the communications revolution of the nineteenth and twentieth centuries has destroyed the initiative of individual diplomats.[36] Today the events of the entire world can be relayed instantaneously to the capital cities, and the relevant decisions can be returned to the diplomat within hours of his initial report. During Napoleon's time it might take weeks for a development to be reported and instructions issued; the diplomat supposedly enjoyed considerable initiative due to the time lag. Such a misconception can be based only on a misunderstanding of the functioning of Napoleon's diplomatic machinery. The chief result of the time lag was not increased local initiative, but rather a slowdown in the pace of events. Important negotiations, such as those at Tilsit, Erfurt, or Bayonne were conducted by Napoleon himself. Less important ones were conducted by the Foreign Minister or a Napoleonic agent, often within hours of Paris. At Châtillon, Caulaincourt reported every evening on the negotiations of that day. Often he had Napoleon's reply by the following morning, dictated at 2 or 3 a.m. and delivered by special courier. In Berlin Napoleon's negotiators had no initiative which today's diplomats would not enjoy, and they had detailed instructions to cover an emergency. Because of the excellence of the information, few international developments took the Napoleonic government by surprise. Almost every war and the probable reaction to it of almost every state was clearly outlined in the diplomatic correspondence months and sometimes years before its outbreak. Also, the slowness of communications can be exaggerated. Most of the diplomatic developments occurred within the borders of today's Common Market.

It did not take long for a special courier to traverse the distance from Paris to Vienna. Only a special crisis could have given a diplomat special initiative, and Napoleon was almost inevitably on the spot during a crisis. It is doubtful if Napoleon's diplomats enjoyed greater initiative than those of the mid-twentieth century, partly because the functioning of the diplomatic machinery has changed little since Napoleon's day.

Chapter 9

Advice and Flattery

There is no mood if it be long sustained more dangerous to the intelligence than the imperative. The exercise of despotic power, with the crushing work that it entailed, was good neither for Napoleon's mind nor for his character. He became less amenable to advice, more irritable, more intolerant of variance, and in the succession of his Foreign Ministers, Talleyrand, Champagny, Maret, each less able and independent than the last, we have an index of the growing divergence between the policy of the Empire and the interests of France.[1]

So wrote H.A.L. Fisher on the eve of World War I. It was a classic statement of one of the cardinal tenets of the liberal interpretation of history, the belief that dictatorship is an inherently evil form of government and is bound to deteriorate through the corruption of power. According to this theory, the dictator gradually moves from the world of reality to a world of illusions. In the course of this evolution he develops a marked preference for flattery and agreement rather than criticism, opposition, and the truth. Gradually he replaces those clear-sighted and independent-minded advisors who speak the truth with flunkeys and flatterers who know only how to obey. Fisher was not the first to enunciate this theory, and he was certainly not the last. In various forms the idea of a progressive deterioration among Napoleon's advisors can be found in the major studies of Napoleon and of French history. Often they agree with Fisher's example of the Ministers of Foreign Affairs; one can often read of the "ineffectual" Champagny replacing the "brilliant" Talleyrand at the helm of Napoleonic diplomacy.[2]

Fisher's account contains one glaring factual error. Napoleon had four rather than three Foreign Ministers. But if Fisher had added the name Caulaincourt to his list, the example would not have had quite the same ring of authenticity. Chandler accepts the general theory of decline, but identifies Caulaincourt as a "possible" exception.[3]

More seriously, this theory of deterioration in the Ministry of Foreign Affairs suffers from two grave weaknesses. In the first place, it ignores the role of the minister in relation to his diplomatic service. In fact, Napoleon's Foreign Ministers were really clerks or bureaucrats. From time to time they submitted advice; more often they merely relayed to Napoleon the observations of his ambassadors. The question of the quality of Napoleon's government cannot therefore be examined merely at the ministerial level, but must also include some study of the advice Napoleon received from his diplomats, whose reports he assiduously read. Second, the theory is not based on an empirical study of the evidence. Fisher and the generations of historians who have followed him have repeated each other's theory and cited the same few examples. They have not read or analyzed the actual advice Napoleon received from his diplomatic service. Such an examination is the only way one can really determine whether Napoleon did progressively replace able ministers with flunkeys, and whether, as a result, the quality of the advice he received gradually declined.

Clearly it would be a gargantuan task to review all the advice Napoleon received from his diplomats in fifteen years. It would also be fruitless, as most of the diplomatic reports contained routine information, the evaluation of which would require several lifetimes of work. One could read all of the dispatches from three successive periods, say 1802, 1807, and 1812; or one could read all of the reports from certain selected ambassadors or missions. A better method is to adopt a topical approach and determine what advice was submitted throughout the period on one specific aspect of diplomacy. The most important matter that can ever confront a diplomatic service is the question of war and peace. Also, Napoleon's policy was characterized by war and the threat of war; he was involved in a series of wars from the beginning to the end of his regime, and in all parts of Europe. Let us examine the advice he received on this issue.

England was the first European country to go to war against Napoleon. During the short span of the Peace of Amiens, he was represented at the

Court of St. James by General Andréossy. Although a close personal friend of Napoleon's, Andréossy was not in any way a blind instrument of his policies. A shrewd observer, he never hesitated to tell his government exactly what he thought. And the ambassador's thoughts differed considerably from those of his master.

Andréossy viewed his mission as the maintenance of peace between England and France. From the very first he concerned himself with informing his government of the size and strength of the peace party in England. The government of Lord Hawkesbury stood for peace, but the survival of that government depended on some degree of success in its foreign policy. The opposition party, that of Pitt, Grenville, and Windham, was more likely to declare war on France. It would exploit Napoleon's expansionism, such as his intervention in Switzerland, in order to come to power.[4] This was a fairly clear statement that the survival of the peace party and hence of peace itself depended on a nonaggressive French policy, and was the first example of Andréossy's attempt to moderate French policy.

Andréossy also reported the effects on English public opinion of French colonial adventures and aspirations. The expedition to San Domingo had caused grave concern over the future of Jamaica. In general the English believed that France had ambitions towards Egypt and India, "the two gold mines of England . . . the sources of their prosperity and industry." Similarly, the growing disquiet caused in England by French continental expansion and the hostile French attitude, as exemplified by the official publication of Sébastiani's report on Egypt, were reported. Andréossy defended the French actions in conversations with the English ministers, but left no doubt in his reports of the harmful effects of French actions on the position of the English peace party.[5]

While reporting on the situation, he also submitted advice on how the war could be avoided. After explaining the English position, he said it was up to Napoleon to decide what sacrifices would be compatible with national honor, suggesting that the maintenance of peace was up to France, although England would appear to be at fault if war broke out. If the fleets were at sea the war could arise out of accidental contacts, so Andréossy suggested that the inaction of the French fleets would be advantageous to the cause of peace. In his fifty-second report he asked how the French government was reacting to English rearmament. Talleyrand had said that France would match these armaments. Andréossy "would not pretend to give advice," but he did point out that an armaments race would increase the likelihood of war. "I will neglect nothing to calm things down, but I need support" a plea, in short, for Napoleon to ignore the English rearmament.[6] In the next report, Andréossy again summarized the English position and concluded that peace was still possible. He suggested that since it was the French position and not the English that was flexible, it was up to Napoleon to make concessions, a position reiterated in the next report even more clearly.[7]

On 4 April 1803 Andréossy again pointed out that French expansion would soon force England to declare war and that it was up to France to reassure the English and initiate conciliatory talks. The advice that France make concessions was finally accepted to a certain extent. The concessions were outlined by Talleyrand in a note of April 9. Andréossy believed that the concessions would be acceptable to the English government, but they came too late: England had already decided that war was preferable to peace.[8] War broke out between France and England in 1803 in spite of the efforts of Ambassador Andréossy. He had done everything he could to maintain peace. The war came because his advice was not heeded soon enough.

In his memoirs, Talleyrand tells us that he, too, advised Napoleon against the policies that led to the war. Duff Cooper states that there is no reason to doubt Talleyrand on this point. On the contrary, there is every reason to question any part of Talleyrand's memoirs that is not supported by documentary evidence. These memoirs are among the least reliable of the period, and this statement cannot be supported from any other source. Nevertheless, Émile Dard also accepts Talleyrand's word on this matter. Dard admits that Talleyrand did not openly oppose Napoleon, but suggests that he submitted his advice orally, adding in self-contradiction, that we do not really know what Talleyrand said to Napoleon in private. Dard suggests that Napoleon would not have tolerated opposition.[9] In fact, Talleyrand had greater opportunity than Andréossy to submit advice, but it was Andréossy and not Talleyrand who opposed the war of 1803 with England. On this matter, Napoleon received excellent advice from his diplomatic service, apparently without comment from his Foreign Minister. And, far from rebuking Andréossy for his views, Napoleon appointed him in 1806 to the extremely important Austrian embassy. Andréossy was still in the diplomatic service in 1814.

Those historians who uphold the legend of the superiority of Talleyrand as Foreign Minister often quote the advice he offered on Austria in 1805. In effect, they have to quote this letter because it is the only documented case of solid advice ever offered by Talleyrand to Napoleon. In the remainder of his letters to Napoleon there is scarcely a one in which he advises Napoleon on policy, unless it is a continuation of this advice on Austria. Talleyrand is supposed to have urged Napoleon to make a "moderate" peace with Austria in 1805. He made his proposal before the Austrian defeat at Ulm and long before Napoleon's brilliant victory at Austerlitz. Since this is the most important surviving evidence of Talleyrand's advice to Napoleon, it must be analyzed in some detail.[10]

According to Talleyrand, there were only four great powers, Prussia being excluded. France was the greatest, and could fight the other three combined. Given all the conflicts of interests, war was inevitable and France would always be involved. A Franco-Prussian alliance was no solution, as Prussian policy was too inconsistent. The way out of the endless conflict was a change in the system so that Austrian interests clashed with those of Russia and England, but not with those of France. Conflict between Austria and France could be avoided by ensuring that their borders did not touch. This could easily be attained by excluding Austria from Italy and Germany and ending all Austrian influence in Switzerland. All the states between Austria and France would be French satellites, but not parts of France.

If Austria lost this territory without compensation, then she would seek wars and alliances to regain her power. Moreover, Austria had always served Europe as a shield against the East. In the past the threat had been Turkey; now it was Russia, and Austria must be reinforced in order to protect Europe from Russia. Therefore, as compensation for her losses and to strengthen her against Russia, Austria was to receive Wallachia, Moldavia, Bessarabia, and part of Bulgaria, all of which belonged to France's ally, Turkey. Turkey would not mind these sacrifices as it was overextended and could, after the withdrawal, consolidate itself and become stronger. Austria would be fully occupied absorbing the new areas and controlling their pro-Russian people. Austria and Russia would become enemies, and thereby make Austria dependent on France. Russia would be thrown back into Asia, where she would eventually become the enemy of England. England would find no allies on the Continent. In this manner a European peace would be achieved.

On paper it was a marvellous plan. It bore certain similarities to Bis-

marck's successful policy, a fact noted by the editor of Talleyrand's letters and copied successively by Cooper, Brinton, and Dard.[11] Talleyrand
said the plan would guarantee peace—he could only have meant peace
in Germany and Italy. The plan guaranteed French hegemony throughout western Europe, and that England would never have accepted. Talleyrand said England would find no major allies on the Continent. He
was not at all clear on why Austria would not join England; and he was
wrong to think that Russian-English rivalries in Asia outweighed the
importance of their mutual trade. He completely ignored Prussia, which
only fifty years earlier had combined with England to inflict a crushing
defeat on Austria and France. Talleyrand claimed Turkey would volun-
tarily give up four provinces to Austria. Yet Turkey had been fighting
desperately for a century to keep them from Russia. Clearly the plan
called for an Austro-Russian war over the Balkans. Austrian control of
the Danube would separate Russia from Constantinople, and access to
the Mediterranean had always been a cardinal goal of Russian foreign
policy. The plan would not end the war with England and, in fact, envisioned a whole series of wars in eastern Europe and even Asia. It would
bring peace on France's European borders.

The word "moderate" is not really applicable to the proposal. In the
preamble Talleyrand asserted that France was already the strongest state
in the world. The program did not envision any territorial expansion for
France, but it would still include the Rhine and Piedmont, which surpassed the "natural frontiers." Surrounding France would be satellites in
Germany and Italy, plus Spain, which was not mentioned. Some of the
satellites could be given to Napoleon's family and could thus create a
French Empire in Germany and Italy. Talleyrand claimed that Austria
would be compensated. In fact, she would be greatly weakened. The new
Austrian areas were poor, but would require expensive conquest, reconstruction, and development; they would always be troublesome, and
their acquisition would necessitate massive expenditure for defense
against Russia. Taken together the terms envisioned the expulsion of
both Russia and Austria from the affairs of central Europe. France and
her new satellites in Italy and Germany, plus Spain and the new "ally"
Austria would hold absolute preponderance in European affairs. It would
have been the peace of total victory in western Europe, not the peace
of the balance of power.

But all of these criticisms miss the main point, and that is that Austria was not in any way prepared to accept the role Talleyrand designed for her. She had no intention of being excluded from Italy and Germany. She was on the offensive in both areas before the Revolution, she remained determined throughout the wars to gain preponderance in southern Germany and northern Italy, and she was largely successful at the Treaty of Vienna. To do this, she fought France five times and was France's most persistent and dangerous continental enemy. Austria exhibited no interest in becoming the new Poland in France's diplomatic system. She could hardly relish the prospect of having a hostile Prussia on the north, a hostile Russia on the east, a hostile Turkey on the south, and a ring of French satellites on the west blocking her from her traditional spheres of influence, power, and wealth. Finally, Austria exhibited no interest in Balkan expansion. Turkey had already been the "sick man of Europe" for almost a century, yet Austria had revealed little desire to conquer or absorb the quasi-independent states of the Balkans. Her interests were in Germany and Italy, not in the East, and no amount of wishful thinking by Talleyrand could alter the reality of Austrian policy.

Talleyrand's famous plan of 1805 was not moderate, it did not ensure European peace, it did not call for a balance of power, and it was not practical. Naturally, Napoleon believed in neither peace, moderation, nor the balance of power, and practicality was never his motto. If he ever had a general European policy, it was for an alliance with Russia, the power whose interests clashed least with France, the power which could gain the most from cooperation with France. Napoleon had always been convinced that Austria would never accept her expulsion from Germany and Italy, and he was right. In spite of this, he toyed for a while with Talleyrand's proposals. Talleyrand was ordered to sound out Austria on the alliance.[12] Austria was to be offered a French alliance and threatened with a Franco-Russian alliance if she did not accept. The negotiations were fruitless, mainly because Austria refused to become a French satellite and refused to reorientate her policy to the East. If one reads the entirety of Talleyrand's correspondence with Napoleon, one can find only this one letter containing full and comprehensive advice on foreign policy. If one analyzes the letter in detail, it becomes impossible to conclude that the advice was very valuable.

One of Napoleon's gravest miscalculations was his decision to intervene in Spain. It was a policy which developed over a period of years; it was also traditional in French diplomacy. The most disastrous of Louis

XIV's wars had been fought to put a Bourbon on the throne of Spain; one of the two most disastrous of Napoleon's wars was designed to put a Bonaparte on the same throne, to maintain the same "pacte de famille." Louis XIV's policy had been largely successful—throughout the eighteenth century Spain had usually been the ally of France. The Revolution broke this alliance, but by 1795 the two powers were allied once more. They remained allied, in theory, until 1814. Besides the family ties, two things cemented the alliance: mutual hatred and fear of England, and mutual desire to conquer and destroy Portugal.

The conquest of Portugal was recommended repeatedly by General Lannes, Napoleon's minister in Lisbon. Lannes was supported by his successor, General Junot, who argued indirectly for war by stressing the importance of Portugal to England and then excluding a peaceful solution.[13] Napoleon accepted the advice of these two ministers. In 1805 the decision was taken to invade Portugal. The advice of these two ministers helped lead Napoleon into the Peninsular War in several ways. In invading Portugal, French troops occupied northern Spain and thus placed France in a position to dominate the entire peninsula. Second, the invasion brought the English army into the peninsula as the defender of some of the people, the Portuguese, against the French armies and all they represented. Third, the Franco-Spanish negotiations over the invasion revealed the weaknesses and intrigues of the Spanish government. Finally, the vast disparity between Spanish resources and Spanish performance brought home to Napoleon how much more effective his Spanish ally could be if only it had a more competent and reliable government.

These doubts about Spain could only have been reinforced by the advice Napoleon received from his ambassador in Madrid, General Beurnonville, who complained several times about the uselessness of the chief minister, Godoy, and about the decadence of the monarchy.[14] The gist of Beurnonville's advice was that Spain had great potential, that this potential could not be realized by the present government, and that Napoleon could easily change that government. These sentiments were more clearly expressed by Beurnonville's successor, Beauharnais: "Spain wants a different system. Everyone waits patiently, hoping that the Emperor will someday turn his attention to this country and put things in order."[15] These general opinions were reinforced by three of Napoleon's agents. The Comte de Montgaillard, who often advised Napoleon on foreign policy, definitely urged the overthrow of the Spanish Bourbons. Tournon told Napoleon that Spain hoped he would intervene in her politics, though Tournon hardly advised the type of intervention Napoleon launched. Murat, too, constantly urged Napoleon to intervene, and deliberately played down the dangers, hoping that he would become King of a new Spanish satellite.[16]

The greatest controversy over the Spanish intervention concerns the role of Talleyrand. There is little documentary evidence that Talleyrand advised Napoleon to overthrow the Spanish Bourbons. The reason for this is not that the evidence never existed, but rather that Talleyrand burned all of it when he returned to the Ministry of Foreign Affairs in 1814. During his ten years as Minister, France had perpetrated several atrocities against the Bourbon family, and Talleyrand could hardly allow any evidence of his complicity to come into the hands of the restored Bourbons or their vengeful followers.[17] He definitely recommended that Napoleon intervene in the peninsula, a fact even he had to admit. He also, apparently, urged Napoleon to overthrow the Spanish Bourbons. As Fugier argues, the evidence for Talleyrand's action is not only contained in the accounts of his contemporaries, such as Napoleon, Pasquier, and Méneval, but it conformed to the whole policy that he was following at that time. This is also the opinion of the French historians Grandmaison and Grasset, who have studied the subject in depth; of such pro-Talleyrand historians as Dard; or a more objective one such as Lefebvre. It can also be documented from Talleyrand's successor, Champagny.[18]

Once the intervention had proved disastrous, Talleyrand pretended innocence and began to suggest that the decisions had been made after he left the Foreign Ministry and were the fault of Champagny and Maret. It was this haughty innocence that drove Napoleon to his famous outburst of January 1809. Before the assembled ministers, Napoleon gave vent to his wrath against Talleyrand. After calling him a thief, a coward, a heathen, and a man who would sell his own father, Napoleon accused him of pretending that he had opposed the "enterprise" in Spain when in fact it was he who had first proposed it and had been the most enthusiastic for it.[19] Napoleon specifically blamed him for the advice on Spain and dared him to reply. Napoleon could hardly have accused him falsely in front of the entire Cabinet. Talleyrand's equally famous reply: "What a pity that such a great man should be so ill-bred" was worthy of his reputation for wit: it was not a satisfactory reply to the accusation. Perhaps the best comment came in 1808 from Napoleon's brother, Joseph, the new King of Spain: "Nobody has told until now the whole truth to Your Majesty." [20]

The man designated to replace Talleyrand at the Ministry of Foreign Affairs was Jean Baptiste Nompère de Champagny. His qualifications for the position were excellent. He had been Minister of the Interior and, before that, ambassador to Austria. In terms of character Champagny was forthright, simple, and honest. He lacked both the cunning slyness of a Talleyrand and the duplicity that frequently accompanied it. In his memoirs Champagny tells us that he was most impressed by Napoleon's attempts to end the Revolutionary chaos and to bring order and prosperity to France. Napoleon offered him a role in this pacification and reconstruction, and he accepted without reservation. [21] He was, then, zealous in his devotion to Napoleon. As a Minister, Champagny was hardworking, obedient, and reliable. He was not the mindless administrative tool that some historians have seen. The several hundred letters he wrote to Napoleon suggest considerable discretion in the execution of orders, and thoughtfulness in the identification of business for Napoleon's decision. [22] In fact, they differ very little from Talleyrand's administrative letters to Napoleon, which were also concerned almost exclusively with the minutiae of administrative routine. Similarly, in the Napoleonic correspondence there is no visible difference in the way Napoleon treated Talleyrand and Champagny.

Champagny's term in office coincided with the longest period of relative peace of the Revolutionary epoch. The peace was based on the alliance between France and Russia which guaranteed French ascendance in western Europe, Russian ascendance in the East. As Minister, Champagny was identified with this alliance—when it broke down he had to be replaced, as did the Russian Foreign Minister, equally identified with the French connection. The period of peace was marred by only two developments, the war of 1809 with Austria and the Spanish affair. When Champagny came into office, the Spanish business was well under way, and he could have little influence one way or another on the course of events there. But he did perform the thankless task of delivering to Napoleon the bad news and the reactions of Europe. It was a task he executed without hesitation.

The most serious development was the capitulation of a French army under General Dupont and the resulting encouragement to the enemies of France throughout Europe. On 6 August 1808 Champagny reported that the news of "Dupont's disaster" was not yet known in Paris "but in general people are speaking of our affairs in Spain in an alarming way." English newspapers carried all the stories from the hostile point of view and were circulated freely throughout the whole of Europe. Several times in 1808 Champagny returned to the developments in Spain. The Dutch courier had come with the "grievous news" of Dupont's surrender, of the evacuation of Madrid by the French, and of a "Spain almost entirely in revolt." Napoleon's return to Paris would soothe "in part" the unease over Spain.[23] There was never any attempt by Champagny to suggest that Spain was not a disaster or to minimize the effects of the revolt on public opinion in Europe. Napoleon is often accused of replacing Talleyrand with flatterers "who told him only what he wanted to hear." Words such as "disaster" or "grievous news" scarcely belong to the vocabulary of flattery, and were designed to convey to Napoleon the truth of the situation rather than to fortify his illusions.

Only one war began during Champagny's tenure at Foreign Affairs. That was the war of 1809 with Austria, and for it, Talleyrand must shoulder the main burden of responsibility. The facts about the origins of this war have long been known. What is curious is that so many historians have been reluctant to accept the conclusion that follows inevitably from these facts. Champagny's role in the diplomacy leading up to the war was quite minimal. As Minister, he kept Napoleon constantly informed of the developments in Austria and the possibility of an Austrian declaration of war. From August 1808 Champagny began reporting on Austrian military preparations and the reactions of France's allies in Germany. He clearly did not believe the statements of the Austrian Foreign Minister, Stadion, or of the Austrian minister in Paris, Metternich, about Austria's peaceful intentions, and he did not believe those French diplomats such as Otto who seemed to think Austria was pacific. In November 1808 Champagny reported that Metternich was returning to Vienna with the intention of maintaining good relations, but Champagny doubted whether he could influence the Austrian government to change its course. In December 1808 and January 1809 Champagny continued to warn Napoleon of Austrian preparations.[24]

It was a war which Napoleon tried desperately to avoid. He was fully involved in Spain, and the diversion of French resources to central Europe could only weaken his influence everywhere and prolong the cancerous struggle in the peninsula. There was, thought Napoleon, a simple way of avoiding a war with Austria. In 1807 France and Russia had made an alliance. Essentially they had divided Europe between them. Each had a huge sphere of influence; each was bound to support the other in her domination of that sphere. Now one of the countries excluded from the spoils was threatening one of the partners. It was in the interests of both to prevent any disturbance to peace in central Europe, for a general war could interfere with French expansion in Spain as well as Russian expansion in the Balkans. This seemed perfectly clear to Napoleon. All he needed was for Russia to tell Austria that any war with France would involve war with Russia. A small Russian mobilization on the Austrian border would add conviction. Austria could not possibly challenge both France and Russia. To obtain such cooperation, Napoleon called for a conference of the two Emperors in the central German town of Erfurt. For reasons never explained, he decided to take Talleyrand as his chief negotiator.

What happened at Erfurt is well known. Every day Napoleon met Alexander and tried to obtain guarantees of Russian cooperation in case of an Austrian attack. Every night Talleyrand met Alexander privately and advised him to avoid any promise of intervention against Austria. Talleyrand was successful. In the agreements of Erfurt there was no mention of possible Russian action against Austria. This welcome news came to the ears of the Austrians, possibly from Talleyrand himself. The result was inevitable. Safe from the threat of Russian intervention, convinced that Napoleon was hopelessly ensnarled in Spain, the Austrians, after a winter of military preparations, attacked France in the spring of 1809 and after a hard campaign were defeated. Since Austria had once more proved that she would not accept French hegemony in Italy and Germany, Napoleon once more set out to weaken her so she could not reverse the results of previous wars she had lost. This time Austria sacrificed more territory in Italy, Germany, and Poland. Part of the latter territory went to the Duchy of Warsaw, whose growth Alexander feared. The seeds of 1812 were therefore contained in the Treaty of 1809.[25]

At no time in this period was Napoleon more poorly served by his diplomatic agents than at Erfurt. And at no time were the results of such disservice more serious to France or to Europe. There can be no doubt that Talleyrand was more responsible for the war of 1809 than any other person. His enemies say so, his defenders accept the fact, and he bragged about Erfurt in his memoirs. Brinton would have us believe that Talleyrand set out to save Austria from "annihilation," a curious twist, as Napoleon's chief interest was in avoiding a war with Austria. There is only one possible explanation for Talleyrand's folly: he must have believed that Austria would win and that the Napoleonic wars could therefore be ended by a quick campaign leading to a new balance of power. The episode upholds the picture of Talleyrand as an independent-minded person; it also casts grave doubts on the quality of that independent mind.

From the failure of the Congress of Erfurt, the relationship between France and Russia steadily deteriorated until Napoleon's ill-fated invasion in 1812. At Erfurt the two Emperors had failed to solve various problems. Napoleon had refused to help Alexander destroy Turkey and Alexander had refused to restrain Austria. The Austrian war of 1809 drew Napoleon's troops back into central Europe, where they threatened both Austria and Russia. From the spoils of that war, Napoleon had to reward his faithful Polish satellite. Then the growth of the Duchy of Warsaw further intensified Alexander's concern, especially as Napoleon would not commit himself on the future of the Duchy. In 1810 Alexander planned an attack on Poland and the French Empire. He abandoned the plan, but Napoleon could neither forgive nor forget. By 1811 Russia had gained all she could from the Tilsit Alliance, namely Finland and part of Turkey. Why continue paying for the alliance through the Continental System if it were not yielding new fruits? Alexander forthwith abandoned the Continental System. Meanwhile, in the interests of the Continental System, Napoleon absorbed the Duchy of Oldenburg, whose independence was specifically guaranteed by Tilsit and whose ruler was related to Alexander. Two less greedy rulers could have solved these problems to their mutual advantage. But Alexander still dreamed of greater conquests and influence in the affairs of Europe; and Napoleon still dreamed of a Europe either subservient or allied. War was inevitable; but what was the opinion of Napoleon's diplomats on all these matters?

As relations deteriorated, Napoleon replaced his "pro-Russian" ambassador in Russia, Caulaincourt, with another close colleague and aide-de-camp, General Lauriston. In one of his first political reports, Lauriston stated that Alexander did not want war. He advised Napoleon on two steps that France would have to take to ensure peace: a reassurance that Poland would not be restored, and a compensation for France's annexation of the Duchy of Oldenburg. Fearing that his isolation might affect his opinions, Lauriston had consulted various people, and was still convinced that Russia would fight only if attacked, an opinion he repeated several times. In case of a military reverse, Russia would follow a scorched-earth policy. This opinion was repeated several times with the added advice that a reduction in the size of the French garrison in Danzig would help reassure Alexander.[26] In mid-July Lauriston replied to an instruction by stating that he was doing all he could to appease the Russians, but that this was somewhat difficult since the Russians rather than he knew all about the French troop movements. He would continue his efforts, but failed to see how he could be more convincing than Caulaincourt had been.[27]

In the autumn of 1811 Lauriston continued to argue that Alexander would not declare war on France, and that peace could be preserved if France offered compensations for Oldenburg and stopped its military preparations.[28] This continued criticism of French policy prompted a strong rebuke from Paris. Lauriston's reply was unequivocal: he had not wanted the appointment and had protested it at the time. He presumed Napoleon had sent him to Russia to learn the truth: "If I wrote anything other than what I have since my arrival, I would deceive my master and betray the truth."[29] No amount of criticism from the Foreign Minister or Napoleon would change his conviction or his determination to report the situation as he saw it. One month later Lauriston again refused to change his opinion to satisfy Paris. By January 1812, with the French troops streaming into Poland, Lauriston reported that some generals, and especially the foreigners in Russian service, wanted war, but that the Russian landowners and most of the generals were opposed to war, as was Alexander.[30]

Napoleon's attack on Russia was repeatedly opposed and criticized by his ambassador to Russia, General Lauriston. In dispatch after dispatch Lauriston had stated that Russia would not start a war, and that the problem was Napoleon's ambiguous attitude towards the restoration of Poland, his annexation of Oldenburg in violation of Tilsit and without compensation, and the continuous French troop movements into eastern Europe. Several times Lauriston had clearly advised Napoleon on how war could be avoided through French concessions, and he had correctly warned Napoleon of the Russian policy of scorched-earth and military retreat. Lauriston had maintained these convictions in the face of con-

tinuous rebukes from Foreign Minister Maret. Nor was Lauriston the
only diplomat to oppose the Russian policy. Champagny argued that he
had opposed some of the policies that led to the breakdown of relations.
There is no supporting evidence for his statement, but it is quite feasible
as he was completely identified with the Russian alliance, and its rupture
coincided with his forced retirement from public life. More important,
Lauriston's predecessor in St. Petersburg, Caulaincourt, was totally opposed to the war and was known to have spent hours arguing with Napoleon over the coming invasion. Nor was he the only person in France
to oppose the invasion of Russia.[31] In Russia Napoleon appointed diplomats who would tell him the truth. They did so, but he ignored every
word they said. For Russia Napoleon could have no one to blame but
himself.

One person who did not oppose the war was Maret, the new Minister
of Foreign Affairs. In a sense, criticism from Maret would have been out
of place. His appointment proved that Napoleon had already decided on
the invasion of Russia. Maret's job was to ensure the success of the new
policy. This he attempted to do through the negotiation of alliances with
Prussia and Austria. Further alliances with Sweden, Turkey, and Persia,
and a complete restoration of Poland might have sealed Russia's fate.
However, the destruction of Russia was not Napoleon's goal, and Maret
did not press for alliances with Russia's traditional enemies. He had always been identified with the Polish policy, so his appointment would
reassure the Polish contingents.[32] But no one expected Maret to influence
his sovereign. He had always been the *premier commis*, the chief executive instrument, of the entire Napoleonic government. He had been present when almost every executive decision had been made; he had never
pretended to exert much influence on those decisions. In this sense Maret
was more of a clerk than either Champagny or Talleyrand, and Napoleon could expect little advice from him. This could be seen as a deterioration of the quality of Napoleon's Foreign Minister, but not as a deterioration in the overall government, for Maret held cabinet rank throughout
the period.

The most honest and frank advice Napoleon ever received from his
diplomatic service came in 1814. The author was the new Foreign Minister, Caulaincourt. As ambassador to Russia, Caulaincourt had distinguished himself as both a man of peace and a man willing to submit his
opinions regardless of the position taken by Napoleon. At that time Na-

poleon had set out to convert Caulaincourt to his policy towards Russia. Napoleon failed utterly; Caulaincourt was and remained a critic of the invasion of Russia. Napoleon could have replaced Caulaincourt with someone more amenable, but he did not. Throughout the invasion and into the campaigns of 1813, Caulaincourt remained in the closest contact with Napoleon, a constant reminder of sound advice unheeded, a constant critic of the continuous wars. Caulaincourt's opposition to the Emperor's policy was well known in public, and the general clamor for peace was one of the factors that brought him to the Foreign Ministry in 1813. As Minister, Caulaincourt continued relentlessly his efforts to convince Napoleon of the necessity of peace.

It is only when history is read backwards that developments appear inevitable. In the winter of 1813–14 Napoleon's abdication, the restoration of the Bourbons, and the loss of France's conquests since 1789 had not yet been determined. Something could be saved from the wreckage—if peace were achieved quickly enough. That was the goal of Caulaincourt. But since complete military defeat had not yet occurred, a few victories, a division in the Allied camp, and even more could be saved. That was the aim of Napoleon. The realist was determined to save a little through concessions; the gambler had dreams of saving all through quick victory. All experience suggested that Napoleon would fight to the bitter end. Caulaincourt must have known that Napoleon would ignore his advice. He could have resigned; he could have encouraged Napoleon's desperate gestures; he could have remained silent. But none of these possibilities were compatible with his character. He had been appointed to negotiate peace, and peace was the only possible guarantee for the survival of France and of Napoleon. Caulaincourt would do all in his power to bring the compulsive gambler to that decision.

There was always a possibility of an Allied peace with Napoleon. None of the Allies wanted France destroyed. None of them relished the prospect of invading France, except perhaps the vengeful Prussians. To the Allies as to many Frenchmen, Bonapartism still seemed the best alternative to rampant Jacobinism or Revolutionary chaos. The King of Rome was the grandson of the Austrian Emperor, and Austria had usually turned dynastic ties to her own advantage. Few of the Allies wanted a Bourbon restoration until that course was thrust upon them by the intransigence of Napoleon and the developments which largely followed his overwhelming defeat in March of 1814.

On the other hand, the Allies were sufficiently united to see the war through to a conclusion, and they were determined to render France incapable of launching a new series of wars. After twenty years of defeats, they finally appreciated that only by combining could they achieve their mutual goals of territorial expansion, the ambitions that France had so skillfully used to divide them against themselves since 1792. Fully cognizant of these facts, Caulaincourt set out in January 1814 to negotiate with the Allies at Châtillon. He had no illusions about the terms they would dictate. His task, as he saw it, lay not in futile bickering over those terms or hopeless attempts to divide the Coalition. It was rather to make his sovereign accept whatever terms were offered, because the only alternative to immediate acceptance was unconditional surrender.

Caulaincourt's first political report contained a blunt statement that France had never been in a more serious situation, plus a request for a list of the sacrifices Napoleon was willing to make.[33] It was the first of many such requests. Throughout January and early February Napoleon pinned his hopes on a military victory. During the same period Caulaincourt repeatedly told Napoleon that even his genius could not defeat the Allies, and that every delay would increase the harshness of the terms. So desperate was the situation that Caulaincourt took the extraordinary step of appealing to Napoleon's closest military advisor, Berthier, and to Napoleon's closest civilian advisor, Maret. Both were implored to convey the truth of the situation to Napoleon, to force him to accept the Allied terms.[34] The victories that made the 1814 campaign a showpiece of military strategy rekindled Napoleon's faith in victory. They had no effect whatever on his Foreign Minister. He thought Napoleon could profit from them by accepting the terms already offered, but the victories would make no difference to the outcome of the campaign.[35]

On February 17 the Allies submitted a proposal for a peace settlement. It was nonnegotiable; France could only reply with a counterproposal. From then on Caulaincourt became desperate in his attempts to obtain from Napoleon a counterproposal containing sufficient concessions to end a war France could not conceivably win. As a minimum, Napoleon would have to surrender Piedmont, Belgium, and Mayence, and do so immediately. The Allies had given France till March 10 to submit their terms. As this date approached, Caulaincourt repeated almost daily his arguments for peace, and developed new ones such as the fear of a Bourbon restoration. He apologized for the tone of his dispatches, but refused to change any of his convictions. He tried to conquer one of the greatest obstacles, Napoleon's pride.

Austria and Prussia have been conquered by you and can now offer an example of resignation that could save you. This virtue benefited both governments, as now they speak as conquerers. Imitate them, Sire! Now, while Paris is not yet invaded and victory has not entirely deserted you. It is necessary to yield at this moment to a united Europe, because peace, I must repeat again, is the desire and necessity of France and safety lies only in peace . . . Can Your Majesty find . . . sufficient motives to take the only step which can save your throne and France?[36]

Such advice, submitted almost daily in increasingly blunt terms, provoked a sharp rebuke from Napoleon. Napoleon disagreed with Caulaincourt's analysis of the situation and with his attitudes, and questioned his loyalty and wisdom. A less determined servant would have given in: Caulaincourt fought back relentlessly. No man, he claimed, was more devoted to Napoleon's dynasty or to France. Even if he succeeded in signing the peace, he would always be condemned by Napoleon and France as the one who had surrendered France's conquests. Napoleon could say what he wanted, but he would not change Caulaincourt's opinion and could never question his loyalty. Caulaincourt saw things as they were, and could see the inevitable consequences of intransigence. The Coalition could not be defeated; Napoleon could not win.[37] In subsequent reports Caulaincourt continued to submit his advice in the frankest language. The Allied deadline came without Caulaincourt's receiving a satisfactory response from Napoleon. The negotiations were terminated; the campaign moved quickly towards its conclusion. As Caulaincourt had predicted, the rejection of the peace terms cost Napoleon his throne and cost France most of the gains of two decades of warfare. Caulaincourt had failed miserably. No man could have made greater efforts.

It is often said that Napoleon came to prefer flattery to hard-headed advice. This substitution supposedly constitutes part of the evidence for deterioration in the government. One of Napoleon's Foreign Ministers did, in fact, flatter him constantly. But unfortunately for the theory of deterioration, it was Talleyrand and not his successors. The most famous example of such flattery was Talleyrand's comparison of his relationship to Napoleon with that of Sully's celebrated devotion to Henry IV, the most popular King in modern French history. Talleyrand quoted the words of Sully: "Since I am attached to your fate, I am yours in life and death." There was seemingly no limit to Talleyrand's devotion: "Permit me to repeat that I love you, that I grieve to leave you, and that my devotion will last till death." There can be no question that this flattery sometimes involved a distortion of the truth, an encouragement to the ambitions of Napoleon. Talleyrand did not oppose the outbreak of the war with England. Instead, in the late summer of 1803, one finds him telling Napoleon: "I see everywhere that Frenchmen are more and more devoted to you, who are their destiny." The establishment of the Empire in 1804, implying significant change in Napoleon's status and an indirect threat to the Holy Roman Empire, was one of the causes of the War of the Third Coalition. Again, there is no evidence that Talleyrand opposed the creation of the Empire or warned Napoleon of the possible repercussions abroad. On the contrary, he appears to have misled him on the general popularity of the change: "I am completely confident that public opinion is entirely favorable to the establishment of your Empire." This was curious advice indeed considering the Republican hostility to the Empire and the fact that some members of the diplomatic service itself, such as Brune and Lannes, were less than enthusiastic about the destruction of the Republic. As late as 1806 we find Talleyrand complaining to Napoleon: "Three days without receiving news of you are like three centuries of anxiety and sadness."[38]

Flattery played an integral part in the formal social intercourse of the day. It was often formalized, as in the endings of letters. In the official correspondence, the diplomats are forever expressing their "boundless gratitude" for some favor, or swearing eternal loyalty to one or another of their rulers. Napoleon had thousands of administrators and generals, each of whom, according to his own letters, was the most devoted, loyal, and zealous of his supporters. Thus one hears from Champagny: "Sire, this year of 1809, like the preceding ones, will add to the glory of Your Majesty. Can I offer congratulations equal to this enormous glory? Such is the dedication of one of Your Majesty's most zealous servants, devoted equally to all your interests."[39] It was his way of saying "Happy New Year"; it would hardly encourage Napoleon's illusions. Maret often indulged in a little flattery, but when he defined himself as Napoleon's most loyal servant, he was not far from the truth. The Duchesse d'Abrantès described Caulaincourt's character as cold and aloof. His correspondence confirms this portrait. It is devoid of any flattery towards his master. It is almost devoid of the little niceties without which diplomatic language would perish. His oft-repeated statement that he was one of Napoleon's most devoted servants was the truth. Sometimes one is left with the impression that Caulaincourt's frank advice might have been more effective if it had been softened by a more diplomatic tone. Subjection to flattery is the fate of all of those who wield power; the differentiation between truth and flattery one of their greatest challenges. From his last Foreign Minister, Napoleon received courtesy but never flattery; from Maret and Champagny he received flattery that was common usage at the time. Only one minister repeatedly exaggerated his admiration for Napoleon and Napoleon's general popularity, and that minister was Talleyrand.

On the issue of war and peace, Napoleon generally received excellent advice from his diplomatic service. He was warned that his policies would lead to war with England, and advised of the measures necessary to avoid that war. He was told that Russia would not attack him in 1812 and that an attack on Russia involved serious risks, and he was advised on the measures he could initiate to avoid a war. This advice was submitted frankly, clearly, and repeatedly by his ambassador to Russia (as had his predecessor) and by other members of the government. In the winter of 1813–14 the possibility existed for Napoleon to save his own throne and some of the conquests of twenty years of French aggression. To do this, he would have to acknowledge overall defeat and negotiate on Allied terms. That was the advice of his Foreign Minister. It was repeated in letter after letter, in spite of all criticism from Napoleon.

Maret did nothing to oppose the invasion of Russia. Champagny may have opposed the development of Napoleon's Russian policy—he could do nothing else as his own political survival depended on the success of the alliance with Russia. Champagny did tell Napoleon the truth about the developments in Spain, and warned him of the coming war with Austria in 1809.

But the most destructive of Napoleon's diplomatic agents appears to have been Talleyrand. On the one hand, there is little or no reliable evidence that Talleyrand opposed the policies that led to the war with England or the Wars of the Third and Fourth Coalitions. On the contrary, Talleyrand probably encouraged the establishment of the Empire and the reorganization of Germany, both of which were threats to Austria. Such policies would be consistent with Talleyrand's position under the Directory, for the expansion of France during Talleyrand's first term as Foreign Minister, and especially the Egyptian expedition, which he supported, led directly to the War of the Second Coalition. In all of Talleyrand's letters to Napoleon, there is only one clear and important example of advice on foreign policy. That was the famous proposal for a "moderate" peace with Austria. In fact, this proposal was neither moderate, nor pacific, nor practical. Furthermore, there can be little doubt that Talleyrand urged Napoleon to intervene in Spain and overthrow the Bourbons. Later, on the basis of a serious misunderstanding of Napoleon's power, Talleyrand created the situation which led to the Austrian war of 1809, a war harmful to the interests of France, of Austria, of Russia, and of Europe. In addition, of the four Foreign Ministers, Talleyrand was the most likely to substitute flattery for the truth.

In conclusion, the idea of a general decline in Napoleon's Cabinet, or in Napoleon's diplomatic service, cannot be supported from the evidence of the advice Napoleon actually received from his diplomats. Of the four Foreign Ministers, it is clearly the last, Caulaincourt, who was most independent-minded and determined to influence Napoleon. It was the first, Talleyrand, who frequently told him what he wanted to hear, and whose advice led to wars.

Conclusion

The growth of bureaucracy has received increasing attention from historians, but is not yet well understood. Years ago political history was studied at the level of heads of state and important personalities. School children memorized the genealogies of ruling dynasties as if this constituted political history. Today, we realize that heads of state and politicians can govern only through massive and complex government machines which are only partly responsive to their wills. It is the degree of this responsiveness that is important. Clearly a state cannot be ruled without a bureaucracy; and it is equally clear that a bureaucracy is an organism in its own right, with a character, traditions, interests, sometimes overwhelming strength. In theory a bureaucracy only executes the will of the political leaders of the country. In practice this is rarely, if ever, the case. A bureaucracy can greatly effect the drafting of new laws through reports, information, and advice, through the constant pressure it exerts on cabinet ministers. If not fully satisfied with the legislation, it can then modify it, sometimes even ignore it. A strong bureaucracy can therefore constitute a check on political authority, and Napoleon is justly regarded as one of the chief architects of centralized and powerful bureaucracy in France.

However flattering it is to Napoleon to suggest that he created the French bureaucracy, the problem of political control of bureaucracy certainly did not begin with him. It was the inability of the Kings of France to rule through the Governors that led to the creation of the Intendants. Later, when it proved impossible for the Revolutionary Assemblies to rule France or to impose their policies on the countryside, they were forced to send individual members of the Assembly to the provinces and to the armies to supervise the execution of their laws. These representatives on mission had near-dictatorial powers; but only mass executions and the Terror paved the way to short-lived success. Several years later, in the more relaxed atmosphere of the Directory, the laws of the government in Paris were again flouted in the countryside of France. Napoleon was able to continue the centralizing policies of the Old Regime and Revolution precisely because those were the policies of the French bureaucracy. In the Old Regime the bureaucracy had been frustrated by the incapacity of the Kings, the power of the privileged classes, and the dead weight of tradition. During the Revolution the bureaucracy was partly frustrated by the diversion of energies into political, religious, social, and international strife. But with Napoleon the bureaucracy found a champion of order, of rationality, of uniformity, and of centralization, a man who would create and direct the enlightened despotism which the bureaucracy wanted to exercise on their *administrés* throughout the length and breath of *une nation unie et indivisable.*

As long as Napoleon's ideas conformed to those of the administration, the bureaucracy could function smoothly. But what if they disagreed? Here was a problem Napoleon's genius and ruthlessness could only partly surmount. The Ministry of Foreign Affairs in Paris was a fully developed bureaucracy. Fortunately, it worked efficiently and obeyed orders. It presented few problems and was largely unaffected by Napoleon. Also, Napoleon could and did read all outgoing mail or instructions, so it could not really thwart his intentions.

The diplomatic or external service was a different matter. These were the men who had to execute foreign policy, who had to represent France and Napoleon abroad, explain French policy to hostile or apprehensive countries, account for the shifts and contradictions in a dynamic and destructive foreign policy. They might be committed to the traditional French policy of alliance with Sweden, Poland, and Turkey. They might be committed, as Talleyrand was, to the recent Franco-Austrian alliance. They might be committed to the old *pacte de famille* and the remaining Bourbons in Spain and Italy. They were probably all sufficiently anti-English to accept Napoleon's policy in that quarter, but how many were sufficiently pro-Russian to make the Tilsit Alliance work? All of these traditions and prejudices could affect their day-to-day conduct at foreign courts or their performance at diplomatic negotiations.

For these reasons, Napoleon, like many other heads of state, had to supervise his external service closely. Apart from the Ministry of War, it was easier for him to supervise diplomacy than any other branch of government because of the inherent simplicity of diplomatic relations, and because he had been engaged in diplomacy since the beginning of the Italian campaign. There Napoleon had, for all intents and purposes, taken over the foreign policy of the Directory and negotiated the termination of the War of the First Coalition. He had directed policy towards the various Italian states, met many French and foreign diplomats, negotiated or dictated several treaties, and developed his own policies towards the Papacy, the satellites, and Austria. He was, then, fully prepared to direct foreign affairs, taking advice where and when he wanted, reserving all decisions for himself. But he could not supervise everything, so he had to deal with the French bureaucracy.

Napoleon attempted to control the French diplomatic service in a number of ways. One was by reducing the Minister of Foreign Affairs to the position of chief clerk. The Foreign Minister's task was to assemble all the diplomatic correspondence for Napoleon to read, to identify major problems and developments, to offer advice, and to ensure that Napoleon's instructions were implemented. He was even specifically ordered to submit daily all the letters that arrived from the ambassadors and ministers.[1] To check on him, Napoleon sometimes had the diplomats correspond directly with himself; and Napoleon usually approved diplomatic instructions before they were dispatched. Napoleon rarely took advice solely from the Foreign Minister. If an issue were important, he would ask for several reports from the Ministry and from other experts, would read the relevant correspondence, and would discuss the issue with his trusted friends, relatives, and advisors.

Many of the most important positions in the diplomatic service were given to Napoleon's agents—his generals, aides-de-camp, relatives, chamberlains, and not to professional diplomats. This was a denial of the career open to talents; it was essential if Napoleon was going to control diplomacy. If an important situation developed, Napoleon frequently sent one of his agents, especially his aides-de-camp, to take control of the negotiations. The best example of this occurred in 1805 when he was trying desperately to prevent Prussia from joining the Third Coalition. The French minister in Berlin, the able professional diplomat Laforest, had begun the negotiations to keep Prussia neutral. Suddenly Napoleon appointed one of his closest friends and advisors, the general and aide-de-camp Duroc. Napoleon's instructions to Talleyrand left no doubts about the position of the professional diplomatic service. Talleyrand was to explain Duroc's position to Laforest: "Tell Laforest that Duroc will play the principal role in these negotiations; that Laforest will negotiate only in his presence; that Duroc will be the principal speaker and, in a word, that Laforest will only take part in the discussions when Duroc asks him."[2]

Each minister was ordered to report all developments in neighboring states. The reports of one minister could thus be checked against those from the ministers in the neighboring states. Several ministers were then criticized for failing to report events which Napoleon learned of from other French diplomats. In addition, Napoleon received information from his military and police agents throughout Europe, and personally interrogated many of the couriers. There was no way the diplomatic service could keep a secret from Napoleon, and failure to execute an order promptly and correctly could lead to immediate recall and disgrace. Some of the recalled diplomats were ordered to explain their conduct to Napoleon, an event which had a sobering effect on any colleagues who might have contemplated some independent actions.

Napoleon's ability as a leader of men stemmed partly from the ruthlessness and determination with which he imposed his will. It stemmed also from his appreciation of human nature. He has been condemned as a cynic, but the results seemed to bear out his judgment. He created the Legion of Honour because, as he said, it is with baubles that men are led. The Legion of Honour and the Napoleonic nobility brought both prestige and considerable financial remuneration. The Senate may have been practically useless as a political body, but a Senator received an enormous salary, prestige, security, influence, an opportunity to take part in public life, or at least, to pretend to take part in the great events. If the diplomat failed to receive a senatorship, there was still the possibility of a seat in one of the other assemblies, an advisory position in local government, or the Council of State. Within the service there were all sorts of rewards such as promotions, a better legation, a *gratification*, a leave, or an inflated expense account. In addition, every French diplomat had children or relatives to look after, and Napoleon could find them a place in a school, the administration, or the army. Napoleon did not coin the saying "Every man has his price," but in its simplicity, its effectiveness, and its crudeness, it could well have been his motto of leadership.

Taken together, these methods, threats, and rewards gave Napoleon effective control of his diplomatic service, and of the other branches of government. Some of the methods, however, such as the appointment of aides-de-camp to supervise negotiations, were crude and *ad hoc* and depended on the availability of persons loyal to him and capable of executing the task. Such improvisation could not satisfy his desire for a more permanent and effective method of controlling the entire bureaucracy. For this he devised the auditoriat of the Council of State. This corps of five hundred young men was recruited from families known to and trusted by Napoleon. In their education, training, and background they formed an administrative elite, far superior to the bureaucrats trained in the previous systems. Most important, Napoleon himself knew them and their families, and their political loyalty was to the Empire and his dynasty. Once they had worked up to the positions of secretary and minister or the equivalent positions in the internal administration, Napoleon no longer had to search for friends and aides-de-camp or relatives to supervise the administration.

The Ministry of Foreign Affairs clearly recognized this threat to its independence and was able to block, in part, the application of this program. This setback notwithstanding, Napoleon did manage, by a subtle combination of all these methods, to gain control of his own diplomatic service and to make of it a highly effective instrument of his own power. The so-called subservience of this administration has sometimes been criticized on the grounds that it made dictatorship possible. Such criticism, favored as it is by the liberal historians, ignores the role of bureaucracy: in dictatorship or democracy, the function of the bureaucracy is to execute policy; in dictatorship or democracy one of the duties of the politician is to control that bureaucracy.

Napoleon inherited much of the administrative structure of his diplomatic service, and he did much to expand and improve upon its bureaucratic characteristics. It remains to determine to what extent the Napoleonic diplomatic service assumed the characteristics of a modern bureaucracy. The study of bureaucracy was really initiated in the early twentieth century by the historian and sociologist Max Weber. It has since been developed by sociologists, and to a lesser extent, by political scientists. It is unfortunate that historians have largely deserted the field of bureaucratic studies, unfortunate for the historians because bureaucratic studies have much to offer, unfortunate for the social scientists because the historian usually begins with facts and searches for explanations, whereas too often the social scientist begins with a theory or a model, then searches for examples or conducts experiments to see if it works. A comparison of the practice of the administration of the diplomatic service with the theory of bureaucratic studies may therefore be of value to both historians and other social scientists.

The most important characteristic of bureaucracy is hierarchical organization. Such an organization was fully developed in the Napoleonic diplomatic service. Within the Ministry, commands ran downwards from the Minister to the *chef*, *sous chef*, first and second *commis*, as far as a ninth *commis*. In the external service there was a hierarchy within each legation consisting of the minister and his first, second, and perhaps third secretary, together with a hierarchy of ranks from ambassador to minister to resident. In both the Ministry and the external service the lowest rank in the pyramid was that of student or attaché. Within this hierarchy clearly defined lines of responsibility ran from the lowest to the highest level, and an equally clear line of command from Napoleon to the diplomatic agents. Since 1814 the number of levels in the pyramid has increased, but its shape has not changed.

The second significant feature of bureaucracy is that the positions are permanent. The duties of each position are defined, and each one is specialized or limited or differentiated from the others. The positions do not depend on the personnel available; they are not created or altered to suit the personnel. Instead, personnel are found or trained to suit the specialized requirements of each position. This was true of both internal and external services. Occasionally an individual's qualifications could affect the organization, as when responsibility for England was transferred to Hauterive's division because of his expertise, but such alterations were not at all important. Also, during wartime, positions could be created in the Ministry for unemployed members of the external service, but they returned to the legations as soon as the war ended.

An established bureaucracy is staffed by professional administrators for whom the bureaucracy is a career. In this respect, all diplomatic services have experienced a slow evolution towards bureaucratic organization largely because diplomacy has often required nonprofessional qualifications such as loyalty, specialized knowledge, political influence, or a prestigious name, and because, unfortunately, diplomatic appointments have often been used as political rewards. Sometimes reward played a part, but more frequently Napoleon appointed ambassadors because of political loyalty, or in the case of many of the generals, because of the respect if not admiration aroused by the memory of their victories. For these reasons ministers and ambassadors were often amateurs in diplomacy. However, the number and proportion of professionals or career diplomats increased progressively throughout the period so that by 1812 two ministers in three were professional diplomats. Also, the secretarial corps was almost entirely staffed by professional diplomats, and the Ministry in Paris was as much as 95% professional. Sometimes the students of bureaucracy identify as a separate characteristic the fact that appointments are made for professional or technical rather than personal reasons. This would seem to be the inevitable corollary of the bureaucracy being a career for the employees. In this respect, then, the diplomatic service was essentially and progressively professional.

Once bureaucratic organization reaches a certain level of sophistication, the execution of specialized duties dictates that the employees have formal training, that they meet the qualifications required to enter the office, and that they be recruited on the basis of some form of objective examination. In this respect, the Napoleonic diplomatic service received a premature initiation into the ways of organized bureaucracy. The auditoriat of the Council of State satisfied all the criteria of a modern system of bureaucratic training. It dictated certain standards of education, entailed formal training both general and specific, required promotion through set phases of training, plus formal examination. In some respects (for example the selection of sub-prefects), it was not until the 1930s that the French administration reestablished such a sophisticated system of training. The establishment of the auditoriat substantiates Napoleon's reputation as an administrative genius of enormous foresight.

A certain degree of stability of personnel is required before employees can fulfill their tasks. Such stability ensures that the bureaucracy contains, at all times, a large number of staff who have acquired extensive experience, who know the rules, procedures, and policies, who can ensure continuity of policy. This stability is necessary in both the overall bureaucracy and in the individual offices. If the administration is stable, then the employees will be acquainted with each other and will have developed the working relationships and understandings without which no group can function effectively. Stability ensures security of office or tenure, giving employees freedom to execute their tasks without fear of a political purge.

The bureaucracy in Paris was highly, almost excessively, stable. There was little transfer between positions or with the external service so that some employees remained in one Division or even one position for decades. For the external service as a whole the career was relatively and increasingly stable. It is this remarkable stability that enabled the diplomatic service to survive the changes from Old Regime to Revolution to Napoleon. At the same time the service was sufficiently flexible to adjust adequately to these changes and to assimilate an amazing number of shifts of policy.

Before a hierarchical organization can function it is necessary that persons be promoted on the basis of merit and seniority. To fill properly the functions at one level, it is essential that employees have successfully held functions at an inferior level, because those are the offices they will now have to supervise and because they can have acquired the necessary knowledge and expertise only at the lower level. This promotion through the ranks also makes continuity of policy possible. Again, the Ministry in Paris operated almost exclusively on this principle, as did, to a large extent, the secretarial corps. At first Napoleon employed a considerable number of ministers who had no experience at lower levels of the service, but gradually the number of ministers promoted through the ranks increased.

A bureaucracy operates on the basis of written rules, procedures, regulations, or precedents. In theory at least, policy is impartially applied and is not subject to personal favoritism or influence. The rule is more important than the administrator or the administered. By its very nature, diplomacy depended on written instructions and written dispatches. In the diplomatic relations of the time, an elaborate protocol had been developed to regulate the relations between a diplomat and a foreign government and the relations between members of the diplomatic service. These rules applied to such matters as precedent at court, the wearing and acceptance of foreign decorations, and the breaking or establishing of diplomatic relations. In the use of written policies and rules, diplomatic services were one of the first branches of government to acquire this characteristic of modern bureaucracy, and this feature was certainly well developed by the Napoleonic period.

The continuous and consistent observation of such rules and policies necessitates the keeping of official records or archives, which are the property of the bureaucracy or the office and not the personal property of the members of the organization. Under Napoleon all diplomatic correspondence and records were regarded as the property of the state. This policy had only recently developed in France: historians working in earlier periods often have to search for records in the attics of decaying chateaus because some eighteenth-century civil servant decided that all his administrative correspondence was his private property. Similarly, there is a complete separation of the office from the incumbent: the diplomat does not own the embassy or its contents. This was only partly true at the time of Napoleon, for a minister was sometimes allowed to keep the plate and china at the end of a mission. But apart from this form of reward, all the material with which the diplomat worked belonged to the state.

The last major characteristic of bureaucracy is that the employees receive a fixed and regular salary which is paid in money and not in kind, and which is graded according to rank and responsibility. This applied perfectly to the Ministry, where the salary increased at each level of the hierarchy, where salaries were the same throughout each level, and where a salary did not change with a change in personnel. In the external service this was also true of the secretarial positions and most of the ministerial ones, but there was some fluctuation in remuneration to specific posts, and this sometimes coincided with a change in minister. In this respect, then, the diplomatic service had achieved a thoroughly modern organization.

The Napoleonic diplomatic service was a developed, sophisticated, and "modern" bureaucracy. It is also possible to argue that in fulfilling these characteristics, the diplomatic service was an "excellent" bureaucracy. In summing up the reasons for the development of bureaucracy, Max Weber argued:

Experience tends universally to show that the purely bureaucratic type of organization . . . is, from a purely technical point of view, capable of attaining the highest degree of efficiency and is in this sense formally the most rational known means of carrying out imperative control over human beings. It is superior to any other form in precision, in stability, in the stringency of its discipline, and in its reliability. It thus makes possible a particularly high degree of calculability of results for the heads of organizations and for those acting in relation to it. It is finally superior both in intensive efficiency and in the scope of its operations, and is formally capable of application to all kinds of administrative tasks.[3]

Weber has been criticized on details, but essentially his argument about the superiority of bureaucratic organization over any possible alternative has survived. One can find it echoed, for example, by F. Morstein Marx, who concludes his discussion of the characteristics of bureaucracy by asserting: "Each of these features represents a response to the basic requirements that the administrative machinery of government function effectively. Indeed, without these features, the machinery would fail to accomplish its purpose. The rise of modern bureaucracy can be understood only when we recognize its superior capacity for attending to the essentials of public administration."[4]

Bureaucracy has consistently evolved throughout the world as the chief instrument through which the modern states responds to its numerous challenges, both internal and external. In its development it has acquired the general characteristics enumerated above, each one in response to specific needs. The complete elimination of any one would render bureaucracy less efficient than it actually is. Perhaps, each characteristic, if carried to excess, would render bureaucracy unworkable. But then, none of them was carried to excess by Napoleon. Basically, Napoleon's diplomatic service constituted a hierarchy of fixed and paid offices, staffed by trained professional diplomats, appointed and promoted on the basis of ability and experience, fulfilling their functions on the basis of established rules and policies. And, every year, the diplomatic service conformed closer to this basic pattern of bureaucratic organization. But Napoleon always reserved the right to appoint persons for special reasons such as political loyalty, to increase their rewards, to promote them ahead of the professionals, or to alter the fixed policies and rules to meet special circumstances. The diplomatic service was, in fact, a successful compromise between the often conflicting goals of good administration and successful politics.

The most important conclusion to emerge from this study is that the diplomatic service constantly improved in quality over the fifteen-year period. Those diplomats trained after 1810 were far better prepared for diplomacy than those who entered the career under Talleyrand. In the Ministry, in the ministerial and secretarial corps, the number and proportion of persons actually trained and prepared for their positions gradually increased. In the early part of the period, the majority of ambassadors were amateurs, sometimes appointed for reasons having little or nothing to do with diplomacy. In the latter part of the period the majority of diplomats were professionals trained for diplomacy, promoted through the ranks, and appointed because of their experience and ability.

There was a gradual increase in the amount of experience shared by the diplomats. In 1802 one could expect France to be represented by a minister with some nine years of experience, assisted by a secretary who had entered the career only four years earlier, and receiving instructions drafted by an employee who had worked in the Ministry for twelve years. By 1812 the ministers had fourteen years of experience, their secretaries ten years, and the employees fifteen.

The instability and chaos of the Revolution spilled over into the Napoleonic period. With the Ministry itself begging for an end to experimentation, change, and confusion, Napoleon established the stability of personnel without which the Ministry could not function properly. From 1801 on, changes in personnel occurred at the normal rate; the employees in effect enjoyed tenure of office. In the external service stability was only gradually attained because of the continuous wars and shifts of policy. By 1810, however, the diplomats appointed to the legations could expect to remain in the service and in any one position for twice as long as their colleagues appointed before 1805. That stability gave them better opportunity to study the affairs of their resident countries and sufficient sense of security to encourage them to voice their opinions to Paris.

The chief function of the diplomatic service was to inform Napoleon; the ultimate test of its quality lies in the evaluation of that advice. It is clear that after 1810 Napoleon was better advised by his diplomats than he had been before. Napoleon was encouraged to launch his disastrous intervention in Spain and Portugal. In contrast, he was repeatedly urged not to invade Russia and was told how he could make concessions to avoid a war. In 1805 Talleyrand submitted a somewhat faulty plan to end the wars between France and Europe. In contrast, in 1813–14 Caulaincourt made every effort to force his reluctant sovereign to sign a peace treaty.

The most important conclusion of this study—that the quality of the diplomatic service steadily improved—contradicts one of the most widely held theories about Napoleon's government. The idea that this government deteriorated is accepted by a variety of schools of thought, by liberal critics such as Cobban, by Marxists such as Lefebvre, by middle-of-the-road Americans like Bruun, and by qualified admirers of Napoleon such as Markham. The contradiction of this theory might seem to place this book in the pro-Napoleonic camp.

But such a conclusion should not be drawn too hastily. One of the first persons to suggest that Napoleon's government declined was Napoleon himself. He was at St. Helena at the time, fabricating the Napoleonic legend which did so much to confirm Voltaire's definition of history as a pack of tricks played upon the dead. There are many facets to the Napoleonic legend, but one of the most important was that Napoleon was not himself responsible for ultimate failure. Along with rising nationalism, the mistakes of his generals, perfidious Albion, and all the rest, his own government could provide a convenient scapegoat. For if his subordinates were progressively less able, and if their advice were increasingly less sound, then clearly these things would account for the defeat. Surrounded by incompetents and submerged in flattery, how could he have done differently? Unfortunately for Napoleon, the evidence of this study partly disproves this scapegoat theory. For if the diplomatic service progressively improved, if it clearly warned Napoleon about the dangers of invading Russia and of continuing the struggle in 1813–14, then Napoleon had no one to blame for his failure but himself. And that conclusion makes it somewhat difficult to classify this study as either pro- or anti-Napoleon. Napoleon created the best diplomatic service of the period and probably one of the best of the nineteenth century. That, in part, identifies him as an administrative genius. His failure to use that service properly, to accept its advice, explains in part his ultimate political failure.

Appendix I

The Ministry of Foreign Affairs

North Division

chef
sous chef
4–8 commis

South Division

chef
sous chef
4–10 commis

Consulates Division

chef
sous chef
3–9 commis
commis chargé de passeports

Archives Division

chef
sous chef
sous chef
analyseur
géographe
directeur des élèves
publicist
bibliothécaire
2–7 commis

Codes Division

chef
chef adjoint
sous chef
2 commis
colleur de chiffre

Finances Division

chef
sous chef
4–6 commis

Appendix II

The Social Origins of the Ministers, Secretaries, and Employees of the Ministry, Shown in Absolute and Percentage Terms for Those Whose Social Origins are Known

Year:		1800	1801	1802	1803	1804	1805	1806	1807	1808	1809	1810	1811	1812	1813
Ministers															
Nobles	number	2	4	8	10	14	5	6	7	9	12	9	10	13	13
	percentage	18	13	23	38	33	21	27	33	37	48	47	47	59	68
Bourgeoisie	number	4	5	9	8	8	9	7	6	6	5	4	4	3	2
	percentage	36	38	37	30	30	39	31	28	25	20	19	19	13	10
Petite bourgeoisie	number	5	4	7	8	10	9	9	8	9	8	7	7	5	4
	percentage	45	31	29	30	36	39	40	38	37	32	33	33	27	21
Secretaries															
Nobles	number	0	1	6	7	7	7	7	9	11	10	9	8	9	6
	percentage	0	10	28	26	26	29	33	47	57	58	52	57	69	54
Bourgeoisie	number	1	2	7	6	6	4	4	3	2	1	1	0	0	1
	percentage	14	20	33	23	23	16	19	15	10	6	6	0	0	9
Petite bourgeoisie	number	6	7	8	13	13	13	10	7	6	6	7	6	4	4
	percentage	85	70	38	50	50	54	47	36	31	35	41	43	31	36
Employees															
Nobles	number	1	1	1	1	1	2	2	3	4	4	4	4	1	1
	percentage	4	3	3	2	2	5	5	9	11	12	11	13	4	4
Bourgeoisie	number	7	8	8	12	12	12	10	9	10	9	10	9	8	7
	percentage	25	25	25	32	32	32	29	26	29	27	29	29	31	28
Petite bourgeoisie	number	20	22	23	24	24	23	22	22	20	20	20	18	17	17
	percentage	71	70	71	64	64	62	64	64	58	61	58	58	65	68

Appendix III

Age and Experience of Diplomats, and Sources of Recruitment of the Ministers

Year:	1800	1801	1802	1803	1804	1805	1806	1807	1808	1809	1810	1811	1812	1813	1814
Average age															
Ministers	45.3	42.6	44.7	43.4	42.6	43.6	43.7	45.7	45.8	45.9	47.1	48.3	44.1	42.3	48.8
Secretaries	28.3	29.7	28.7	30.6	30.5	32.1	32.2	31.5	32.0	32.7	33.1	33.9	31.6	31.0	
Employees	43.0	42.0	43.4	44.8	43.8	44.7	46.6	45.8	45.3	46.3	46.6	48.7	48.0	49.0	48.8
Average experience															
Ministers	11.4	10.2	9.6	8.9	7.5	7.4	8.1	9.6	9.3	11.1	13.6	14.5	14.1	12.2	13.3
Secretaries	4.5	6.1	4.2	4.7	4.8	5.8	6.7	7.4	7.6	8.7	9.6	10.1	10.3	9.9	12.7
Employees	11.7	11.1	11.7	12.7	12.5	13.2	13.7	14.1	12.9	12.9	13.8	14.4	15.2	15.2	17.0
Recruitment of ministers															
Number of ministers	11	16	24	27	28	23	22	21	24	24	21	21	22	20	4
Generals: number	3	5	6	8	8	4	5	5	7	4	3	3	1	2	1
percentage	*27.2*	*31.3*	*25.0*	*30.0*	*28.6*	*17.4*	*22.7*	*23.8*	*29.2*	*16.7*	*14.3*	*14.3*	*4.5*	*10.0*	*25.0*
Diplomats: number	6	6	9	11	11	9	10	10	11	14	14	16	15	14	3
percentage	*54.5*	*37.5*	*37.5*	*40.7*	*39.2*	*39.1*	*45.4*	*47.6*	*45.8*	*58.3*	*66.6*	*76.2*	*68.2*	*70.0*	*75.0*
Imperial Household: number	1	3	3	2	2	3	2	1	1	2	1	1	5	5	
Administration: number								2	2	3	3	1	1	1	1

Appendix IV

French Legations and Dates of Occupancy

Amsterdam: Batavian Republic, Holland, 1799 to September 1810.

Berlin: Prussia, 1799 to October 1806; December 1808 to March 1813.

Berne: Helvetic Republic, Swiss Confederation, 1799 to 1814.

Cassel: Hesse-Cassel, Circle of the Upper Rhine, Kingdom of Westphalia, 1799 to October 1806; December 1808 to November 1813.

Constantinople: Turkey, Ottoman Empire, Levant, January 1803 to 1814.

Copenhagen: Denmark, 1799 to May 1814.

Danzig: July 1808 to January 1811; August 1812 to January 1813.

Darmstadt: Hesse-Darmstadt, March 1801 to October 1813.

Dresden: Saxony, Upper Saxony, 1799 to September 1806; December 1806 to October 1813.

Florence: Tuscany, Etruria, September 1801 to October 1807.

Frankfort: Frankfort, Confederation of the Rhine, May 1801 to October 1813.

Genoa: Ligurian Republic, June 1800 to June 1805.

Hamburg: Circle of Lower Saxony, Hanseatic Cities, June 1802 to December 1810.

Karlsruhe: Baden, Circle of Swabia, January 1800 to November 1813.

Lisbon: Portugal, March 1802 to October 1805.

London: Great Britain, November 1802 to May 1803.

Lucca: October 1801 to April 1809.

Madrid: Spain, 1799 to May 1813.

Malta: August 1802 to October 1803.

Mecklenburg: Mecklenburg-Schewerin and Mecklenburg-Strelitz, April 1811 to March 1813.

Milan: Cisalpine Republic, Italian Republic, June 1802 to March 1805.

Munich: Bavaria, August 1802 to November 1813.

Naples: Naples, Sicily, Two Sicilies, April 1801 to April 1806; September 1806 to January 1814.

Parma: March 1801 to October 1802.

Ragusa: July 1806 to September 1808.

Ratisbon: German Diet, 1799 to September 1806.

Rome: Papal States, April 1801 to June 1808.

Saint Petersburg: Russia, April 1802 to June 1804; December 1807 to July 1812.

Salzburg: June 1803 to November 1805.

Stockholm: Sweden, August 1801 to August 1804; October 1810 to November 1811.

Stuttgart: Württemberg, July 1803 to October 1813.

Teheran: Persia, December 1807 to December 1810.

Turin: Piedmont, Sardinia, August 1800 to April 1801.

Valais: June 1804 to December 1810.

Vienna: Austria, October 1801 to October 1805; January 1806 to March 1809; December 1809 to August 1813.

Warsaw: Grand Duchy of Warsaw, February 1808 to February 1813.

Washington (*Philadelphia*): United States of America, October 1800 to 1814.

Weimar: Saxon Princes, December 1811 to October 1813.

Würzburg: January 1806 to 1813.

Appendix V

The Diplomatic List

The first task in the study of a diplomatic service is the establishment of an accurate and comprehensive diplomatic list. The task is not easy. The names of both places and persons are apparently in constant flux. Moustier becomes Demoustier; D'Aubusson de la Feuillade can be found under D, A, or F. An embassy such as that at Karlsruhe may be identified as Karlsruhe, Baden, Swabia, or Circle of Swabia. The mission in Hamburg was attached to the Hanseatic Cities, or the Circle of Lower Saxony, and in one source is listed under the individual cities. By way of clarification, embassies are classified here by cities rather than countries.

The official French diplomatic lists began in 1853. Before that one has to rely on the *Almanach Royal, National,* or *Impérial.* The *Almanach* contains a basic list of ministers and secretaries and, for the Ministry, the *chefs* and *sous chefs.* However, its limitations are many. It was an annual publication and lists only one person for each post regardless of whether there was a change during the year. No *Almanach* was published in 1814.

The *Reporterium der Diplomatischer Vertreter aller Länder* is concerned only with those persons who were in charge of missions. Secretaries are mentioned only if and when they held the position of chargé d'affaires, and no distinction is drawn between those appointed *ad interim* and those *en titre.* The *Reportorium* contains some errors which detract from its usefulness. It suffers a little from being too technical: for instance, dividing Saint Aignan's mission to the Saxon Princes into its component parts introduces a degree of hopeless confusion into the German embassies.

The budgets of the Ministry give a useful picture of the embassy network, and of the ministers and secretaries in the external service. But the figures given are in no way precise. Payments were often made to the nearest quarter of a year, and some diplomats such as Cacault were paid long after they had left their posts. Only two of the miscellaneous personnel were paid, and the budget for 1813 is missing. The service records in the personnel dossiers were usually drawn up by the diplomats themselves. As the immediate objective was often a pension, lengths of service were maximized. Didelot gives himself nine years two months; his actual term was seven years five months. The political correspondence gives the most accurate information on the lengths of missions, especially for those who were in charge. The series "Décrets et Arrêtés" contains most, but not all, of the appointments, plus several nominations which were not confirmed. All of these sources have been used in compiling the following list, which is divided into heads of mission, secretaries, and employees of the Ministry.

Abbreviations used

amb.	ambassador
m.	minister
m. plen.	minister plenipotentiary
en.	envoy
ext.	extraordinary
ch.	chargé d'affaires *en titre*
sec.	secretary
I sec., 2 sec.	first, second secretary
res.	resident.

Part One: Permanent Heads of Mission

D'Aguesseau, Henri Jean Baptiste Cardin
    m. plen. and en. ext., *Copenhagen*, May 1802 to May 1805
Alquier, Charles Jean Marie
    amb., *Madrid*, February 1800 to December 1800
    amb., *Naples*, April 1801 to April 1806
    amb., *Rome*, May 1806 to February 1808
    m. plen. and en. ext., *Stockholm*, October 1810 to November 1811
    m. plen. and en. ext., *Copenhagen*, November 1811 to May 1814
Andréossy, Antoine François
    amb., *London*, November 1802 to May 1803
    amb., *Vienna*, November 1806 to March 1809
    amb., *Constantinople*, July 1812 to November 1814
Aubusson de la Feuillade, Pierre Raymond Hector
    m. plen., *Florence*, September 1806 to October 1807
    amb., *Naples*, January 1808 to August 1809
Bacher, Jacques Justin Théobald
    ch., *Ratisbon*, 1799 to September 1806
    ch., *Frankfort*, September 1806 to December 1811

Beauharnais, François
   m. (later m. plen.), *Florence*, April 1805 to May 1806
   amb., *Madrid*, December 1806 to April 1808
Beurnonville, Pierre Riel de
   m. plen. (later m. plen. and en. ext.), *Berlin*, January 1800 to February
      1802
   amb., *Madrid*, October 1802 to May 1806
Bignon, Louis Pierre Édouard
   m. plen., *Cassel*, August 1803 to October 1806
   ch., *Warsaw*, May 1811 to June 1812
   m. plen. and en. ext., *Warsaw*, January 1813 to February 1813
Bonaparte, Lucien
   amb., *Madrid*, December 1800 to July 1801
Bourgoing, Jean François
   m. plen., *Copenhagen*, August 1800 to August 1801
   m. plen. and en. ext., *Stockholm*, August 1801 to April 1803
   m. plen., *Dresden*, May 1807 to July 1811
Bourrienne, Louis Antoine Fauvelet de
   m. plen., *Hamburg*, May 1805 to December 1810
Brune, Guillaume Marie Ann
   amb., *Constantinople*, January 1803 to December 1804
Cacault, François
   m. plen., *Rome*, April 1801 to July 1803
Caulaincourt, Armand Augustin Louis de
   amb. ext. and m. plen., *St. Petersburg*, December 1807 to May 1811
Champagny, Jean Baptiste Nompère de
   amb., *Vienna*, October 1801 to October 1804
Clarke, Henri Jacques Guillaume
   m., *Florence*, September 1801 to June 1804
Dejean, Jean François Aimé
   m. plen., *Genoa*, June 1800 to February 1802
Demoustier, Clément Édouard
   m. plen. and en. ext., *Karlsruhe*, March 1811 to February 1812
   m. plen. and en. ext., *Stuttgart*, February 1812 to April 1813
Derville-Maléchard, Claude Joseph Parfait
   ch., *Lucca*, August 1803 to August 1806
   m. plen., *Valais*, August 1806 to December 1810
Desaugiers, Jules Joseph (*jeune*)
   ch., *Mecklenburg*, April 1811 to March 1813
Didelot, François Charles Luce
   m. plen., *Stuttgart*, July 1803 to May 1806

m. plen., *Copenhagen*, May 1807 to June 1811
Dupont-Chaumont, Antoine
　m. plen., *Amsterdam*, August 1805 to March 1808
Durant de Mareuil, Joseph Alexandre Jacques
　m. plen., *Dresden*, June 1805 to September 1806
　m. plen., *Stuttgart*, May 1807 to December 1810
　m. plen., *Naples*, April 1811 to January 1814
Eschasseriaux, Joseph
　ch., *Valais*, 1804 to August 1806
　m. plen., *Lucca*, August 1806 to April 1809
Fesch, Joseph
　amb., *Rome*, July 1803 to May 1806
Gardane, Claude Mathieu
　m. plen., *Teheran*, December 1807 to February 1809
Germain de Montfort, August Jean
　m. plen. and en. ext., *Würzburg*, 1813
Gouvion St. Cyr, Laurent
　amb., *Madrid*, November 1801 to August 1802
Hédouville, Gabriel Marie Théodore Joseph de
　m. plen. and en. ext., *St. Petersburg*, April 1802 to June 1804
Hédouville, Théodore Charles Joseph de
　m. plen., *Ratisbon*, July 1805 to July 1806
　m. plen., *Frankfort*, July 1806 to October 1813
Helflinger, Jean Frédéric
　ch., *Dresden*, November 1799 to February 1800
　ch., *Darmstadt*, March 1801 to March 1812
Hirsinger, Yves Louis Joseph
　res., *Frankfort*, May 1801 to August 1806
　m. plen., *Würzburg*, August 1806 to January 1812
Jourdan, Jean Baptiste
　m. plen., *Turin*, August 1800 to April 1801
Junot, Jean Andoche
　amb., *Lisbon*, April 1805 to October 1805
Laforest, Antoine Réné Charles Mathurin
　m. plen., *Munich*, August 1802 to April 1803
　m. plen. and en. ext., *Berlin*, May 1803 to October 1806
　amb., *Madrid*, May 1808 to May 1813
Lamoussaye, Louis
　res., *Danzig*, August 1812 to January 1813
Lannes, Jean
　m. plen. and en. ext., *Lisbon*, March 1802 to July 1804

Larochefoucauld, Alexandre François
    ch., *Dresden*, April 1801 to January 1805
    amb., *Vienna*, January 1805 to November 1806
    amb., *Amsterdam*, April 1808 to May 1810
Latour-Maubourg, Juste Pons Florimand de Fay
    m. plen., *Würzburg*, 1813
    m. plen., *Stuttgart*, April 1813 to October 1813
Lauriston, Jacques Alexandre Bernard Law de
    amb. ext., *St. Petersburg*, May 1811 to July 1812
La Valette, Antoine Marie Chaumont
    ch., *Dresden*, February 1800 to March 1801
Lezai-Marnesia, Adrien
    m. plen., *Salzburg*, November 1803 to November 1805
    m. plen., *Würzburg*, January 1806 to May 1806
Macdonald, Jacques Étienne Joseph Alexandre
    m. plen. and en. ext., *Copenhagen*, July 1801 to December 1801
Massias, Nicolas
    ch., *Karlsruhe*, August 1800 to May 1808
    res., *Danzig*, July 1808 to January 1811
Mercy d'Argenteau, François Joseph Charles
    m. plen., *Munich*, July 1812 to November 1813
Montholon-Sémonville, Charles Tristian
    m. plen., *Würzburg*, January 1812 to October 1812
Moreau St. Mery, Méderic Louis Elie
    res., *Parma*, March 1801 to October 1802
Narbonne-Lara, Louis Marie Jacques Almeric de
    m. plen. and en. ext., *Munich*, March 1810 to November 1811
    amb., *Vienna*, March 1813 to August 1813
Ney, Michel
    m. plen., *Bern*, October 1802 to January 1804
Nicolai, Armand François Marie Cristian
    m. plen., *Karlsruhe*, January 1812 to November 1813
Otto, Louis Guillaume
    m. plen. and en. ext., *Munich*, October 1803 to January 1810
    amb., *Vienna*, January 1810 to March 1813
Petiet, Claude Louis
    m. ext., *Milan*, June 1800 to March 1805
Pichon, Louis André
    ch., *Philadelphia*, October 1800 to September 1804
Portalis, Joseph (*fils*)
    m. plen., *Ratisbon*, October 1804 to July 1805

de Pradt, Dominique de Riom
  amb., *Warsaw*, June 1812 to December 1812
Raymond, Jean
  ch., *Ragusa*, July 1806 to September 1808
Reinhard, Charles Frédéric
  m. plen., *Bern*, February 1800 to September 1801
  m. plen., *Hamburg*, June 1802 to June 1805
  m. plen., *Cassel*, December 1808 to November 1813
Rivals, Louis Marc
  m. plen., *Cassel*, 1799 to August 1803
Saint Aignan, Nicolas Auguste Marie Rousseau
  m. plen., *Weimar*, December 1811 to October 1813
Saint Marsan, Philippe Antoine Asinari de (San Marsano)
  m. plen., *Berlin*, December 1808 to March 1813
Salicetti, Antoine Cristophe
  en. ext., *Lucca*, October 1801 to July 1802
  m. plen., *Genoa*, June 1802 to June 1805
Sébastiani della Porta, Horace François
  amb., *Constantinople*, September 1806 to April 1808
Sémonville, Charles Louis Huguet de
  m. plen., *Amsterdam*, January 1800 to February 1805
Serra, Jean Charles François
  res., *Warsaw*, February 1808 to March 1811
  m. plen. and en. ext., *Stuttgart*, April 1811 to November 1811
  m. plen. and en. ext., *Dresden*, January 1812 to October 1813
Serurier, Louis Charles
  m. plen., *Washington*, February 1811 to January 1816
Talleyrand, Auguste Louis
  m. plen., *Karlsruhe*, April 1808 to September 1808
  m. plen., *Bern*, December 1808 to December 1813
Turreau de Garambouville, Louis Marie
  m. plen., *Washington*, November 1804 to February 1811
Vandeul, Denis Simon Caroillan de
  m. plen., *Darmstadt*, March 1812 to October 1813
Verninac, Raymond
  m. plen., *Bern*, September 1801 to September 1802
Vial, Honoré
  m. plen., *Malta*, August 1802 to October 1803
  amb., *Bern*, February 1804 to June 1808
Victor, Claude Perrin
  m., *Copenhagen*, May 1805 to August 1806

Part Two: Secretaries

Artaud, Jean Alexandre François de Montor
    sec., *Rome*, March 1801 to September 1803
    sec., *Rome*, September 1804 to June 1805
    sec., *Florence*, June 1805 to December 1807
Bignon, Louis Pierre Édouard
    1 sec., *Berlin*, December 1799 to August 1803
Bogne de Faye, Pierre François Jean
    sec., *Munich*, September 1805 to March 1812
Bottu, ———
    sec., *Turin*, June 1800 to January 1801
Cabre, Auguste Honoré Michel Sabartier de
    sec., *Stockholm*, May 1811 to December 1812
Caillard, Bernard Antoine Jean (*neveu*)
    2 sec., *Berlin*, September 1799 to June 1801
    1 sec., *Stockholm*, June 1801 to September 1804
    1 sec., *Berlin*, September 1804 to March 1808
    1 sec., *Berlin*, February 1809 to May 1811
    1 sec., *Madrid*, May 1811 to mid-1813
Chasteau, Edme Thérèse Jean Baptiste de
    sec., *Stuttgart*, November 1812 to October 1813
Chateaubriand, François Auguste Réné de
    1 sec., *Rome*, June 1803 to December 1803
Chateau-Giron, Réné Charles Hyppolyte Le Prestre
    1 sec., *St. Petersburg*, February 1802 to September 1804
Crenzé, Auguste
    sec., *Parma*, December 1800 to September 1802
David, Pierre Laurent Jean Baptiste Étienne
    sec., *Malta*, June 1802 to December 1807
Demoustier, Clement Édouard
    sec., *Dresden*, October 1801 to February 1811
Derville-Maléchard, Claude Joseph Parfait
    sec., *Milan*, July 1800 to March 1802
Desaugiers, Felix Auguste (*ainé*)
    1 sec., *Copenhagen*, September 1799 to December 1811
Desaugiers, Jules Joseph (*jeune*)
    2 sec., *Copenhagen*, September 1799 to March 1810
    sec., *Stockholm*, March 1810 to December 1810
Desmazières, Thomas Louis
    2 sec., *Amsterdam*, September 1799 to September 1805

Desportes, Felix
  1 sec., *Madrid,* December 1800 to December 1801
Dodun, Claude Laurent Marie
  2 sec., *Vienna,* September 1801 to June 1803
  1 sec., *Vienna,* June 1803 to June 1809
Durant (St. André), Esprit André
  2 sec., *Madrid,* February 1800 to February 1801
  sec., *Naples,* February 1801 to September 1802
  sec., *Copenhagen,* January 1812 to May 1814
Fitte, Xavier
  sec., *Bern,* February 1800 to September 1801
  sec., *Lisbon,* December 1801 to September 1804
Gabriac, Alphonse Joseph Paul Marie Ernest de Cadoine
  sec., *Naples,* May 1811 to December 1813
Gandolphe, Saveur Joseph
  sec., *Bern,* September 1801 to December 1803
  sec., *Rome,* December 1803 to September 1804
Gardane, Paul Ange Louis
  1 sec., *Teheran,* May 1807 to December 1808
Garonne, ———
  3 sec., *Vienna,* January 1810 to March 1813
  2 sec., *Vienna,* March 1813 to August 1813
Groisbois, Claude François Xavier Hué de
  sec., *Naples,* January 1808 to March 1813
Hédouville, Théodore Charles Joseph de
  2 sec., *Rome,* December 1803 to June 1805
Hermand, François Antoine
  1 sec., *Madrid,* November 1801 to March 1806
Jacob, ———
  1 sec., *Madrid,* May 1800 to December 1800
Jordan (Duplessis), Augustin
  sec., *Salzburg,* June 1803 to September 1806
  sec., *Würzburg,* October 1806 to June 1811
Lablanche, Xavier Olivier de
  2 sec., *Vienna,* June 1804 to January 1806
  1 sec., *Constantinople,* May 1806 to December 1809
  1 sec., *Vienna,* January 1810 to August 1813
Lacuée, ———
  1 sec., *Vienna,* June 1801 to June 1803
Lagrange, Ange François Le Fievre de
  3 sec., *Vienna,* March 1806 to January 1810
  2 sec., *Vienna,* January 1810 to March 1812

Lajard, Felix
    2 sec., *Berlin,* May 1803 to May 1807
    3 sec., *Teheran,* May 1807 to October 1808
    2 sec., *Teheran,* November 1808 to December 1810
    sec., *Dresden,* May 1811 to May 1812
    1 sec., *Warsaw,* June 1812 to February 1813
Lamare, Pierre Bernard
    2 sec., *Constantinople,* September 1802 to November 1806
Latour-Maubourg, Juste pons Florimand de Fay
    2 sec., *Constantinople,* November 1806 to August 1812
Lefebvre, Edouard Pierre Michel
    1 sec., *Florence,* August 1801 to September 1802
    sec., *Naples,* September 1802 to May 1806
    sec., *Rome,* June 1806 to June 1808
    sec., *Cassel,* October 1808 to May 1811
    sec., *Berlin,* May 1811 to March 1813
Malartic, Charles Jean Baptiste Alphonse de
    sec., *Stuttgart,* February 1809 to May 1811
    sec., *Cassel,* May 1811 to November 1813
Marandet, Alexandre Leopold
    sec., *Munich,* December 1801 to September 1805
Marcieu, Alberic Jean Eugène de
    sec., *Dresden,* July 1812 to October 1813
Marivault, Antoine Delacoux
    1 sec., *Amsterdam,* January 1800 to July 1805
Mergèz, George Nicolas
    2 sec., *Washington,* December 1802 to December 1803
Mériage, Louis Auguste François
    2 sec., *Vienna,* March 1806 to April 1809
Parandier, Pierre
    1 sec., *Constantinople,* September 1802 to May 1806
Pétry, ————
    sec., *Washington,* December 1802 to 1814
Portalis, Joseph (*fils*)
    sec., *London,* September 1802 to June 1803
    1 sec., *Berlin,* August 1803 to September 1804
Posuel de Verneaux, Pierre Marie
    3 sec., *Vienna,* June 1801 to March 1804
    2 sec., *Vienna,* March 1804 to January 1806
Prévost, Achille Felicité
    3 sec., *St. Petersburg,* October 1807 to July 1812

Raillane, ———
   sec., *Turin*, January 1801 to April 1801
Raymond, Jean
   sec., *Stuttgart*, April 1803 to February 1806
Rayneval, Maximilien François Joseph Marie Gérard de
   2 sec., *St. Petersburg*, February 1802 to September 1804
   sec., *Lisbon*, October 1804 to September 1807
   1 sec., *St. Petersburg*, December 1807 to July 1812
Recordin, ———
   3 sec., *Constantinople*, September 1802 to May 1806
Rousseau, Jean Baptiste Louis Jacques (*fils*)
   2 sec., *Teheran*, May 1807 to October 1808
Rouyer, ———
   sec., *Bern*, December 1803 to 1814
Rumigny, Marie Hypollyte Gueully de
   sec., *Stuttgart*, May 1811 to May 1812
   2 sec., *Warsaw*, June 1812 to February 1813
St. Genèst, Louis Courbon de
   sec., *Cassel*, January 1806 to November 1807
   2 sec., *St. Petersburg*, November 1807 to July 1812
Salignac-Fénélon, Jean Raymond Sigsmond Alfred
   2 sec., *Stockholm*, July 1801 to September 1804
   sec., *Ratisbon*, October 1804 to December 1806
   sec., *Frankfort*, January 1807 to October 1813
Serurier, Louis
   sec., *Cassel*, April 1800 to June 1805
   sec., *Amsterdam*, June 1805 to September 1810
Siméon, Joseph Balthazar
   2 sec., *Florence*, September 1801 to September 1802
   1 sec., *Florence*, September 1802 to June 1805
   sec., *Rome*, June 1805 to June 1806
   sec., *Stuttgart*, July 1806 to September 1808
Sinetti, ———
   3 sec., *Vienna*, February 1812 to August 1813
Tculon, ———
   sec., *Hamburg*, June 1802 to June 1806
Thiebault, ———
   2 sec., *Madrid*, December 1801 to January 1803
Vandeul, Denis Simon Caroillan de
   2 sec., *Berlin*, June 1801 to January 1803
   2 sec., *Madrid*, January 1803 to December 1810

Part Three: The Ministry

Angelucci, ———
  commis, *Consulates*, June 1810 to July 1811
Barbie du Bocage, Jean Denis
  géographe, *Archives*, December 1802 to May 1814
Barbry, ———
  commis, *Finances*, September 1799 to September 1800
Barthel, Jean Frédéric
  commis, *North*, September 1799 to May 1814
Baudard, ———
  chef adjoint, *Codes*, 1809 to August 1811
  sous chef, *Archives*, September 1811 to May 1814
Bendit, ———
  chef du bureau de l'ouest, *South*, June 1812 to 1813
Besson, Louis Marc
  commis, *Archives*, November 1799 to May 1814
Beuscher, Jean Marie
  commis, *North*, September 1799 to December 1807
  commis, *Codes*, January 1808 to May 1814
Bonnet, ———
  commis, *Archives*, September 1799 to August 1800
Bourdois, ———
  commis, *Consulates*, September 1802 to April 1804
Bourjot, Auguste François Charles
  commis, *North*, September 1799 to September 1800
  secrétaire intime, *North*, September 1800 to April 1807
  sous chef, *South*, May 1807 to March 1812
  sous chef, *North*, April 1812 to May 1814
Brenier, Henri
  commis, *South*, January 1804 to 1813
  sous chef, *South*, 1813 to May 1814
Bresson, Jean Baptiste Marie François
  chef, *Finances*, November 1799 to May 1814
Brulé, Nicolas
  chargé de passeports, *Consulates*, September 1799 to May 1814
Buache, Louis Charles
  géographe, *Archives*, September 1799 to November 1802
Butet, Antoine Alexandre
  commis, *Consulates*, September 1799 to May 1814
Caillard, Antoine Bernard
  chef, *Archives*, December 1799 to April 1807

Caillard (*jeune*), ———
  commis, *Archives*, September 1801 to May 1814
Campy-Gambier, Pierre François Louis
  chef, *Codes*, September 1799 to May 1814
Cansorville, ———
  commis, *North*, March 1800 to May 1801
Carbonnier, Pierre Louis
  commis, *South*, September 1799 to December 1803
Challaye, ———
  commis, *North*, July 1807 to May 1814
Cornillot, Charles Nicolas
  commis, *Codes*, September 1799 to May 1814
Couteaux, Alexandre Claude
  commis, *Consulates*, September 1800 to May 1810
Damour, Augustin Jean
  commis, *Consulates*, December 1802 to February 1805
  secrétaire intime, *Codes*, February 1805 to July 1807
  sous chef, *Codes*, August 1807 to May 1814
D'asnières de la Châtaigneraye, Jean Baptiste François Auguste
  commis, *North*, June 1806 to September 1811
Deffaudis, ———
  commis, *Consulates*, June 1806 to May 1814
Delaboutraye, ———
  commis, *Consulates*, June 1806 to May 1814
Delaflèchelle, Jacques Gilles
  sous chef, *Finances*, September 1799 to May 1814
Denois, ———
  commis, *South*, January 1811 to May 1814
Desages, ———
  commis, *Consulates*, February 1810 to May 1814
Desnaux, ———
  commis, *Codes*, September 1799 to May 1808
Deviefville, ———
  commis, *South*, February 1805 to 1809
Dietrick, ———
  commis, *Codes*, September 1799 to November 1799
  commis, *North*, November 1799 to March 1800
Drouin, Jacques
  commis, *North*, September 1799 to September 1800
Duault, ———
  commis, *North*, September 1800 to May 1814

Durant (St. André), Esprit André
  sous chef, *North*, September 1802 to March 1812
Durant (de Mareuil), Joseph Alexandre
  chef, *North*, January 1800 to March 1805
Durant, ———
  commis, *Finances*, January 1814 to May 1814
Ferandel, Jean Jacques François
  commis, *Consulates*, September 1799 to January 1810
Feuchère, ———
  commis, *Consulates*, August 1811 to May 1814
Finet, ———
  colleur de chiffre, *Codes*, September 1799 to May 1814
Flury, ———
  sous chef, *Consulates*, January 1806 to May 1814
Galon-Boyer, Jean François
  sous chef, *Archives*, September 1799 to October 1802
Goffinet, ———
  commis, *South*, September 1799 to 1813
Goujon, ———
  commis, *South*, October 1799 to 1809
  commis, *Archives*, 1809 to May 1814
Grandmaison, ———
  commis, *Finances*, September 1799 to August 1800
Guérard, François Marie
  commis, *North*, September 1799 to May 1807
  commis, *Archives*, June 1807 to May 1814
Guilleauformons, ———
  commis, *Codes*, 1809 to May 1814
Guillois, François Joachim
  commis, *Finances*, September 1799 to June 1811
Guyétard, Emmanuel
  commis, *South*, September 1799 to April 1805
  commis, *North*, April 1805 to May 1807
  commis, *South*, June 1807 to November 1811
D'Hauteforts, ———
  commis, *Archives*, 1809 to March 1811
Hauterive, Blanc
  chef, *North*, September 1799 to January 1800
  chef, *South*, January 1800 to April 1807
  chef, *Archives*, May 1807 to May 1814
D'Hermand, Emmanuel Louis Joseph
  chef, *Consulates*, September 1799 to May 1814

Joly, Jean Baptiste Charles
    commis, *Consulates*, September 1799 to May 1814
Jorelle, François
    commis, *Archives*, September 1799 to May 1814
Labesnardière, Jean Baptiste
    sous chef, *Consulates*, September 1799 to March 1805
    chef, *North*, March 1805 to May 1814
Laborie, ———
    secrétaire intime, *North*, September 1800 to August 1801
Lajard, Félix
    commis, *South*, September 1802 to May 1803
Lajonchère, ———
    secrétaire intime, *North*, February 1805 to 1809
    commis, *North*, 1809 to March 1812
Laubepin, Moucher Battefort de, Marie François Emmanuel
    commis, *South*, November 1803 to December 1810
Lebartz, ———
    commis, *Codes*, November 1799 to October 1807
Mahélin, Augustin Jean
    commis, *Finances*, September 1799 to April 1802
Martin, ———
    commis, *South*, 1809 to May 1814
Masson, Étienne Nicolas
    commis, *Finances*, December 1802 to May 1814
Mathias, André
    commis, *South*, December 1802 to May 1806
    bibliothécaire, *Archives*, June 1806 to 1809
Mathieu, Jacques
    sous chef, *North*, September 1799 to September 1802
    publiciste, *Archives*, September 1802 to July 1805
Monnier, ———
    chef du bureau du centre, *North*, June 1812 to 1813
Osmond, ———
    secrétaire intime, *South*, September 1800 to August 1807
Pelé, ———
    commis, *Finances*, April 1802 to May 1814
Picard, Paul Alexandre
    commis, *Finances*, September 1799 to May 1814
Pichon, Louis André
    sous chef, *South*, September 1799 to September 1800
Posuel de Verneaux, Pierre Marie
    secrétaire intime, *South*, August 1807 to June 1811

Quiret, Antoine Joseph
  commis, *Finances*, September 1799 to June 1800
  commis, *Consulates*, June 1800 to May 1814
Renard, ———
  commis, *North*, July 1807 to May 1814
Roederer, Antoine Marie (*fils*)
  secrétaire intime, *South*, September 1800 to November 1805
Rosenstiel, Henri Charles
  publiciste, *Archives*, April 1802 to May 1814
Rosenstiel, (*fils*)
  commis, *Consulates*, June 1806 to May 1814
Roth, ———
  commis, *South*, December 1799 to September 1803
Roux de Rochelle, Jean Baptiste Gaspard
  commis, *South*, September 1799 to September 1800
  sous chef, *South*, September 1800 to April 1807
  chef, *South*, May 1807 to May 1814
Rumigny, Marie Hyppolite Queully de
  commis, *South*, November 1803 to May 1811
Sautereau, Claude
  analyseur, *Archives*, September 1799 to May 1812
Sauvage, ———
  commis, *Consulates*, September 1799 to May 1814
Ségur, ———
  commis, *South*, January 1814 to May 1814
Tessier, Nicolas Antoine Queux
  directeur des élèves, *Archives*, September 1799 to July 1807
  sous chef, *Archives*, August 1807 to May 1814
Viela, ———
  commis, *Archives*, 1809 to May 1814
Vitry, François Antoine
  commis, *Finances*, July 1800 to May 1814

Notes

Abbreviations and Short Titles Used

AAE	Archives des Affaires Étrangères
AAEDP	Dossiers du personnel, AAE
Comptabilité	Fonds et Comptabilité, AAE
M & D	Mémoires et Documents, Fonds France, AAE
O & R	Organisation et Réglements du Ministère, AAE
Décrets	Décrets et Arrêtés, AAE
AN	Archives Nationales
AN AP	Archives Privées AN
AGDP	Dossiers du personnel, Archives de la Guerre
Corr.	*Correspondance de Napoléon Ier publiée par ordre de l'Empereur Napoléon III.*
Brotonne, *Dernières Lettres*	Léonce de Brotonne, *Dernières Lettres Inédites de Napoléon Ier*
Chuquet, *Inédites*	Arthur Chuquet, *Inédites Napoléoniens.*
Chuquet, *Ordres*	Arthur Chuquet, *Ordres et Apostilles de Napoléon, 1799–1815*
Lecestre	L. Lecestre, *Lettres Inédites de Napoléon Ier, an VIII–1815*
Mikhailovich	Grand Duke P. Mikhailovich, *Les Relations de la Russie et de la France d'auprès les rapports des ambassadeurs*
RHD	Revue d'Histoire diplomatique

Introduction

1. Godechot, *L'Europe et l'Amerique*, p. 34.
2. Parker, "Two Administrative Bureaux under the Directory and Napoleon," *French Historical Studies*, 4, no. 2 (1965), 151.
3. Godechot, *Les Institutions de la France sous la Révolution et l'Empire*, p. 559.
4. Levi-Mirepoix, *Le Ministère des Affaires Étrangères*; Chastenet, *Le Quai d'Orsay*; Masson, *Le Département des Affaires Étrangères*; and Outrey, "Histoire et Principes de l'administration française des affaires étrangères."
5. Cambon, *The Diplomatist*, p. 36.

Chapter 1. The External Service

1. Mattingly, *Renaissance Diplomacy*, pp. 60–76.
2. Latour-Maubourg to Maret, 22 October 1813, AAE, Correspondance Politique (hereinafter cited only by the name of the country), Württembourg 48, f. 54.
3. Mattingly, *Renaissance Diplomacy*, pp. 24–31; Satow, *Guide to Diplomatic Practice*, pp. 164–70; Horn, *British Diplomatic Service*, pp. 42–47; and Picavet, *La Diplomatie Française*, pp. 73–75.
4. Décrets, vols. 7, 9, and 10 are the sources for all the information on rank, except where otherwise indicated.
5. Napoleon to Savary, 16 September 1807, Corr. 16:13163.
6. Beauharnais to Talleyrand, 19 April 1805 (29 Germinal Year XIII), and reply, 25 April 1805 (4 Floréal Year III), Toscane 157A, ff. 155–56 and 173–74.
7. Report to Napoleon, AN AF IV 1706F.
8. Talleyrand to Massias, 14 December 1803 (22 Frimaire Year XII), Bade 5, ff. 304–5.
9. Napoleon to Talleyrand, 13 March 1806, Décrets, vol. 9, f. 114.
10. Maret to Napoleon, 31 May 1811, Pologne 327, f. 263.
11. AAEDP 2, ff. 43 and 69; Talleyrand to Doucet and Laville, March and April 1803 (Germinal Year XI), Württembourg 39, ff. 84–85; AAEDP 18, ff. 46–48; and Larochefoucauld to Talleyrand, 2 June 1802 (13 Prairial Year X), AE B III 466.
12. Perse 9, ff. 150–51.
13. AAEDP 7, f. 368.
14. AAEDP 2, f. 55.
15. AAEDP 53, f. 26.
16. Verninac to Talleyrand, 13 September 1801 (26 Fructidor Year IX), Suisse 475, ff. 324–25.
17. AAEDP 18, ff. 46–48.
18. Broglie, *Souvenirs*, 1:213.
19. Perse 9, ff. 150–51.
20. Beurnonville to Caulaincourt, 31 December 1801 (10 Nivôse Year X), AN 95 AP 4; Adams, *Memoirs*, 2:141.
21. Lauriston to Caulaincourt, 12 March 1811, AN 95 AP 22, dos. 6.
22. Talleyrand to Caillard, 28 August 1804 (10 Fructidor Year XII), Suède 292, f. 392.
23. Décrets, vol. 10, ff. 30 and 36.
24. Sardaigne 200, f. 89.
25. Massias to Talleyrand, 23 February 1800 (4 Ventôse Year VIII), Bade 4, f. 179.

Chapter 2. The Ministry in Paris

1. Masson, *Le Département*. One must also mention the work of Outrey, "Histoire et Principes de l'administration française des Affaires étrangères." This study, which covers the entire development of the Ministry in 113 pages, is based mainly on the *arrêtés* of organization.

2. Masson, *Le Département*, p. 363.

3. The main source for this chapter is the pay records of the employees of the Ministry called the "État des emplois au Ministère des Relations Extérieures, pour servir au paiement de leurs appointements," found in Comptabilité, vols. 18–21. The employees were paid monthly, and the pay roll is divided into six divisions with the surname, rank, and yearly salary.

4. Comptabilité, vol. 19, ff. 34–35, miscellaneous personnel paid for the Year XIII.

5. O & R, vol. 2, ff. 50–55.

6. Masson, *Le Département*, p. 470.

7. O & R, vol. 1, f. 351.

8. O & R, vol. 2, ff. 32–55.

9. Deutsch, *Napoleonic Imperialism*, p. 253.

10. Outrey, *Histoire*, p. 495.

11. Masson, *Le Département*, p. 486; O & R, vol. 2, ff. 50–55, article 11.

12. Masson, *Le Département*, p. 486.

13. Ibid., p. 488.

14. Decree of 27 November 1810, O & R, vol. 2, f. 22.

15. Holtman, *Napoleonic Propaganda*, mentions in chapters 3 and 4 the propaganda work of the Foreign Minister and of Hauterive in controlling the press and writing articles and pamphlets.

16. Talleyrand's instructions to Hauterive, Floréal Year XIII, in O & R, vol. 1, f. 350; O & R, vol. 2, f. 21; Décrets, vol. 10, ff. 109, 121, 123, 124, 134.

17. Napoleon to Talleyrand, 27 August 1805 (9 Fructidor Year XIII), M & D 1776, f. 33; Picard to Bresson, 28 June 1814, AAEDP 57, f. 132; O & R, vol. 2, f. 21; O & R, vol. 1, ff. 320–21.

18. Napoleon to Hauterive, 13 July 1805 (24 Messidor Year XIII), M & D 1775, f. 117.

19. The whole subject of the Council of State and of the position of the Office des Relations Extérieures is described by Durand in *Le Conseil d'État*.

20. O & R, vol. 1, ff. 332–30; and M & D 518, ff. 300–303.

21. For example, Duff Cooper, *Talleyrand*, pp. 162–63; Madelin, *Talleyrand*, pp. 141–45.

22. Napoleon to Champagny, 1 April 1811, M & D 1778, f. 121; Champagny, *Souvenirs*, pp. 125–27; Napoleon to Champagny, 17 April 1811, Corr. 22: 17614.

23. From 19 April to 18 May 1813, Caulaincourt wrote twenty-seven diplomatic letters. AN 95 AP 12, dos. 95.
24. The main sources for these figures are the pay records, dictionaries, and Masson, *Le Département*.

Chapter 3. The Diplomats

1. The information for this chapter comes from a variety of sources, including biographical dictionaries; diplomatic, military, and prefectoral dossiers; correspondence; the series AN AF IV; the Fonds Masson; and Masson, *Le Département*. Appendices II and III give the statistical background.
2. The generals were Andréossy, Beurnonville, Brune, Caulaincourt, Clarke, Dejean, Dupont, Gardane, Gouvion, Hédouville, Jourdan, Junot, Lannes, Lauriston, La Valette, Macdonald, Narbonne, Ney, Sébastiani, Turreau, Vial, and Victor.
3. Mowat, *Diplomacy of Napoleon*, p. 117; Deutsch, *Napoleonic Imperialism*, p. 183.
4. Ministers inherited from the Revolution, with the approximate number of years of diplomatic experience: Bacher (27), Bourgoing (21), Cacault (23), Helflinger (17), Hirsinger (10), Laforest (28), Otto (27), Reinhard (8), and Rivals (5).
5. Ministers promoted from secretary, with the approximate number of years of experience at the time of the ministerial appointment: Bignon (7), Demoustier (10), Derville (2), Desaugiers *jeune* (17), Hédouville (2), Latour-Maubourg (13), Portalis (3), Raymond (4), Serurier (12), and Vandeul (11).
6. Ministers with six years' experience or more during the Napoleonic period: Alquier (13), Andréossy (7), Beurnonville (6), Bourrienne (7), Didelot (9), Larochefoucauld (8), Massias (11), Sémonville (6), Auguste Talleyrand (6), Turreau (7), and Vial (6).
7. Roederer, *Oeuvres*, 4:308.
8. Napoleon to Clarke, 15 September 1802 (28 Fructidor Year X), Corr. 8: 6392.
9. AAEDP 22, f. 48.
10. Secretaries with fifteen years in office: Bogne, Caillard, Durant, Desaugiers *ainé*, Desaugiers *jeune*, Desportes, and Lefebvre.
11. Cobban, *Social Interpretation of the French Revolution*, chap. 6, "Who Were the Revolutionary Bourgeois?" and Richardson, *French Prefectoral Corps* for a discussion of the types of nobility and the methods of ennoblement and the problems concerning the identification of nobles.
12. The main source of information on the Old Regime nobility are the genealogical dictionaries listed in the bibliography and the various personnel dossiers.

13. Cobban, *History of France*, 2:26.
14. Madelin, *Consulate and the Empire*, vol. 2, chap. 25.
15. The birthplaces are known for sixty-six of the ministers, thirty-seven of the secretaries, and forty-four of the employees.
16. The 47th parallel has been used as the dividing line between the north and the south of both France and Europe.
17. Talleyrand to Gouvion St. Cyr, 30 June 1802 (30 Prairial Year X), Espagne 662, f. 447.
18. Horn, *British Diplomatic Service*, p. 122.
19. Napoleon to Maret, 20 April 1813, M & D 1791, f. 46.
20. Champagny to Bruntzen, January 1808, Hollande 612, ff. 3–4.
21. Lucien Bonaparte to Napoleon, 29 June 1801 (9 Messidor Year IX), quoted in Jung, *Lucien Bonaparte*, 1:92.
22. AAEDP 49, f. 57.
23. Fénélon to Talleyrand, 8 August 1804 (29 Thermidor Year XIII), Suède 292, f. 378.
24. Corr. 11:9167, Décision, 31 August 1805 (13 Fructidor Year XI); AAEDP 30, f. 246.
25. Talleyrand to Turreau, 18 February 1804 (28 Pluviôse Year XII), États Unis 56, f. 374.
26. AAEDP 39, ff. 88–89.
27. AAEDP 24, ff. 71, 60.
28. AAEDP 11, ff. 12–13; Bourgoing, *Souvenirs*, p. 14.
29. AAEDP 58, f. 13.
30. AAEDP 52, ff. 5–6.
31. AAEDP 9, f. 152.
32. AAEDP 40, ff. 338, 339, 341, 343, 345.
33. AAEDP 39, ff. 81–82.
34. Décrets, vol. 10, f. 85 (Lagrange), and AAEDP 50, f. 47 (Mériage).
35. AAEDP 33, f. 281.
36. Napoleon to Talleyrand, 14 January 1806, M & D 1776, ff. 83–84.
37. Verninac, AAEDP 68, ff. 133, 135, 136, 137, 138, 139; Rivals, AAEDP 60, f. 89; Nicolai, AAEDP 54, ff. 75, 77, 78.
38. La Valette, *Mémoires*, vol. 2, chap. 17.

Chapter 4. Appointments and Dismissals

1. Godechot, *Institutions*, p. 483.
2. Chaptal, *Souvenirs*, p. 364.
3. Savary, *Mémoires*, 3:94–95.
4. Bourgoing, *Souvenirs*, p. 398.
5. Cobban, *History of Modern France*, 2:55.
6. The main sources for this chapter are the Napoleonic correspondence, series

AN AF IV 1671 to 1706F, the political correspondence, the personnel dossiers, and the dictionaries and memoirs, which have to be used with great caution.

7. Napoleon to Talleyrand, 30 October 1801 (8 Brumaire Year X), M & D 1773, f. 40 (Gouvion); 12 April 1807, Corr. 15:12354 (Gardane); 16 May 1802 (26 Floréal Year X), M & D 1773, f. 96 (Vial); 7 November 1806, M & D 1778, f. 7 (Andréossy).

8. AGDP, MF 24, f. 2.

9. Talleyrand to Larochefoucauld, 7 November 1806, Autriche 379, f. 407.

10. Dry, *Soldats Ambassadeurs sous le Directoire.*

11. Talleyrand to Beurnonville, about 16 September 1802 (29 Fructidor Year X), quoted in Graux, *Beurnonville*, p. 322.

12. Méneval, *Mémoires*, 1:189; Junot, *Mémoires*, 2:234.

13. Bourrienne, *Mémoires*, 2:102; and Las Casas, *Mémorial de Sainte Hélène*, vol. 3, part 6, p. 268.

14. Méneval, *Mémoires*, 1:353; Roederer, *Oeuvres*, 3:348; Miot de Melito, *Memoirs*, 1:389; and Junot, *Mémoires*, 3:256.

15. Napoleon to Talleyrand, 30 November 1800 (9 Frimaire Year IX), M & D 1771, f. 201; Napoleon to Champagny, 27 February 1808, M & D 1780, f. 47.

16. Chateaubriand, *Mémoires*, 3:214.

17. Napoleon to Champagny, 5 December 1810, M & D 1778, f. 2; Bignon, *Souvenirs*, pp. 219–22; Napoleon to Maret, 11 December 1812, Corr. 24: 19384; Napoleon to Champagny, 31 October 1807, M & D 1780, f. 4.

18. Napoleon to Talleyrand, 23 August 1805 (5 Fructidor Year XIII), M & D 1776, ff. 24–25; and Champagny to Napoleon, 5 September 1810, AF IV 1706F.

19. Talleyrand to Napoleon and reply, 7 August 1804 (19 Thermidor Year XII), M & D 1775, f. 55; Champagny to Napoleon, December 1809, AF IV 1675, plaq 7 (ii), f. 796; Champagny to Napoleon, 16 December 1810, AF IV 1706F; and Napoleon to Maret, 4 April 1813, Corr. 25:19800.

20. Napoleon to Talleyrand, 14 August 1805 (23 Thermidor Year XIII), M & D 1776, f. 16.

21. Report, Champagny to Napoleon, 18 September 1808, AN AF IV 1706F.

22. Napoleon to Maret, 5 August 1811, M & D 1789, f. 77; Report, Maret to Napoleon, November 1811, AN AF IV 1706F.

23. Report, Champagny to Napoleon, 15 September 1810, AN AF IV 1706F.

24. AAEDP 67, f. 331.

25. Napoleon to Champagny, 17 August 1807, M & D 1779, f. 58; Napoleon to Talleyrand, 26 March 1806, M & D 1777, f. 9.

26. Napoleon to Talleyrand, 29 September 1800 (7 Vendémiaire Year IX), M & D 1771, f. 175; Napoleon to Champagny, 2 September 1808, M & D 1781, f. 98.

27. Larochefoucauld to Talleyrand, 15 April 1806, Autriche 378, f. 209; Clarke

to Talleyrand, 6 November 1801 (15 Brumaire Year X), Toscane 153B, f. 189.

28. Bourgoing to Talleyrand, 13 September 1800 (26 Fructidor Year VIII), Danemark 176, f. 189; Napoleon to Talleyrand, 6 August 1804 (18 Thermidor Year XII), Corr. 9:7906.

29. Maret to Lajard, 10 October 1811, Saxe 8, f. 303.

30. Aubusson to Talleyrand, 12 December 1807, AAEDP 3, f. 159; Napoleon to Louis Bonaparte, 12 October 1808, Corr. 17:14374.

31. Beurnonville to Caulaincourt, 21 December 1801 (30 Frimaire Year X), AN 95 AP 4, f. 44.

32. Savary to Napoleon, 21 October 1807, AN AF IV 1697, dos. 1; and Napoleon to Champagny, 17 February 1811, M & D 1788, f. 58.

33. Lauriston to Maret, 29 September 1811, Mikhailovich, 6:112.

34. Lannes to Talleyrand, 27 November 1801 (6 Frimaire Year X), Portugal 122, f. 498, and 17 April 1802 (27 Germinal Year X), AF IV 1689, dos. 2, f. 19.

35. Victor to Talleyrand, 5 February 1805 (16 Pluviôse Year XIII), Danemark 178, f. 332; Aubusson to Talleyrand, 12 December 1807, AAEDP 3, f. 159.

36. Beurnonville to Napoleon, 29 September 1801 (8 Brumaire Year X), AN AF IV 1690, dos. 2, f. 13.

37. Champagny to Napoleon, 22 September 1807, AN AF IV 1706E, dos. 2, f. 7; and Caulaincourt, *Memoirs*, 1:53–54.

38. Talleyrand to Cacault, 8 April 1803 (18 Germinal Year XI), Rome 935, f. 47; Bignon, *Souvenirs*, p. 3; Champagny to Bignon, 12 December 1810, Pologne 327, ff. 361–62.

39. Napoleon to Roederer, 16 March 1802 (25 Ventôse Year X), Corr. 7:5995; and Lezai-Marnesia, *Souvenirs*, pp. 83–84.

40. Bourgoing, *Souvenirs*, p. 52; Ernouf, *Maret*, p. 224.

41. Ernouf, *Maret*, p. 378.

42. Chateaubriand, *Mémoires*, p. 214.

43. Hermand to Talleyrand, 7 October 1801 (15 Vendémiaire Year X), AAEDP 38, f. 329; AAEDP 39, f. 236.

44. Brotonne, *Dernières Lettres*, Décision, 28 February 1806, 1:*363; and report Champagny to Napoleon, December 1809, AN AF IV 1675, plaq. 7 (ii), ff. 797–98, 800–801.

45. Napoleon to Maret, 22 April 1811, Corr. 22:17657.

46. Note by Sémonville on his embassy, AN AF IV 1682, dos. 2, f. 308; Durant to Champagny, 22 August 1808, Württembourg 43, f. 400; AAEDP 22, ff. 48–49; Maret to Otto, 9 March 1813, Autriche 395, f. 254; AAEDP 55, f. 252.

47. Brotonne, *Dernières Lettres*, Décision, 28 February 1806, 1:*363.

48. AAEDP 48, ff. 25–26; AAEDP 42, f. 228.

49. AAE *École diplomatique*: Lajonchère, Villemarest, and Mabon.

50. D'Aguesseau to Talleyrand, 21 May 1802 (1 Prairial Year X), Danemark

177, f. 369; and Bourgoing to Talleyrand, 5 January 1800 (15 Nivôse Year IX), Danemark 177, f. 10.

51. Talleyrand to Clarke, 9 April 1803 (19 Germinal Year XI), Toscane 155, f. 101.

52. Report on *élèves*, AAE *École diplomatique*, vol. 1, f. 82.

53. AAEDP 22, ff. 114–16.

54. Méneval, *Mémoires*, pp. 146–47; Fain, *Mémoires*, p. 28.

55. Champagny to Bignon, 12 December 1810, Pologne 326, ff. 361–62; Napoleon to Champagny, 5 December 1810, M & D 1788, f. 2; Bignon, *Souvenirs*, p. 5.

56. Champagny to Napoleon, 6 March 1810, AN AF IV 1799, dos. 2, f. 5; Brotonne, *Dernières Lettres*, Décision, 28 February 1806, 1:*363.

57. Suède 291, f. 184.

58. Napoleon to Talleyrand, 12 April 1807, Corr. 15:12354.

59. Bourgoing, *Souvenirs*, pp. 14, 52.

60. Caulaincourt, *Memoirs*, 2:351.

61. Maret to Bignon, 29 May 1812, Pologne 330, ff. 78–79.

62. Lucien Bonaparte to Talleyrand, 2 July 1801 (13 Messidor Year IX), Espagne 661, ff. 314–15; Lannes to Talleyrand, 22 May 1804 (2 Prairial Year XII), Portugal 125, f. 78.

63. Napoleon to Talleyrand, 9 April 1803 (19 Germinal Year XI), M & D 1774, f. 46; Napoleon to Fesch, 16 May 1806, Corr. 12:10239; Napoleon to Champagny, 17 August 1807, M & D 1779, f. 58.

64. Napoleon to Maret, 11 December 1812, Corr. 24:19384.

65. Napoleon to Maret, 11 March 1811, M & D 1788, f. 83; Maret to Didelot, 4 November 1811, AAEDP 24, f. 73; Napoleon to Champagny, 23 October 1806, M & D 1779, f. 121; Didelot to Talleyrand, 28 December 1806, AAEDP 24, ff. 69–70.

66. Talleyrand to Napoleon, 22 July 1801 (3 Thermidor Year IX), Suisse 475, ff. 225–26; Champagny, *Souvenirs*, p. 97.

67. Maret to the Duke of Würzburg, 3 November 1812, AAEDP 52, f. 235; Méneval, *Mémoires*, 3:19.

68. Pichon, *De l'État de la France*.

69. Portugal 122, f. 381.

70. Napoleon to Champagny, 20 August 1809, M & D 1783, ff. 21–22.

71. Napoleon to Talleyrand, 24 August 1804 (4 Fructidor Year XII), M & D 1775, f. 63; Napoleon to Champagny, 12 October 1807, M & D 1779, f. 113.

72. Talleyrand to Desportes, 29 November 1801 (6 Frimaire Year X), AAEDP 23, f. 463; AAEDP 38, ff. 38–40; AAEDP 67, f. 331.

73. Napoleon to Maret, 16 February 1812, M & D 1790, f. 45.

74. Aubusson to Napoleon, 24 October 1807, AN AF IV 1701, dos. 4; Napoleon to Champagny, 6 February 1808, M & D 1780, f. 50; *Rapport à son Excellence le Ministre des Relations Extérieures* par Hauterive.

75. There is far more documentary evidence about appointments and dismissals than could possibly be quoted in this chapter: further examples of all aspects of this chapter can be found in my original thesis, "The French Diplomatic Service 1799–1814," University of London, 1970.

Chapter 5.   Diplomatic Training

1. Hauterive's report to the Council of State, March 1806, O & R, vol. 1, ff. 360–68.
2. AAEDP 11, f. 11; Bourgoing, *Souvenirs*, pp. 16–20.
3. M & D 518, ff. 300–303; 519, f. 5.
4. M & D 519, f. 5.
5. Talleyrand to Napoleon, 1800 (Year VIII), AAE *École diplomatique* vol. 1, ff. 79–80.
6. Talleyrand to Castellane, 5 September 1801 (18 Fructidor Year IX), Suisse 475, f. 273.
7. AAE *École diplomatique*, vol. 1, ff. 87–89, 90–91.
8. This plan of study is found in AAE *École diplomatique*, vol. 1, ff. 83–5.
9. Latour du Pin to Champagny, 1 April 1809, AAEDP 43, f. 131.
10. AAEDP 50, ff. 49–50.
11. Bignon to Talleyrand, 11 October 1804 (19 Vendémiaire Year XIII), Hesse Cassel 18, f. 246; Hollande 609, ff. 130–41; Serurier to Champagny, 6 March 1808, Hollande 612, ff. 79–81.
12. Rivals to Talleyrand, 10 April 1803 (20 Germinal Year XI), Hesse Cassel 17, f. 271.
13. Danemark 184, ff. 455, 505.
14. Durand, *Les Auditeurs au Conseil d'État*, pp. 31, 156–57; Richardson, *Prefectoral Corps*, pp. 132–33.
15. O & R 1, ff. 360–68.
16. Napoleon to Talleyrand, 31 May 1806, M & D 1777, f. 42.
17. Saint Jean d'Angély's speech is found in AN AF IV 1335, f. 12.
18. AAE *École diplomatique*, vol. 1, ff. 211–23.
19. AN AF IV 1335, f. 2 (4) (Chasteau), f. 66 (Brunet), f. 57 (Marquet).
20. AAE *École diplomatique*, vol. 1, ff. 123–28.
21. Durand, *Les Auditeurs au Conseil d'État*, p. 158. Durand mentions the *auditeurs d'ambassade* in Warsaw and Vienna, the minister in Stuttgart, and the chargé d'affaires in Danzig. He also mentions that the *auditeur* Vincent was chargé d'affaires in Warsaw. This is incorrect, as Vincent was never accredited.
22. Masson, *Le Département*, pp. 454–55.
23. Bruun, *Europe and the French Imperium*, p. 67.
24. O & R vol. 1, ff. 366–67.
25. AAE *École diplomatique*, vol. 1, f. 95.

26. Hauterive to Maret, 2 November 1812, 3 March 1813, AAE *École diplo-matique*, vol. 1, ff. 224, 227.
27. Maret to Caulaincourt, 24 November 1813; report Hauterive to Caulain-court, 29 November 1813; and Caulaincourt to Maret, 2 December 1813; in AAE *École diplomatique*, vol. 1, ff. 228, 229–31, 232.

Chapter 6. The Diplomatic Career

1. The main sources of information for this chapter are the financial records of the Ministry and the records of decrees which were necessary for all pay-ments save those made secretly.
2. Napoleon to Davout, 1 January 1811, Corr. 21:17257, copy to Champagny, M & D 1788, f. 31; and Napoleon to Maret, 13 June 1811, M & D 1789, f. 37.
3. Bignon, *Histoire de la France*, 19:316.
4. Hirsinger to Talleyrand, 27 June 1805 (5 Messidor Year XIII), AAEDP 38, ff. 393–94; Helflinger to Talleyrand, 16 February 1800 (27 Pluviôse Year VIII), Saxe 74, f. 155; AAEDP 49, dossier Massias; and Beurnonville to Talleyrand, 5 March 1800 (14 Ventôse Year VIII), 24 May 1800 (4 Prai-rial Year VIII), AAEDP 8, ff. 248, 249–50, 251.
5. De Pradt to Maret, 6 June 1812, Pologne 330, ff. 129–30; and Bignon, *Souvenirs*, p. 227.
6. Bourgoing to Champagny, 6 October 1808, AAEDP 11, ff. 49–51; report Champagny to Napoleon, September 1808, AN AF IV 1706F; Serra to Maret, 19 April 1813, Saxe 84, f. 69, 21 May 1813, Saxe 84, ff. 144–45; report, Maret to Napoleon, 11 June 1813, Saxe 84, f. 190.
7. The main sources for this section are the *Armorial du Premier Empire*, the *Almanach National* and *Impérial*, and the dictionaries.
8. Alquier to Napoleon, 9 April 1810, AN AF IV 1799, dos. 2, f. 5; Napoleon to Champagny, 15 March 1810, Décrets, vol. 10, f. 36.
9. Quoted in Markham, *Napoleon*, p. 95.
10. The main sources for the section on the Legion of Honour are AN AF IV 1037, 1038, 1039, and the *Almanach*.
11. Circular letter to diplomats, 24 June 1804 (5 Messidor Year XII), M & D 519, f. 62; Lacepède to Napoleon, AN AF IV 1038 dos. 3, f. 8.
12. Maret to Napoleon, 2 January 1813, AN AF IV 1706F.
13. Champagny to Napoleon, 1 August 1810, AN AF IV 1706F.
14. Bacher to Talleyrand, 18 November 1803 (24 Brumaire Year XII), AAEDP 3, ff. 393–94; 1 June 1802 (12 Prairial Year X), Allemagne 717, f. 131; 2 October 1804 (10 Vendémiaire Year XIII), Allemagne 727, f. 233.
15. Durant to Talleyrand for Demoustier, 10 July 1805 (21 Messidor Year XIII), Saxe 75, f. 217; Lannes to Talleyrand for Fitte, 7 June 1804 (18 Prairial Year XII), AN AF IV 1689, dos. 2, f. 81.

16. Ney to Champagny, 28 April 1808, Suisse, f. 71; Champagny to Ney, 9 May 1808, Suisse 487, f. 83; and Lacepède to Napoleon, 20 May 1808, AN AF IV 1038, dos. 4, f. 64.

17. Recommendation for Hédouville, AN AF IV 1038, dos. 3, f. 8.

18. Reinhard to Talleyrand, 6 July 1804 (17 Messidor Year XII), Hambourg 118, f. 4.

19. Laforest to Champagny, 1 January 1811, Laforest, *Correspondance*, 4:685.

20. Demoustier to Maret, Württembourg 48, f. 324.

21. Clarke to Talleyrand, 18 March 1803 (27 Ventôse Year XI), AAEDP 18, f. 57.

22. Hirsinger to Talleyrand, 9 June 1804 (20 Prairial Year XII), Allemagne 216 f. 284; Talleyrand to Hirsinger, 2 July 1805 (13 Messidor Year XIII), Allemagne 216, f. 285; Bourgoing to Talleyrand, 7 May 1802 (17 Floréal Year X), Suède 291, ff. 350–51; Bourgoing to Talleyrand, 2 July 1802 (13 Messidor Year X), Suède 291, f. 378.

23. Durant to Champagny, 21 August 1807, Württembourg 43, f. 171; reply, 28 August 1807, ff. 175, 329, 340.

24. Serra to Champagny, 21 January 1811, Pologne 327, f. 13; Serra to Maret, 6 May 1811, 18 October 1811, and reply 3 November 1811, Württembourg 46, ff. 211–13, 236, 423, 438.

25. Siméon to Champagny, 11 May 1807, 16 August 1807, 20 June 1808, 16 July 1808, and reply 16 August 1808, Württembourg 43, ff. 93, 104, 164–65, 367–68, 327–28, 395.

26. Andréossy to Maret, 13 August 1812, Turquie 226, ff. 41–42.

27. Demoustier to Maret, 6 March 1813, Württembourg 48, f. 182; Maret to Demoustier, 11 April 1813, Württembourg, f. 294; and leave granted, Saxe 75, f. 15.

28. Talleyrand to Massias, 28 September 1800 (6 Vendémiaire Year IX), Bade 4, f. 205.

29. Report Champagny to Napoleon, 25 May 1810, M & D 1770 f. 146.

30. Napoleon to Champagny, 25 November 1808, Corr. 18:14505; Champagny to Bignon, 2 December 1808, Bade 8, f. 524; and reply f. 525; and report Champagny to Napoleon, January 1809, Brotonne, *Dernières Lettres*, 1: *858, Décision.

31. Clarke: AAEDP 18, ff. 46–48; Beauharnais: Napoleon to Talleyrand, 20 October 1804 (28 Vendémiaire Year XIII), M & D 1775, f. 94.

32. Laforest to Maret, 20 July 1811, Laforest *Correspondance*, 5:686–93; Larochefoucauld to Talleyrand, 25 October 1806, Autriche 379, f. 373.

33. Champigny to Talleyrand, 15 January 1800 (25 Nivôse Year VIII), Hollande 603, f. 337; Aubusson to Talleyrand, 12 December 1807, AAEDP 3, f. 159; Didelot to Napoleon, 28 December 1806, AAEDP 24, f. 7.

34. Larochefoucauld to Talleyrand, AAEDP 43, f. 57.

35. Bacher to Talleyrand, 16 March 1806, Allemagne 731, f. 172.

36. Marivault to Talleyrand, 19 April 1805 (29 Germinal Year XIII), and 30

April 1805 (10 Floréal Year XIII), Hollande 609, ff. 107–8, 116; Talleyrand to Van der Goes, 24 May 1804 (4 Prairial Year XIII), Hollande
609, f. 162; Talleyrand to Marivault, 27 May 1805 (7 Prairial Year XIII),
Hollande 609, f. 163; Talleyrand to Serurier, 27 May 1805 (7 Prairial Year
XIII), f. 161.

37. Levaulx to Champagny, 3 January 1809, AN AF IV 1689, dos. 1; Décrets,
vol. 9, f. 152; AAEDP 33, f. 281.

38. Napoleon to Talleyrand, 12 April 1807, Corr. 15:12354; Rousseau to Talleyrand, 12 September 1805 (25 Fructidor Year XIII), Perse 8, f. 376;
Corancez to Talleyrand, 12 January 1806, Perse 9, ff. 13–17.

39. Decree of 25 November 1810, Décrets, vol. 10, f. 50.

Chapter 7. Duties and Functions

1. William J. Roosen, "The Functioning of Ambassadors under Louis XIV,"
French Historical Studies, 4 (1970).

2. Lachs, *The Diplomatic Corps*, chap. 2; and Horn, *British Diplomatic Service*,
chap. 10.

3. Lannes to Talleyrand, 12 November 1803 (20 Brumaire Year XII), Portugal
124, ff. 366–67.

4. Saxe 81, f. 318.

5. Napoleon's instructions to Prince Eugène, June 1805, M & D 1770, ff. 93–
94; Napoleon to Murat, 30 September 1809, Corr. 19:15887.

6. Champagny to Bignon, 12 December 1810, Pologne 326, between ff. 361
and 362.

7. Instructions to Bignon, 24 April 1811, 21 May 1811, Pologne 327, ff. 71–3,
168.

8. Bignon to Champagny, 29 March 1811, 5 March 1811, 20 April 1811, Pologne 327, ff. 75–77, 134–35, 162–63.

9. Bignon to Maret, 8 May 1811, Pologne 327, ff. 213–16.

10. Maret to Bignon, 13 August 1811, Pologne 328, f. 11.

11. Napoleon to Maret, 20 December 1811, M & D 1790, f. 12; Maret to Bignon, 31 December 1811, Pologne 328, f. 482; Bignon to Maret, 18 January
1812, 21 January 1812, Pologne 329, ff. 50–60, 76–77.

12. Napoleon to Champagny, 13 February 1809, 3 March 1809, M & D 1782, ff.
51, 61.

13. Napoleon to Champagny, 24 January 1810, M & D 1784, f. 54.

14. Napoleon to Champagny, 2 August 1810, M & D 1786, f. 66; Circular to
ministers, 6 August 1810, M & D 519, f. 190.

15. Instructions to Lauriston, 11 September 1811, Mikhailovich, 7:352.

16. Circular to ministers of 16 March 1812, referred to in Nicolai to Maret, 29
March 1812, Bade 12, f. 264.

17. Maret to Nicolai, 20 March 1813, Bade 13, f. 100.

18. Nicolai to Maret, 29 March 1812, Bade 12, f. 264.
19. Victor to Talleyrand, 15 May 1805 (25 Floréal Year XIII), Danemark 179, ff. 11–13.
20. Richard Cobb has noted a similar demand for information on the part of the Old Regime government, and alludes to a similar result: The French government was certainly the *most*—if not the *best*—informed government in eighteenth-century Europe . . . The old government was as much a victim of its insatiable curiosity, of its voracity for information, much of it trivial, as of its consequent overconfidence." *A Second Identity* (Oxford, 1969), p. 148.
21. Napoleon to Didelot, 2 October 1805 (9 Vendémiaire Year XIV), Corr. 11:9310.
22. Instructions to Larochefoucauld, 2 January 1805 (12 Nivôse Year XIII), Autriche 376, f. 185.
23. The advice submitted on the question of war and peace is the subject of Chapter 9.
24. Archives Nationales, AE B III, cartons 464–73.
25. Corr. 6:4917, 17 June 1800 (29 Prairial Year VIII).
26. Napoleon's instructions in the *arrêté* of 4 Messidor Year VIII (23 June 1800), Gênes 177, f. 229; Dejean to Talleyrand, 2 July 1800 (13 Messidor Year VIII), Gênes 177, ff. 239–42; Dejean to Talleyrand, 1 June 1800 (12 Prairial Year VIII), Gênes 178, f. 112.
27. Instructions to Salicetti, Lucques 1, ff. 306–12 and 316–17; and Salicetti to Talleyrand, 5 January 1802 (15 Nivôse Year X), Lucques 1, ff. 342–43.
28. Napoleon to Talleyrand, 13 April 1802 (23 Germinal Year X), M & D 1773, f. 87; Napoleon to Bourgoing, 19 April 1809, Corr. 18:15095; Victor to Talleyrand, 22 October 1805 (30 Vendémiaire Year XIV), Danemark 178, ff. 408–10.
29. Instructions to Serra, Pologne 324, ff. 329–30.
30. Bignon, *Souvenirs*, pp. 50–51, 91; Bignon to Champagny, June–July 1811, Pologne 327, ff. 410–17; 20 July 1811, Pologne 327, f. 318; 26 September 1811, Pologne 328, ff. 182–83; 1 October 1811, Pologne 328, ff. 191–92.
31. Instructions to de Pradt, Pologne 330, ff. 326–29.
32. Napoleon to Maret, 11 July 1813, M & D 1791, f. 125; Maret to Nicolai, 27 February 1813, Bade 13, ff. 70–71; Vandeul to Maret, 21 April 1812, Hesse Darmstadt 5, ff. 79–80.
33. Dejean to Talleyrand, 4 August 1800 (16 Thermidor Year VIII), Gênes 177, ff. 286–88; Napoleon to Reinhard, 18 May 1800 (29 Floréal Year VIII), Corr. 6:4821; Napoleon to Champagny, 21 February 1809, Corr. 18:14793; Instructions to Bignon, 2 February 1809, Bade 9, ff. 20–21; Maret to Reinhard, 20 April 1813, Lecestre, *995.
34. Bignon, *Souvenirs*, p. 50; Instructions to Bignon, 31 December 1811, Pologne 328, ff. 484–85; Bignon to Maret, 22 January 1812, Pologne 329, ff. 92–104.

35. Instructions to Lannes, Portugal 125, f. 246; Instructions to Alquier, Naples 127, ff. 140–47.
36. For example, Salicetti in Genoa reported on tariffs, contraband, and leaks in the Continental System. Salicetti to Talleyrand, 5 August 1802 (17 Thermidor Year X), Gênes 178, ff. 389–90.
37. Napoleon to Clarke, 20 May 1803 (30 Floréal Year XI), Corr. 8:6743.
38. Talleyrand to Gardane, 26 August 1807, Perse 9, ff. 226–27.
39. Napoleon to Champagny, 26 May 1808, M & D 1781, f. 18; 5 May 1808, M & D 1780, f. 104; 4 July 1810, M & D 1786, f. 10; 7 October 1810, M & D 1787, f. 24; 19 August 1807, M & D 1779, f. 63; 4 January 1809, M & D 1782, f. 3.
40. Dejean to Talleyrand, 27 July 1800 (8 Thermidor Year VIII), Gênes 177, ff. 270–72; 4 August 1800 (16 Thermidor Year VIII), Gênes 177, f. 280.
41. Instructions for Sémonville, Hollande 603, ff. 317–18; Serra's report to Champagny, Pologne 327, ff. 98–100; Lannes to Talleyrand, 25 March 1802 (4 Germinal Year X), Portugal 123, f. 56.
42. Holtman, *Napoleonic Propaganda.*
43. Napoleon to Talleyrand, 2 November 1803 (10 Brumaire Year XII), Corr. 9:7242; Napoleon to Talleyrand, 20 March 1804 (29 Ventôse Year XII), Corr. 9:7633; Napoleon to Talleyrand, 15 March 1807, M & D 1778, f. 69; Napoleon to Champagny, 25 April 1810, M & D 1785, f. 56; Napoleon to Champagny, 18 February 1810, M & D 1784, f. 95.
44. Vandeul to Maret, 21 November 1812, Hesse Darmstadt 5, f. 168; Mercy d'Argenteau to Maret, 29 March 1812, Bavière 188, ff. 89–92; de Pradt to Maret, 30 June 1812, Pologne 330, f. 445; Napoleon to Champagny, 13 January 1809, M & D 1782, f. 12.
45. Instructions to Durant, 20 February 1811, Naples 135, ff. 86–89; instructions to Serra, Pologne 324, ff. 329–30.
46. Hédouville to Maret, 6 February 1812, AN AE B III, 465.
47. Rule on passports, Allemagne, Petits Principautés, Salzburg 60, ff. 285–90.
48. Napoleon to Talleyrand, 24 July 1806, M & D 1777, f. 78.
49. Maret to Lauriston, 25 July 1811, Mikhailovich, 7:334–35.
50. Talleyrand to Fouché, 24 July 1804 (5 Thermidor Year XI), Suisse 475, f. 213; instructions to Bourrienne, Hambourg 118, f. 295.

Chapter 8. The Functioning of the Diplomatic Service

1. Napoleon to Joseph Bonaparte, Corr. 6:5131, 5200, 5204, 5315.
2. Talleyrand to Didelot, 19 March 1803 (28 Ventôse Year XI), Württembourg 39, f. 77.
3. There is only one letter of credit in the archives—that of Bernadotte, who did not accept his appointment.
4. Serra to Champagny, 30 November 1807, Pologne 324, f. 316.

5. Décrets, vol. 9, f. 95.
6. Napoleon to Talleyrand, 17 May 1806, M & D 1777, f. 31.
7. Napoleon to Champagny, 1 November 1809, M & D 1783, f. 107.
8. Napoleon to Champagny, 25 February 1811, M & D 1788, f. 63; 13 March 1810, M & D 1785, f. 11.
9. AN AF IV 1682, Hollande, dos. 1, ff. 41–46.
10. Bavière 179, f. 214.
11. AN 95 AP 10, dos. 4.
12. Napoleon to Champagny, 25 December 1810, M & D 1788, f. 25.
13. Napoleon to Maret, 18 September 1812, Corr. 24:19208.
14. Napoleon to Talleyrand, 28 February 1806, M & D 1776, f. 100.
15. AN AF IV 1706F.
16. Napoleon to Talleyrand, 7 April 1805 (17 Germinal Year XIII), M & D 1775, f. 99.
17. Nineteen letters from Napoleon to Champagny, 24 April 1810, M & D 1785, ff. 34–53.
18. Napoleon to Hauterive, 28 October 1809, M & D 1783, f. 104; Driault, *Napoléon en Italie*, p. 561; Handlesman, *Napoléon et la Pologne*, p. 8.
19. AN AF IV 1231, dos. 2, folder 3, ff. 10–13.
20. Godechot, *Institutions*, p. 563; Adams, *Memoirs*, 2:259.
21. Examples of instructions written by Napoleon: Corr. 15:12563; Corr. 10: 8350; M & D 1773, ff. 16–19.
22. Napoleon to Champagny, 1 April 1811, M & D 1788, f. 121.
23. Dejean to Talleyrand, 27 July 1800 (8 Thermidor Year VIII), Gênes 177, f. 268.
24. Napoleon to Champagny, 10 August 1808, M & D 1781, f. 88.
25. Brotonne, *Dernières Lettres*, vol. 1, *1225, Décision, 30 December 1810.
26. Quotation from Napoleon to Maret, 13 May 1813, copy in M & D 1791, f. 54; Napoleon's criticism of Maret in Napoleon to Maret, 28 April 1813, Corr. 25:19923; 1 May 1813, M & D 1791, f. 51; 8 July 1813, copy in M & D 1791, f. 122; 27 July 1813, copy in M & D 1792, f. 9.
27. Napoleon to Lannes, 16 April 1804 (26 Germinal Year XII), Corr. 8:7689.
28. Napoleon to Talleyrand, 28 May 1806, M & D 1777, f. 39.
29. Serra to Champagny, 20 June 1808, Pologne 324, ff. 470–73.
30. Napoleon to Fesch, 30 January 1806, Corr. 11:9717.
31. Napoleon to Didelot, 2 October 1805 (9 Vendémiaire Year XIV), Corr. 11: 9310.
32. Napoleon to Champagny, 1 April 1808, M & D 1780, f. 78.
33. Napoleon to Talleyrand, 24 August 1805 (6 Fructidor Year XIII), M & D 1336, f. 27.
34. Clarke to Talleyrand, 13 May 1802 (23 Floréal Year X), Toscane 154, ff. 160–64; Napoleon to Talleyrand, 22 May 1802 (2 Prairial Year X), M & D 1773, ff. 98–99.
35. Talleyrand to Bignon, 2 July 1805 (13 Messidor Year XIII), 17 August

1805 (29 Thermidor Year XIII), 5 November 1805 (10 Brumaire Year XIV), Hesse Cassel 19, ff. 140–41, 189, 286; Talleyrand to Saint Genèst, 10 February 1806 and reply 25 February 1806, Hesse Cassel 20, ff. 15, 26–28; Talleyrand to St. Genèst, 18 March 1806, f. 41.
36. Horn, *British Diplomatic Service*, pp. 217ff.

Chapter 9. Advice and Flattery

1. Fisher, *Napoleon*, p. 191.
2. Lockhart, *Napoleon*, p. 322; Lefebvre, *Napoléon*, p. 394; Bruun, *Europe and the French Imperium*, p. 66; Knapton, *Revolutionary and Imperial France*, p. 117; Cobban, *History of Modern France*, 2:25, 55; Lovie and Paulluel-Guillard, *L'Episode Napoléonien*, p. 94.
3. Chandler, *Campaigns of Napoleon*, p. 747.
4. Andréossy to Talleyrand, 19 November 1802 (28 Brumaire Year XI), 28 November 1802 (7 Frimaire Year XI), 23 December 1802 (2 Nivôse Year XI), 9 January 1803 (19 Nivôse Year XI), Angleterre 600, ff. 86–88, 109, 124–25, 145–46.
5. Andréossy to Talleyrand, 26 January 1803 (6 Pluviôse Year XI), 8 February 1803 (19 Pluviôse Year XI), 15 February 1803 (26 Pluviôse Year XI), Angleterre 600, ff. 158, 166–67, 173–74.
6. Andréossy to Talleyrand, 7 January 1803 (26 Nivôse Year XI), Angleterre 600, f. 237.
7. Andréossy to Talleyrand, 17 March 1803 (26 Ventôse Year XI), 21 March 1803 (30 Ventôse Year XI), Angleterre 600, ff. 238–39, 257.
8. Andréossy to Talleyrand, 14 April 1803 (24 Germinal Year XI), 7 May 1803 (17 Floréal Year XI), and 15 May 1803 (25 Floréal Year XI), Angleterre 600, ff. 293–94, 331–34, 369–70.
9. Talleyrand, *Mémoires*, p. 290; Duff Cooper, *Talleyrand*, pp. 110–11; Dard, *Napoléon et Talleyrand*, pp. 64–68.
10. Talleyrand to Napoleon, 17 October 1805 (25 Vendémiaire Year XIV), published by Bertrand, *Lettres Inédites à Napoléon*, *CXI.
11. Duff Cooper, *Talleyrand*, p. 122; Dard, *Napoléon et Talleyrand*, pp. 109–10; Brinton, *Lives of Talleyrand*, pp. 137–42.
12. Talleyrand to Napoleon, 12 March 1807, Bertrand, *CCL.
13. Lannes to Napoleon, 4 April 1803 (14 Germinal Year XI), Portugal 124, ff. 54–57; Lannes to Talleyrand, 12 April 1803 (22 Germinal Year XI), Portugal 124, ff. 71–72; Lannes to Talleyrand, 6 June 1803 (17 Prairial Year XI), Portugal 124, ff. 122–23; Lannes to Talleyrand, 8 August 1803 (20 Thermidor Year XI), Portugal 124, ff. 240–47; Junot to Talleyrand, 4 May 1805 (14 Floréal Year XIII), and 13 August 1805 (25 Thermidor Year XIII), Portugal 125, ff. 294–95, 337–41.
14. Grandmaison, *L'Espagne et Napoléon*, pp. 46–48.

15. Beauharnais to Talleyrand, 12 July 1807, Espagne 671, f. 376, quoted in Grandmaison, *L'Espagne et Napoléon*, pp. 89–90.
16. Lovette, *Napoleon and the Birth of Modern Spain*, 1:87, 105–6; Fugier, *Napoléon et l'Espagne*, 2:307–13; Grasset, *La Guerre d'Espagne*, 1:224–25.
17. See Fugier, *Napoléon et l'Espagne*, 1:xiii; Dard, *Napoléon et Talleyrand*, pp. 168–69.
18. Fugier, *Napoléon et l'Espagne*, 2:314–16; Grandmaison, *L'Espagne et Napoléon*, pp. 95–96, 125; Grasset, *La Guerre d'Espagne*, pp. 224–25; Dard, *Napoléon et Talleyrand*, pp. 164–72; Lefebvre, *Napoléon*, p. 262; Champagny, *Souvenirs*, pp. 96–98; Méneval, *Mémoires*, 2:135; Pasquier, *Mémoires*, 1:329; Savary, *Memoirs*, (London edition) 1:part 1, p. 139; Madelin, *Talleyrand*, 146–47; Lovie, *L'Episode Napoléonien*, p. 102.
19. Grandmaison, *L'Espagne et Napoléon*, pp. 237–38, 258.
20. Quoted in Lovette, *Birth of Modern Spain*, 1:729.
21. Champagny, *Souvenirs*, p. 83.
22. AN AF IV 1706E, dos. 2, 6.
23. Champagny to Napoleon, 6 August 1808, 12 August 1808, AN AF IV 1706E, dos. 3.
24. Champagny to Napoleon, 6 August 1808, 8 August 1808, 9 August 1808, 4 November 1808, 14 December 1808, AN AF IV 1706E, dos. 3; 6 January 1809, dos. 4.
25. The story of Erfurt can be found in any survey of the period such as Lefebvre, *Napoléon*, pp. 276, 281, 298; Fugier, *La Révolution française et l'Empire Napoléonien*; Dard, *Napoléon et Talleyrand*, chap. XI; Brinton, *Talleyrand*, pp. 149–52.
26. Lauriston to Champagny, 29 May 1811, 22 June 1811, 16 July 1811, quoted in Mikhailovich, 6:14–20.
27. Lauriston to Champagny, 15 July 1811, Mikhailovich 6:40.
28. Lauriston to Maret, 14 August 1811, 27 September 1811, quoted in Mikhailovich, 6.
29. Lauriston to Maret, 29 September 1811, Mikhailovich, 6:112–16.
30. Lauriston to Maret, 19 October 1811, 16 January 1812, 11 March 1812, 25 March 1812, Mikhailovich, 6:133–35, 186–91, 228, 250–51.
31. Chateaubriand, for example, says that Duroc, Caulaincourt, and de Ségur opposed the war. Chateaubriand, *Mémoires*, 6:11; Champagny, *Souvenirs*, pp. 125–26.
32. Ernouf, *Maret*, p. 289.
33. Caulaincourt to Napoleon, 8 January 1814, M & D 668, ff. 98–99.
34. Caulaincourt to Napoleon, 3 February 1814, Caulaincourt to Berthier, 3 February 1814, Caulaincourt to Maret, 14 February 1814, M & D 668, ff. 222, 170, 235.
35. Caulaincourt to Napoleon, 14 February 1814, M & D 668, ff. 233–34.
36. Caulaincourt to Napoleon, 3 March 1814, M & D 668, ff. 346–51.
37. Caulaincourt to Napoleon, 5 March 1814, M & D 668, f. 356.

38. Talleyrand to Napoleon, 13 September 1801 (26 Fructidor Year IX), 28
    June 1801 (9 Messidor Year IX), 9 August 1803 (21 Thermidor Year
    XI), 27 July 1804 (8 Thermidor Year XII), 11 October 1806, in Bert-
    rand, *XII, *VI, *XXXIV, *LXVIII, *CCI.
39. Champagny to Napoleon, 31 December 1808, AN AF IV 1706E, dos. 3.

Conclusion

1. Napoleon to Talleyrand, 28 February 1806, M & D 1776, f. 100.
2. Napoleon to Talleyrand, 24 August 1805 (6 Fructidor Year XIII), M & D
   1776, f. 28.
3. Max Weber, quoted in Merton, *Reader in Bureaucracy*, p. 24.
4. Marx, *The Administrative State*, p. 34.

Bibliography

Archival Primary Sources

A. *Archives des Affaires Étrangères*, Paris

1. *Correspondance Politique*
   Allemagne: 716, 717, 722, 726, 727, 728, 729, 730, 731, 732, 733.
   Allemagne, Petites Principautés: 60, 61, 65, 66, 68, 69.
   Angleterre: 596, 600.
   Autriche: 371, 372, 376, 379, 385, 394.
   Bade: 4, 5, 6, 7, 8, 9, 10, 11, 12, 13.
   Bavière: 179, 180, 181, 185, 186, 188.
   Danemark: 176, 177, 178, 179, 180, 184.
   Danzig: 57.
   Espagne: 658, 659, 660, 661, 662, 663, 669, 670, 673, 674.
   États-Unis: 56, 63.
   Gênes: 177, 178, 179.
   Hambourg: 115, 117, 118, 119.
   Hesse-Cassel: 16, 17, 18, 19, 20.
   Hesse-Darmstadt: 2, 3, 5.
   Lucques: 1, 4.
   Mecklenbourg, Supplément: 4, 5.
   Hollande: 603, 609, 612.
   Naples: 127, 131, 132, 135, 136.
   Parme: 46, 47.
   Perse: 8, 9, 10.
   Pologne: 323, 324, 326, 327, 328, 329, 330, 331, 332, 333, 334, 335.
   Portugal: 122, 123, 124, 125.
   Prusse: 226, 231, 235, 236, 237, 238, 239, 240, 242.
   Rome: 930, 935, 939.
   Russie: 141, 144.
   Sardaigne: 279, 280.
   Saxe Ducale: 1.

Saxe Électorale et Royale: 74, 75, 76, 80, 81, 82, 83, 84.

Suède: 291, 292, 293.

Suisse: 471, 472, 473, 475, 478, 482, 487.

Toscane: 153, 153bis, 154, 155, 156, 157, 157bis, 158, 158 bis.

Toscane Supplément, Archives de la légation française à Florence: 7, 8, 9.

Turquie: 205, 206, 207, 208, 209, 212, 216, 226.

Westphalie: 1.

Württembourg: 38, 39, 40, 41, 42, 43, 46, 47, 48.

2. *Dossiers du Personnel*, 1ère Série (dossiers des agents ayant cessé leurs fonctions avant le 1er janvier 1816), 69 volumes.

3. *Fonds et Comptabilité*, Série III, Finances du Ministère, 18, 19, 20, 21.

4. *Mémoires et Documents*, Fonds France

335	1795–1814	circulars, miscellaneous information.
1414	1796–1802	memoirs on finances, state of the Republic.
1415	1803–1805	reports on finances.
463	1715–1813	foreign policy reports.
518	1744–1800	organization of the Ministry in 1800.
519	1801–1813	circulars.
652	1792–1805	state of Europe and the Republic.
668	1813–1814	Congress of Châtillon.
1875	1792–1815	peace treaties, letters.

Papiers Bonaparte, letters of Napoleon to his Foreign Ministers, volumes 1771 to 1792.

5. *Organisation et Réglements du Ministère*, 114, 115.

6. *Décrets et Arrêtés*, 7, 9, 10, 11.

7. *École Diplomatique*, 3 volumes.

B. *Archives Nationales*, Paris

1. AF IV, Archives du pouvoir exécutif de 1799 à 1815

1037, 1038, 1039, Legion of Honour.

1040, Titles and Dotations.

1227, Conseils Privés.

1229–1230, Conseils des Ministres.

1231, Conseils administratives.

1304, 1305, 1326A, 1335, 1336, 1337, Council of State.

1459, requests for pensions.

1671 to 1701, External Relations.

1702, 1703, 1704, 1705, 1706A, 1706B, 1706C&D, treaties.
1706F, miscellaneous.

2. A III, archives du pouvoir exécutif de la Directoire, 28, 52–55.

3. (AE) B III, Consular affairs, 197, 198, 199, 200, 219, 464, 465, 466, 467, 468, 469, 470, 471, 472, 473.

4. F₁B₁, dossiers des préfets: Aubernon (155–9), Derville-Maléchard (158–17), Didelot (158–22), Heim (162–4), Lamoussaye (166), Racault de Reuilly (172–7), Roederer (172–13), St. Genèst (173–3), Verninac (176–8).

5. O², Maison de l'Empereur, 56.

6. A P Archives Privées, Andréossy (179), Beauharnais (251), Beurnonville (174), Bignon (136), Joseph Bonaparte (176AP3), Lucien Bonaparte (176AP4), Brune (179), Cacault (165), Jourdan (194), Lauriston (201), Maret (204), Ney (137AP2, 3), Nicolai (3), Salicetti (212), Sémonville (115), Talleyrand (215), Victor (217), and Caulaincourt (25).

C. *Archives de la Guerre*, Paris

1. Dossiers administratives
   Marshals: Beurnonville (MF 28), Brune (MF 9), Gouvion St. Cyr (MF 24), Jourdan (MF 4), Lannes (MF 10), Lauriston (MF 31), Macdonald (MF 20), Ney (MF 12), Victor (MF 19), Clarke (MF 29).
   Generals: Andréossy (GD 343), Caulaincourt (GD 407), Dejean (GB 998), Hédouville (GD 269), Junot (GD 364), Vial (GD 381).
   Officers (Classement général alphabétique): dossiers Lagrange, Mériage, and Posuel de Verneaux.
D. *Fonds Masson*, Bibliothèque Thiers, Paris, cartons 520–529.

Printed Primary Sources

A. *Napoleonic Correspondence*

Brotonne, Léonce de. *Dernières Lettres Inédites de Napoléon Iᵉʳ*. 2 vols. Paris, 1903.
———. *Lettres Inédites de Napoléon Iᵉʳ, 1799–1815*. Paris, 1898.
Chuquet, Arthur. *Inédites Napoléoniens*. 2 vols. Paris, 1913–19.

————. *Ordres et apostilles de Napoléon, 1799–1815*. 4 vols. Paris, 1911–12.

Correspondance de Napoléon Ier publiée par ordre de l'Empereur Napoléon III. 32 vols. Paris, 1858–70.

Lecestre, L. *Lettres Inédites de Napoléon Ier, an VII–1815*, 2 vols. Paris, 1897.

Thompson, J. M. *Napoleon's Letters*. Oxford, 1934.

B. *Printed Documents*

Almanach National, Impérial, Royal. Paris.

Browning, O. *England and Napoleon in 1803: Dispatches of Lord Whitworth*. London, 1883.

Bulletin des Lois, 3rd. series. 9 vols. 4th. series, 20 vols.

Dunant, Émile. *Les Relations diplomatiques de la France et de la République Hélvetique, 1798–1803. Recueil de documents tirés des archives de Paris*. Basel, 1901.

Hauterive, Blanc. *Conseils à un élève du Ministère des Relations Extérieures*. Paris, n.d.

————. *De l'État de la France à la Fin de l'an VIII*. Paris, Brumaire an IX (October 1800).

————. *Faits, Calculs et Observations sur les Dépenses d'une grande Administration de l'État*. Paris, 1828.

————. *Rapport à son Excellence, le Ministre des Affaires Étrangères sur M. Artaud, secrétaire de Légation à Florence*. Paris, 1808.

Laforest, Antoine. *Correspondance, 1808–13*. ed. G. de Grandmaison. 7 vols. Paris, 1905–7.

Marmottan, Paul. *Documents sur le Royaume d'Étrurie, 1801–7*. Paris, 1900.

Mikhailovich, Grand Duke P. *Les Relations de la Russie et de la France d'après les rapports des ambassadeurs*. 6 vols. St. Petersburg, 1905.

Talleyrand, Charles Maurice. *Lettres Inédites à Napoléon, 1800–09*, ed. by P. Bertrand. 2nd. ed. Paris, 1889.

C. *Memoirs*

Adams, John Q. *Memoirs of John Quincy Adams, Comprising Portions of His Diary from 1795 to 1848*. Philadelphia, 1874–77.

Barras, Paul. *Mémoires*. 4 vols. Paris, 1895–96.

Beugnot, Jacques C. *Mémoires du comte Beugnot, 1799–1815*, Paris, 1868.

Bignon, L.P.E. *Souvenirs d'un diplomat, la Pologne, 1811–13*. Paris, 1864.

Bonaparte, Joseph. *Mémoires et correspondance politique et militaire*. 10 vols., Paris, 1853–54.

Bonaparte, Lucien. *Lucien Bonaparte et ses Mémoires*, ed. by H.F.T. Jung. 3 vols. Paris, 1882.

Bourgoing, Paul C.A. *Souvenirs d'histoire contemporaine*. Paris, 1864.

Bourrienne, Louis Antoine Fauvelet de. *Mémoires de Monsieur de Bourrienne sur Napoléon, le Directoire, le Consulat, l'Empire, et la Restauration*. 10 vols. Paris, 1829.

Broglie, Achille L. Victor de. *Souvenirs, 1795–1870*. 4 vols. Paris, 1886.

Caulaincourt, Armand Augustin Louis de. *Mémoires du général de Caulaincourt*. 3 vols. Paris, 1933.

Champagny, J.B. Nompère comte de. *Souvenirs*. Paris, 1846.

Chaptal, J.A.C. *Mes Souvenirs sur Napoléon publiés par son arrière-petit-fils le vicomte Antoine Chaptal*. Paris, 1893.

Chateaubriand, François Réné, Vicomte. *Mémoires d'outre tombe*, 12 vols. Paris, 1849.

Czartoryski, Adam, Prince. *Mémoires du Prince Adam Czartoryski et correspondance avec l'empereur Alexandre Ier*. 2 vols. Paris, 1887.

Fain, A.J.F. *Manuscrit de 1812*. 2 vols. Paris, 1827.

————. *The Manuscript of 1814*. London, 1823.

————. *Manuscrit de 1813*. 2 vols. Paris, 1824.

————. *Mémoires de Baron Fain*. Paris, 1908.

Junot, Laure, Duchesse d'Abrantès. *Mémoires de Madame la Duchesse d'Abrantès*. 18 vols. Paris, 1831–35.

————. *Souvenirs d'un ambassade et d'un séjour en Espagne et en Portugal de 1808–1811*. Paris, 1837.

Las Cases, M.J.E.A.D. *Mémorial de Sainte Hélène*. 4 vols. Paris, 1823–24.

La Valette, Antoine, comte. *Mémoires et Souvenirs publiés par sa famille et sur ses manuscrits*. 2 vols. Paris, 1831.

Lezai-Marnesia, Albert. *Mes Souvenirs à mes enfants*. Blois, 1851.

Macdonald, Étienne. *Souvenirs*. Paris, 1892.

Marmont, Duc de Raguse. *Mémoires*. 9 vols. Paris, 1857.

Méneval, Claude François, baron. *Mémoires pour servir à l'histoire de Napoléon Ier, 1802–1815*. 3 vols. Paris, 1894.

Miot de Mélito. *Memoirs*. 2 vols. London, 1881.

Molé, Count. *Le comte Molé, 1781–1855, sa vie, ses mémoires*. ed. le Marquis de Noailles. Paris, 1922.

Mollien, François Nicolas. *Mémoires d'un ministre de Trésor Public, 1780–1815*. 4 vols. Paris, 1845.

Ney, Michel. *Memoirs of Marshal Ney Published by His Family*, London, 1833.

Pasquier, Étienne-Denis. *Histoire de mon temps: Mémoires du Chancelier*

Pasquier, *publiés par M. le Duc d'Audiffret-Pasquier.* 6 vols. Paris, 1893–95.

Pichon, Léon. *De l'État de la France sous la domination de Napoléon Bonaparte.* Nouvelle édition. Paris, 1814.

Pradt, Dominique de. *Histoire de l'ambassade dans le Grand Duché de Varsovie en 1812.* Deuxième édition. Paris, 1815.

Rambuteau, comte de. *Mémoires du comte de Rambuteau, publiés par son petit-fils, comte P.M.E.S. Lombard de Buffières de Rambuteau.* Paris, 1905.

Roederer, P.L. comte de. *Oeuvres.* 8 vols. Paris, 1853–59.

Savary, A.J.M.R. *Mémoires du duc de Rovigo.* 4 vols. London, 1828.

Ségur. Paul Philippe. *Un aide de camp de Napoléon: Mémoires du Général comte de Ségur.* 3 vols. Paris, 1894.

Stapfer, P.A. *Bonaparte, Talleyrand, et Stapfer.* Zurich, 1869.

Talleyrand-Périgord, Charles Maurice. *Mémoires publiés avec un préface et des notes par le duc de Broglie.* 5 vols. Paris, 1891–92.

Villemain, C. *Souvenirs contemporaines d'histoire et de litterature.* Paris, 1854.

Secondary Sources

A. *Works of Reference*

Bajot, Louis M. *Chronologie Ministérielle de trois siècles.* 4th. ed. Paris, 1844.

Balteau, J., et al. *Dictionnaire de Biographie française.* 9 vols. In progress, Paris, 1933–.

Biographia delg' Italiani viventi o sia Storia per ordine alfabetico. 2 vols. Lugano, 1818.

Biographie de tous les ministres depuis 1791. Paris, 1825.

Biographie universelle et portative des contemporains. 5 vols. Paris, 1834.

Bittner, L., and L. Gross. *Répertoire des Représentants Diplomatiques de tous les Pays depuis la paix de Westphalie.* Vol. 3. Berlin, 1936.

Chaix d'Est Ange. *Dictionnaire des familles françaises anciennes ou notables à la fin du XIXe siècle.* 20 vols. Evreux, 1903–29.

Chevalier, J.J. *Histoire des Institutions et des Régimes Politiques de la France moderne, 1789 à 1958.* 3rd. ed. rev. Paris, 1967.

Concordance des calendries grégoriens et républicains. Paris, 1963.

Coiffier de Verseux. *Dictionnaire biographique et historique des hommes de la Révolution française.* 3 vols. London, 1800.

Cussy, F. *Dictionnaire du Diplomatie.* Leipzig, 1846.

Frangulis, ed. *Dictionnaire Diplomatique comprenant les biographies des diplomates du moyen age à nos jours.* Vol. 5. Paris, n.d.

Godechot, Jacques. *L'Europe et l'Amerique à l'Époque Napoléonienne* (Nouvelle Clio). Paris, 1967.

————. *Les Institutions de la France sous la Révolution et l'Empire*. Paris, 1951.

Guiffrey, Jules, ed. *Les Conventionnels*. Paris, 1889.

Jougla, Henri. *Grand Armorial de France*. 7 vols. Paris, 1934–52.

Kuscinski, Auguste. *Les Députés à l'Assemblée Législative de 1791*. Paris, 1900.

————. *Les Députés au Corps Législatif*. Paris, 1906.

Laîne. P.L. *Annuaire de l'Ancienne Noblesse*. Paris, 1935.

————. *Dictionnaire verdique des origines des maisons nobles de la France*. Paris, 1918.

Melchior-Bonnet, B., ed. *Dictionnaire de la Révolution et de l'Empire*. Paris, 1965.

Poullet, Prosper. *Les Institutions françaises de 1795 à 1814*. Bruxelles, 1907.

Révérend, Albert. *Armorial du premier Empire*. 4 vols. Paris, 1894–97.

————. *Les Familles Titrées et Anoblies au XIXᵉ Siècle*, 6 vols. Paris, 1901–6.

Robert, A., and C. Cugny, eds. *Dictionnaire des Parlementaires français de 1789 à 1889*. 5 vols. Paris, 1889–90.

Saint-Allais, N. Vitron de. *Nobiliaire Universel de France*. 21 vols. Paris, 1872–77.

Six, Georges. *Dictionnaire biographiques des généraux et amiraux français de la Révolution et de l'Empire*. 2 vols. Paris, 1934.

Valynseele, Joseph. *Les Maréchaux de la Restauration et de la Monarchie de Juillet*. Paris, 1962.

————. *Les Maréchaux du premier Empire, leur familles et leur descendance*. Paris, 1957.

————. *Les Princes et Ducs du premier Empire non Maréchaux, leur famille et leur descendance*. Paris, 1959.

Woelmont de Brumagne, baron de. *La Noblesse Française*. 5 vols. Paris, 1928.

————. *Notices Généalogiques*. 9 vols. Paris, 1923–35.

B. *Biographies*

Artaud de Montor, Chevalier. *Histoire de la vie et des travaux politiques du Comte d'Hauterive, 1784–1830*. 2nd. ed. Paris, 1839.

Brinton, Crane. *The Lives of Talleyrand*. London, 1937.

Dard, Émile. *Un confident de l'empereur, le Comte de Narbonne*. Paris, 1943.

Derrécagaix, Victor B. *Le Maréchal Berthier, Prince de Wagram et de Neuchatel*. Paris, 1904.

Duff-Cooper, A. *Talleyrand.* London, 1932.
Ernouf, A.A. *Maret, duc de Bassano.* Paris, 1878.
Fisher, H.A.L., *Napoleon.* London, 1912.
Gay de Vernon, J.L.C. *Vie du Maréchal Gouvion St. Cyr.* Paris, 1856.
Godechot, J. *Napoléon.* Paris, 1969.
Graux, L. *Le Maréchal Beurnonville.* Paris, 1929.
Kircheisen, F. *Napoleon.* London, 1931.
Lacour-Gayet, G. *Talleyrand.* 5 vols. Paris, 1928–32.
Lannes, Charles. *Le Maréchal Lannes, duc de Montebello.* Tours, 1907.
Markham, F.M.H. *Napoleon.* London, 1963.
Madelin, Louis. *Talleyrand.* London, 1948.
Mesmay, J.T. de. *Horace Sébastiani: soldat, diplomat, homme d'état, Maré-chal de France, 1772–1851.* Paris, 1948.
Savant, J. *Napoleon.* London, 1958.
Tarlé, E. *Napoleon.* 3rd. ed. Moscow, 1937.
Thompson, J.M. *Napoleon Bonaparte, His Rise and Fall.* Oxford, 1952.
Thomas, C. *Le Maréchal Lannes.* Paris, 1891.

C. *Diplomatic and Administrative History*

Baschet, Armand. *Histoire du Dépôt des Archives des Affaires Étrangères.* Paris, 1875.
Cambon, Jules. *The Diplomatist.* London, 1931.
Chastenet, Jacques. *Le Quai d'Orsay, Les Oeuvres Libres, No. 97.* Paris, 1954.
Chinoy, E. *Society.* 2nd. ed. New York, 1967.
Deffaudis, A. *Diplomacy of France.* Paris, 1863.
———. *Ministère des Affaires Étrangères.* Paris, 1849.
Deffaudis, M. *Questions diplomatiques et particulièrement des travaux et de l'organisation du ministère des Affaires Étrangères.* Paris, 1849.
Durand, Charles. *Les auditeurs du Conseil d'Etat de 1803 à 1815.* Aix en Provence, 1958.
———. *Le Conseil d'État napoléonien, l'emploi des conseillers d'État et des maîtres des requêtes en dehors du Conseil.* Aix en Provence, 1952.
———. *Études sur le Conseil d'État napoléonien.* Paris, 1949.
———. *L'Exercise de la fonction législative de 1800 à 1814.* Aix en Provence, 1955.
Freund, Julien. *The Sociology of Max Weber.* New York, 1969.
Horn, D.B. *The British Diplomatic Service, 1689 to 1789.* Oxford, 1961.
Illchman, Warren F. *Professional Diplomacy in the United States, 1799 to 1939.* Chicago, 1961.
Lachs, Phyllis S. *The Diplomatic Corps under Charles II and James II.* Ph.D. thesis, Bryn Mawr College, 1963.

Lévi-Mirepoix, Emmanuel de. *Le Ministère des Affaires Étrangères.* Angers, 1934.

Marx, F.M. *The Administrative State: an Introduction to Bureaucracy.* Chicago, 1957.

————, ed., *Elements of Public Administration.* 2nd, ed. Englewood Cliffs, 1959.

Masson Frédéric. *Le Département des Affaires Étrangères pendant la Révolution, 1789–1804.* Paris, 1877.

Merton, R.K., ed. *Reader in Bureaucracy.* Glencoe, Ill., 1952.

Mouzelis, N.P. *Organization and Bureaucracy.* Chicago, 1968.

Nicolson, H. *Diplomacy.* 2nd. ed. Oxford, 1950.

————. *The Evolution of Diplomatic Method.* London, 1954.

Outrey, Amédée. "Histoire et principes de l'administration française des affaires étrangères," *Revue française de science politique,* Paris, 1953–54.

Parker, H.T. "Two Administrative Bureaux under the Directory and Napoleon," *French Historical Studies,* vol. 4, no. 2, 1965.

Picavet, C.G. *La Diplomatie Française au temps de Louis XIV, 1661–1715.* Paris, 1930.

Piccioni, Camille. *Les Premiers Commis des Affaires Étrangères au XVII et XVIII Siècles.* Paris, 1928.

Richardson, Nicolas *The French Prefectoral Corps, 1814–1830.* Cambridge, 1966.

Régnier, Jacques. *Les Préfets du Consulat et de l'Empire.* Paris, 1907.

Robson, A., ed. *The Civil Service in Britain and France.* London, 1956.

Satow, Sir Ernest. *A Guide to Diplomatic Practice.* 4th ed. London, 1957.

Savant, Jean. *Les Préfets de Napoléon.* Paris, 1958.

Sharp, W.R. *The French Civil Service: Bureaucracy in Transition.* New York, 1931.

Spaulding, E.W. *Ambassadors Ordinary and Extraordinary,* Washington, 1961.

Walsh, H.H. *The Concordat of 1801.* New York, 1967.

Weber, Max. *From Max Weber, Essays in Sociology,* trans., ed., and with an introduction by H.H. Gerth and C.W. Mills. New York, 1946.

D. *International Relations*

Arvengas, Jean. "Le Baron Massias, diplomat et philosophe 1764–1848. Sa mission à Carlsruhe 1800–1808 et son rôle dans l'enlevement du duc d'Enghien en 1804," *RHD,* 1953–54.

Bignon, P.E. *Histoire de la France depuis le 18ᵉ brumaire.* 14 vols. Paris, 1829–41.

Butterfield, H. *The Peace Tactics of Napoleon, 1806–1808.* Cambridge, 1929.

Connelly, Owen. *Napoleon's Satellite Kingdoms.* New York, 1965.

Coquelle, Pierre. "L'Ambassade du Maréchal Brune à Constantinople, 1803–1805," *RHD*, 1904.

———. "Andréossy, ambassadeur à Constantinople, 1812–1814," *RHD*, 1906.

———. "Latour-Maubourg, chargé d'affaires à Constantinople, 1809 à 1812," *RHD*, 1905.

———. "La Mission d'Alquier à Stockholm, 1810–1811," *RHD*, 1909.

———. *Napoleon and England, 1803–1813.* London, 1904.

Deutsch, H.C., *The Genesis of Napoleonic Imperialism.* Cambridge, Mass., 1938.

Driault, Édouard, "L'histoire de la politique exteriéur de Napoléon Ier", *RHD*, 1901–2.

———. "Napoléon à Finkenstein, avril-mai 1807," *RHD*, 1899.

———. *Napoléon en Italie, 1800–1812.* Paris, 1906.

Dunan, Marcel, ed. *Napoléon et l'Europe.* Paris, 1961.

Dunan, Raymond, "L'Ambassadeur Otto de Mosley, 1803–1810," *RHD*, 1955.

Fisher, H.A.L. *Napoleonic Statesmanship in Germany.* Oxford, 1903.

Fugier, André. *Napoléon et l'Espagne, 1799–1808.* 2 vols. Paris, 1930.

———. *Napoléon et L'Italie.* Paris 1947.

———. *La Révolution française et l'Empire napoléonien.* Paris, 1954.

Grandmaison, Geoffroy de. *L'Ambassade française en Espagne 1789–1804.* Paris, 1892.

———. *L'Espagne et Napoléon, 1804–1815.* 3 vols. Paris, 1908–31.

Guillon, Édouard. *Napoléon et la Suisse, 1803–1815.* Paris, 1910.

Hales, E.E.Y. *Napoleon and the Pope.* London, 1962.

Handlesman, Marcel. *Napoléon et la Pologne, 1806–1807.* Paris, 1909.

Krakowski, Édouard. "La Pologne et Lithuanie en 1812: Le Conflit des ambassades françaises de l'Abbé de Pradt et du Baron Bignon," *RHD*, 1937.

Lefebvre, Armand. *L'Histoire des Cabinets de l'Europe pendant Le Consulat et l'Empire.* 3 vols. Paris, 1845–47.

Lovette, Gabriel. *Napoleon and the Birth of Modern Spain.* 2 vols. New York, 1965.

Marchand, Jean. "Un Ambassadeur de Napoléon, le comte A. de Larochefoucauld," *RHD*, 1934.

Marmottan, Paul. *Bonaparte et la République de Lucques.* Paris, 1896.

———. *Le Royaume d'Étrurie, 1801–1807.* Paris, 1896.

Mowat, R.B. *The Diplomacy of Napoleon.* London, 1924.

Potiemkine, V. *Histoire de la Diplomatie.* 2 vols. Paris, 1946.

Puryear, V.J. *Napoleon and the Dardanelles.* Berkeley, 1951.

Rain, Pierre. *La Diplomatic française.* vols. 1 and 2. Paris, 1947–50.

Sorel, Albert. *L'Europe et la Révolution française.* 8 vols. Paris, 1885–1904.

Vandal, Albert. *Napoléon et Alexandre Ier.* 3 vols. Paris, 1891–96.

E. *General History*

Anderson, M.S. *Europe in the Eighteenth Century.* London, 1961.

Bruun, Geoffrey. *Europe and the French Imperium, 1799–1814.* New York, 1938 and 1965.

Chandler, David. *The Campaigns of Napoleon.* London, 1967.

Cobban, A.B.C. *A History of France.* 3 vols. London, 1961.

Dard, Émile. *Napoleon and Talleyrand.* Paris, 1935; London, 1937.

Dry, A. *Soldats Ambassadeurs sous le Directoire.* 2 vols. Paris, 1906.

Ford, F.L. *Robe and Sword: The Regrouping of the French Aristocracy after Louis XIV.* Cambridge, Mass., 1953.

Geyl, P. *Napoleon—For and Against.* London, 1949.

Gershoy, L. *The French Revolution and Napoleon.* New York, 1964.

Godechot, Jacques, et al. *The Napoleonic Era in Europe.* New York, 1971.

Grasset, A. *La Guerre d'Espagne, 1807–1813.* 3 vols. Paris, 1914.

Goodwin, A. *The European Nobility in the Eighteenth Century.* London, 1953.

Hecksher, E.F. *The Continental System.* Oxford, 1922.

Holtman, Robert E. *Napoleonic Propaganda.* Baton Rouge, 1950.

————. *The Napoleonic Revolution.* New York, 1967.

Hampson, N. *The First European Revolution, 1776–1815.* London, 1969.

Lefebvre, G. *Napoléon.* 5th. ed. Paris, 1965.

Lockhart, G. *The History of Napoleon.* London, 1906.

Lovie, J., and A. Palluel-Guillard. *L'Episode Napoléonien: Aspects Extérieures, 1799–1815.* Paris, 1972.

Madelin, Louis. *The Consulate and the Empire.* 2 vols. N.Y., 1967.

Markham, F.M.H. *Napoleon and the Awakening of Europe.* London, 1954.

Ponteil, Félix. *Napoléon Ier et l'organisation autoritaire de la France.* Paris, 1956.

Six, G. *Les Généraux de la Révolution et de l'Empire.* Paris, 1947.

Index